PRACTICAL PHILOSOPHY OF SPORT

R. Scott Kretchmar, PhD

Penn State University

Human Kinetics

Library of Congress Cataloging-in-Publication Data

Kretchmar, R. Scott (Robert Scott)
    Practical philosophy of sport / R. Scott Kretchmar.
      p. cm.
    Includes index.
    ISBN 0-87322-619-4
    1. Sports--Philosophy. 2. Physical education and training-
-Philosophy. I. Title.
    GV706.K74 1994   93-27142
    796'.01--dc20   CIP

ISBN: 0-87322-619-4

Passage on page 256 from the *Rochester Times-Union*, "McQuaid Turns Down #1" by D. Patrick, November 12, 1981, reprinted here by permission of the publisher.

Developmental Editor: Marni Basic
Assistant Editors: Lisa Sotirelis, Dawn Roselund, and John Wentworth
Copyeditor: Jay Thomas
Proofreader: Karen Leszczynski
Indexer: Theresa Schaefer
Production Director: Ernie Noa
Typesetter and Text Layout: Yvonne Winsor
Text Design: Keith Blomberg
Cover Design: Jack Davis
Illustrations: Keith Neely
Interior Photos: see Photo Credits
Printer: Braun-Brumfield

Printed in the United States of America   10 9 8 7 6 5 4

Human Kinetics
Web site: www.humankinetics.com

United States: Human Kinetics, P.O. Box 5076, Champaign, IL 61825-5076
800-747-4457
e-mail: humank@hkusa.com

Canada: Human Kinetics, 475 Devonshire Road, Unit 100, Windsor, ON N8Y 2L5
800-465-7301 (in Canada only)
e-mail: orders@hkcanada.com

Europe: Human Kinetics, Units C2/C3 Wira Business Park, West Park Ring Road
Leeds LS16 6EB, United Kingdom
+44 (0) 113 278 1708
e-mail: hk@hkeurope.com

Australia: Human Kinetics, 57A Price Avenue, Lower Mitcham, South Australia 5062
08 8277 1555
e-mail: liahka@senet.com.au

New Zealand: Human Kinetics, P.O. Box 105-231, Auckland Central
09-523-3462
e-mail: hkp@ihug.co.nz

For Robert T. Kretchmar (1917-1961)

Contents

PART III Improving Life Through Our Profession: Applications of Philosophic Thinking

Chapter 8   Making Changes That Matter

Chapter 9   The Significance of Games and Play

Acknowledgments

This book is the product of the efforts and insights of many people. As memory has allowed, I have attempted to credit those individuals whose ideas I have borrowed. Undoubtedly, however, I have forgotten the source of some of the concepts I discuss here. To any I have overlooked, I offer my apologies.

Particular gratitude should be directed to Warren Fraleigh—friend, mentor, and the individual who gave me my first job in the philosophy of sport. Also, thanks must be given to Bill Harper and Klaus Meier, who read an earlier version of this book and whose good advice I probably should have taken even more to heart than I did; to Marni Basic, my editor at Human Kinetics, for her kind and patient assistance; to Luanne Fox and Alan Hardman, who proofread the text and double-checked my references; and to my colleagues in the Philosophic Society for the Study of Sport, who have taught, encouraged, stimulated, and corrected me over the years. Finally, deep appreciation is due my wife, Janet, and my two children, Matt and Jen, for their patience and support during this project.

Preface

This book has been written during a time of great need and opportunity in the physical education profession. Unsure of its mission, unable to articulate its importance, and lacking political clout, physical education has been a victim of budget cuts in many schools across the country. Division I college athletics and professional sports, apparently interested more in wins and profits than in education, ethics, and community responsibility, are often perceived as lacking integrity. Even sports medicine has been drawn into debates about drugs and drug testing, dangerous or extreme therapies, and high health care costs.

These circumstances would not be so unsettling if professionals in sport, exercise science, and physical education had a sound philosophic basis on which to stand while working for reforms and improvements. However, no persuasive philosophy of physical education dominates the landscape. No widely followed philosophic leaders have drawn authoritative maps to help individuals find their destination. Very little philosophy is systematically or seriously taught in major programs in exercise science.

Thus, without the ammunition and focus provided by a well-reasoned philosophy, some graduates are left to their own resources. They must assume that fitness is important, or that sport is somehow good for people, or that movement skills can free individuals in significant ways. They must find professional direction and establish priorities by trial and error, or on the basis of personal opinions and previously held biases. Little wonder, then, that uncertainty and tentativeness characterize the professional travels of many people today.

I have written this book to stimulate philosophic thinking and foster a spirit of confidence in the profession—in sport, dance, exercise, games, and play. I want to help readers find a personal sense of mission—even excitement—to bring to their coaching, teaching, dance, or sports medicine careers. I want them to see their vocation not as a mere job, but as a true calling—a place where they can change people's lives for the better in vitally important ways.

The Book's Purpose

The book invites readers to do philosophy, to actually hike along a philosophic trail. This journey has been designed with three objectives in mind: (1) to help readers develop their philosophic skills, (2) to provide them with some answers to philosophic questions, and (3) to assist them in developing a personal philosophy of sport, exercise science, and physical education. The first objective is important because readers are bound to encounter novel problems that require philosophic analysis. They must have the skill and ability to think clearly on their own. The second objective is equally important because philosophy, if it is worth its salt, must lead to real answers that are illuminating and useful. Finally, the development of a personal philosophy, the third objective, can provide professionals with both a cause and a compass—with a reason for being devoted to their field and guidelines for channeling that commitment in the right direction.

I designed this book for undergraduate students majoring in exercise and sport science who have had little or no formal training in philosophy. It should be useful for first- or second-year students in introductory courses as well as juniors or seniors who are thinking of going on to graduate school or who are about to begin their professional careers.

Using this text in an introductory course has the advantage of presenting students with value questions and ideals early in their studies. It should help young major students understand why they chose this profession, whether they have (or can develop) any passion for it, and what uniquely valuable contributions they might make in it. It should also encourage new majors to be philosophically inquisitive as they proceed through their studies and into their vocations.

The book can also be used in a junior- or senior-level current issues course where students are required to reflect on previous studies while looking for solutions to contemporary professional problems. Many such courses have students develop a personal philosophy as a capstone experience in their undergraduate education. This book was designed to help readers produce just that sort of statement.

This volume is very different from many other introductory and current issues texts because it focuses squarely on values and ethics. Value decisions, I am convinced, come first and are among the most important commitments that human beings make. They guide, stimulate, and inspire us. Thus, they deserve extended treatment and considerable reflective time and energy.

This book keeps first things first. Readers are required to focus on the values that should make this profession an exciting one, on the purposes that make one physical education career choice better than another one for a given person, and on the ethics that help professionals solve day-to-day problems of right and wrong. If readers are thinking of devoting their lives to this field (or have already done so), they had better know that such devotion is well placed, and they had better be able to explain why it is warranted! In addition, if readers are interested in making the best decisions in their work, they had better know what is good, bad, and in between and then be able to defend their judgments to colleagues, parents, principals, school boards, medical personnel, business leaders, and whoever else has an interest in their work.

Finally, I wrote this volume for individuals headed toward any one of the many careers available in the field: academic research, teaching, coaching, administration and management, fitness, rehabilitation, physical therapy, recreation, sports medicine, gerontology, and other activity-related professions. It is also intended to be useful for individuals who are now involved in, or about to join, the many institutions related to exercise science: the fitness and entertainment industries, business, education, communications, social service, medicine, recreation, and health.

The Book's Trail

The book should be read from start to finish in the order in which it is presented. Part I (chaps. 1-3) is designed to help readers get started on their travels. This portion of the journey is fundamental; it cannot be bypassed. Without some assessment of the readers' philosophic attitudes and skills and without at least a partial understanding of philosophy and its methods, it would be difficult, if not foolhardy, to venture on. Additionally, all ethics and all value judgments are based on understandings and assumptions about people—about their nature, their likes and dislikes, their potential, their highest purposes. Without at least some understanding of what people are or should be, readers would have a very difficult time answering questions about how physical education can best help them.

In chapter 1, readers will take a Philosophic Readiness Inventory in order to measure their philosophic curiosity, confidence, and commitment. They will also take a brief look at how philosophic questions differ from those asked by other kinds of scholars in physical education and get some experience in using three methods used by many philosophers. They will test out these methods while attempting to answer the question, What is at the heart of good sportsmanship?

Chapter 2 describes four attractive but dangerous forms of dualistic descriptions of human life. Readers will attempt to understand why the mind is often thought of as separate from and more valuable than the body. They will examine arguments against mind-body dualism and see why it is a mortal enemy of the movement-related professions. An alternative, holistic, interpretation of persons is presented in chapter 3. This view is one that respects creativity, insight, and brilliance in active and sedentary, verbal and nonverbal, and reflective and nonreflective activities. Readers will also examine some potentially dramatic implications of a holistic vision of persons for their professional lives.

Part II (chaps. 4-7) is devoted to examining the needs of individuals and society and imagining how sport, exercise science, and physical education might address these needs. This is the heart of the book, the place where some of the most difficult and important philosophic judgments will be made. It is where readers will examine the different values of sport, dance, exercise, games, and play and attempt to shape a profession around the most important ones.

In chapter 4 readers will look for what is right and wrong with contemporary society and individual lives in it. On the basis of this diagnosis, readers will speculate on how physical education might respond. This sociologically oriented chapter is included to prevent later philosophic reflections from becoming too abstract, idealistic, and irrelevant for addressing actual human needs in a world headed into the 21st century.

Chapter 5 demonstrates that philosophers must not react blindly to the needs of society. Here readers will pick up some reflective tools that will allow them to work on answers to questions like these: What is good for people in general? Apart from immediate, local, or temporary needs, what values are best? Near the end of this chapter, readers will encounter four values traditionally cited by physical educators in answer to these questions. Chapter 6 looks at these four values as extrinsic values (values that are means to beneficial ends), and an attempt is made to rank them. Similarly, chapter 7 examines the values as intrinsic values (values that are beneficial in themselves). Two rankings are proposed: the four values as intrinsic values and an overall ranking that takes into account the extrinsic and intrinsic aspects of the values.

Part III (chaps. 8-11) focuses on making changes, on actually improving human existence and society through the profession. Here readers examine the practical implications of the philosophic reflections of Parts I and II. First, in chapter 8, they will examine the differences between mainstream (liberal) and peripheral educational change and see how they (as sport managers, physical education teachers, coaches, fitness specialists, or other movement-related professionals) might qualify as mainstream change agents. They will also see why they should want to be identified in this way.

In chapter 9 readers will focus on the content of physical education and attempt to determine its significance. Charges that games and play are only for children, for example, are addressed and countered. By considering insights about the significance of physical education, the holistic nature of persons, the activity-related needs of society, the most important intrinsic values of activity, and the potential for being mainstream change agents, readers will examine a variety of practical implications relating to personnel, curriculum, and methodology.

In chapter 10 readers will come upon the implications of mainstream, liberal physical education for their day-to-day behavior as professionals and the actions of people in sport and other movement activities. In more traditional terms, this is the chapter about ethics and sportsmanship. Readers will look for solutions to ethical problems that permit, as often as possible, win-win solutions. Finally, in chapter 11, readers will review the trail of their philosophic reflections to see where they have been and why they visited those places. More importantly, they will be encouraged to write a personal philosophy of sport, exercise science, and physical education.

Organization Within Chapters

Each chapter (except the last) is organized as follows. First, readers will encounter a practical example that introduces them to the general topic of the chapter. This is followed by a list of questions that are raised by the example. Because these questions are related to the content of the chapter, readers should be able to answer them after they have journeyed down the trail that follows. Next, the purpose of each chapter is described in relationship to analyses made in previous chapters. This is followed by a listing of the specific goals of the chapter and a second set of questions, which are designed to arouse the readers' curiosity.

The major part of each chapter is devoted to a philosophic analysis of the issue at hand. This is where readers are expected to make some philosophic headway, to uncover some answers, to come to some tentative conclusions. At one or more points in each chapter, readers will find Summary Breaks that allow them to take stock of what has been discovered and what more needs to be known. In addition they will be asked to engage in some Philosophic Exercises that are designed to improve their philosophic skills and supplement the analysis provided.

Near the end of each chapter, a Review and a preview ("Looking Ahead") are provided. This is followed by some review questions ("Checking Your Understanding"), Key Terms that were used in the chapter, and Further Readings for supplementary study.

Introduction

This volume is not intended to provide a tidy philosophy of sport, one full of recipes and pat answers. I plan to challenge you to rethink old assumptions and examine long-held biases. I hope as well to encourage you to think very seriously about the value of your studies and work. The book is intended to be personal, challenging, perhaps even disturbing in places.

Definitions

During the course of our philosophic journey, I will refer to three things related to our profession: a subject matter, an academic field, and a number of related vocations. Unfortunately, the boundary lines of all three are indistinct. Even experts do not agree on the nature of our subject matter (Is it human movement? Sport? Exercise? Or something else?), the structure of our academic field (Is there a difference between the discipline and the profession? Are we an art, or a science, or both? Is the learning of movement skill appropriate as an academic major?), and the scope of our vocations (Do dance-related vocations belong to our field or another one? Are health-oriented jobs more closely related to health education departments than kinesiology or exercise science units?).

To make matters worse, these three things are called by different names. For example, some people prefer *kinesiology* as the name for the academic field. Others like *exercise and sport science*. Still others think that *physical education* deserves to be retained.

These debates, while they may be interesting and important, should not distract us here. I will start out by providing some working definitions to make sure that we are thinking of the same thing when I use certain words or titles to refer to our subject matter, our academic field, and related vocations.

I suggest that we define our subject matter as *human movement, with a focus on five of its intentional or purposeful forms: sport, dance, exercise, games, and play*. Because this is such a lengthy description, I will frequently use the term *sport* to refer to our subject matter in general. Thus when you see this word in the pages ahead, try to picture exercise and other forms of vigorous movement, not only competitive activities. Of course, when I am trying to make a point specifically about contests like basketball or volleyball, I will attempt to alert you to this. Nevertheless, *sport* will frequently be used broadly and generically to refer to many movement activities.

I suggest that our academic field involves *the systematic study of human movement and many of its cultural forms*. Valid sources of information include experience in performance itself, reflection, and empirical experimentation. Useful content is produced by the arts and humanities and by the social, behavioral, and physical sciences. Once again, this is a long and somewhat complex description. Thus, for the sake of economy (and because the academic field must be named something), I will call it *exercise science*. Therefore, it is important for you not to think of the terms *exercise* and *science* in their narrow senses.

By the term *vocation* I mean *the wide variety of things that movement professionals do for which a higher education (not just vocational training) is required*. Vocations related to the subject matter of sport (and other movement forms) and the discipline of exercise science (or whatever else it may be called) include sport management, coaching, teaching, athletic training, cardiac rehabilitation, physical therapy, dance therapy, sport psychology, biomechanics, sport journalism, exercise gerontology, exercise physiology, and a host of others. But once again, it would be cumbersome to name each of these professional specialties every time I want to refer to the work we do. Consequently, I will often use the term *physical education* to refer to the vocations of the field in general. So when you see this term, think of the wide variety of tasks that movement professionals do, not just teaching in schools.

Visions and Destinations

In this book I attempt to strike a balance between idealism and practicality. I fully expect philosophy to play a role as we work to solve very real, day-to-day problems. But I do not want its power to be compromised by realists whose feet are stuck so firmly in the clay that they routinely reject fresh ideas with dreary and closed-minded statements like "It will never work!" or "We have never done it like that around here before."

On the other hand, I expect philosophy to promote dreaming, speculating, and following exciting ideas to their logical conclusions. But I do not want its reflective power to be diminished by idealists whose feet never touch the ground and who often express indifference to practical matters with short-sighted questions: Who cares if this will never work? Why even bother to draw out the practical implications of this idea?

With these concerns in mind, this book offers a dual vision.

A Hopeful, Idealistic Vision

This book is optimistic about you as an individual. It assumes that you will not be fulfilled simply by getting a job, buying a house and a car, perhaps raising a family, living out your work life, and then retiring with a degree of comfort and security. Rather it assumes that a healthy degree of idealism resides in you—that you want a calling, that you want to spend your days doing something that you believe in, that you want to reach your professional goals with care and some distinction, that you want to affix your personal signature to what you craft and fashion.

This book is also optimistic about what you can accomplish. It assumes that you need not limit yourself to projects that are rational, safe, traditional, or simply doable. Rather it assumes that apparently outlandish ideas can sometimes be made to work. It assumes that it may occasionally be more valuable to follow a wonderful dream with only a degree of success than to adopt a routine task that is easy to accomplish.

This idealistic face of this book will have you dealing with questions like these:

• Can physical educators lead directed, inspired, and committed professional lives

without the guidance and insight provided by philosophy?

• What is a person and, more importantly, what are the characteristics of good people—of human beings who have reached their full potential as humans?

• Among the many values of sport, which ones best help people to reach their potential, to experience the good life? For example, is a long and healthy life closer to this objective than a meaningful or creative existence?

• Can physical educators, coaches, and other activity professionals provide basic education, like English or math teachers do? Why is a positive answer to this question so important?

• How should morally outstanding people behave in their profession and in sport? What is ideal sportsmanship?

A Realistic, Practical Vision

This book is realistic about you as an individual. It acknowledges the fact that you may need a job and will have to make yourself marketable. It assumes that you have roots in a culture and are constrained by your traditions. It understands that you are part of the status quo and that anyone's personal ability to change and adapt or pursue any new philosophic vision is finite.

This volume is also realistic about what you can do. It assumes that much change occurs in degrees and is constrained by the current state of affairs and well-fortified vested interests. It understands that the status quo carries its own momentum that is often difficult to slow down. It acknowledges the fact that much change is dependent on wisely used power and political action, not just good ideas.

The realistic aspect of this book will have you asking the following sorts of questions:

• Does philosophy provide real answers to real-life problems? For instance, could it affect who should be hired, what activities are recommended by physical therapists or taught by physical education teachers, and the methods by which instruction occurs?

• Are physical educators typically given little professional status because they supposedly deal more with human bodies than minds? If we wanted to eliminate mind-body dualism from our thinking, how would we go about it?

• What are society's greatest needs today, and in what ways can we address them? For example, is the win-at-all-cost atmosphere that surrounds some sport a genuine problem? If so, what can be done about it?

• What are the inherent values of different physical education outcomes? Is fitness, for example, more likely to contribute to the good life than a high level of motor skill is? What would a profession designed around motor skill and play look like?

• How can we best promote sportsmanship? What should you do about an opponent's serve in tennis when you are not sure if it was "in" or "out" and there are no line judges around?

A Personal Destination

At the end of this partly idealistic and partly practical philosophic journey, you will be encouraged to pull your ideas together in the form of a personal philosophy of your profession. This is to be written in pencil, not ink, because your reflections should be revised and refined throughout your career. Nevertheless, if you have not already done so carefully and in earnest, it is important that you start thinking, questioning, and writing by the time you finish this book. Your philosophic statement, as incomplete as it may be,

will serve as an antidote for one of the illnesses of our society.

Many of us today are pressured in our society to get a job and to be productive, period! Perhaps you have not been encouraged to give much thought to the value of different types of work or to different meanings of success. You may not have been allowed to follow your own unique talents, interests, or loves. The important thing, or so you may have been led to believe, is to get a job and to become a productive member of society.

Try to imagine what it would be like to live in a land where every able-bodied person travels. In fact, traveling is so important in this place that people do little else from sunup to sundown. The only problem is that nobody has a road map, and, to make matters worse, there are no map-makers in this society who can supply them. But the absence of maps and the general disregard for selecting one destination over another does not prevent or even discourage traveling. Most people simply travel the same roads taken by their parents, teachers, coaches, or some celebrity. Those without strong family traditions or role models simply follow the person in front of them. Everybody assumes that those who originally established traveling patterns knew where they were going.

As a newcomer to this land, you are urged to get on an avenue and begin traveling yourself. If you remain at the side of the road much longer, you will run the risk of falling behind and appearing to be an outsider who does not like to travel. You may be vaguely uneasy about starting your journey without an idea of where you are going, and you do not much like the notion of traveling without a roadmap. However, this is a place where maps are thought to be unnecessary and destinations are nothing more than where a traveler happens to be at the end of the day.

What should you do about this? I hope that you will refuse to get on any highway until you have had an opportunity to think, question, doubt, and examine; until you have had a chance to become committed to reaching a specific destination; until you see that aimless and passionless productivity may be worse than no productivity at all; until you sense in your very bones that philosophic reasoning can and should affect everything that you do. Writing a personal philosophy will give you an opportunity to identify, with ever greater clarity as you repeat this process throughout your career, the best destinations for you and your field.

Part I
Getting Started

Philosophy is valuable not only for the theories and propositions it produces but also for the thinking skills it requires. Like all skills, thinking can be done well or poorly, and it proceeds along fairly well-defined pathways. In this part I describe these pathways and identify some of the first questions that you will encounter in any philosophy of sport, exercise science, and physical education.

It is important that you learn the fundamentals and begin with some basic issues. In chapter 1 you are introduced to philosophy, provided with some tips on how to think philosophically, and then given an opportunity to do some philosophy yourself. These skills are then used in chapters 2 and 3, where you examine attitudes about the supposed mental and physical aspects of persons and the related importance of mental and physical education.

Chapter 1

Developing Philosophic Skills

The author: Why are our physical education majors required to take so much science? Might we not be preparing a generation of technicians who are unable to appreciate the human side of physical education, coaching, sport management, or sports medicine?

Professor Jones: You know the condition of our curriculum. There is not enough time now to acquaint physical education majors with the expanding scientific content in our field. And besides, science reigns supreme. Science measures real things and produces facts. Would you rather have students sitting around sharing *opinions* in some philosophy class?

The author: How can you say that philosophers do nothing more than share opinions, and what makes you think that historical, literary, and philosophic information is not expanding too?

Professor Jones: I don't want to get into some never-ending argument about that, but I will say that a three-credit course on history and principles should provide more than enough time to do whatever it is that you folks need to do.

Why is Professor Jones so unsympathetic to the humanities? Does he simply lack philosophic curiosity? Or is it more that he has little confidence in the validity of the philosophic process? Or could it be that he thinks that philosophic answers lack practical application? Is it true that philosophers do little more than share opinions?

IN THIS CHAPTER, YOU WILL

- **become acquainted with philosophy,**
- **assess your readiness to think philosophically,**
- **acquire skill in asking philosophic questions,**
- **improve your ability to pursue philosophic answers, and**
- **work through a philosophic analysis.**

Philosophy means literally "the love of wisdom." Because wisdom affects every choice we make and everything we do, philosophy is a broad and fundamental discipline. Philosophy may be mystifying because it deals primarily with ideas—things that we cannot touch, weigh, or put under a microscope and see. For some, this makes philosophy difficult to describe and to do. For many of these same people, it makes philosophy difficult to trust.

But philosophy should be neither mystifying nor untrustworthy. It is not even all that difficult to do. In fact, you have been thinking philosophically your whole life, and many of you have probably been doing it very well. Nevertheless, we need to look at the field of philosophy to eliminate any misunderstandings that may exist and try an analysis to remove any uncertainty or fear that may remain. For many of you this will be an adventure that will allow you to address some questions about the field of philosophy:

Why is it important to ask philosophic questions in the first place?

How do you compare with other students in terms of your philosophic curiosity, confidence, and commitment?

Why is physical education such a science-intensive field? Is this an entirely good thing?

Can you think well enough philosophically to avoid the criticism that your conclusions are nothing more than mere opinions?

Acquiring Skill in Asking Philosophic Questions

The **philosophic process** is the art and science of wondering about reality, posing questions related to that wonder, and pursuing answers to those questions reflectively. It is an art and a science because the philosophic skills of wondering, posing questions, and searching for answers are grounded partly on repeatable methods that can be objectified and explained (science) and partly on intuitions, tendencies, and flashes of insight that can neither be fully predicted nor accounted for (art).

Why Even Ask Philosophic Questions?

The shortest answer to this question, and one that is not entirely misleading, is "Because they are there." Much like Sir Edmund Hillary, who gave a similar response to questions about his motives for climbing Mount Everest, you have undoubtedly come upon philosophical dilemmas and found at least some of them to be interesting. Hillary did not invent Mount Everest, nor did he artificially manufacture an interest in climbing it. In some ways, Hillary could not help himself from wanting, even needing, to climb this challenging mountain. It is possible that Everest controlled Hillary rather than the other way around.

Similarly, philosophic questions beg for attention. What should you do with your life? Should you devote yourself to one of the physical professions when society seems to value mental activities more highly? What role should movement play in human existence? How important is winning? Should biological health be the ultimate goal of physical education? Should young children be placed in high-intensity athletic environments? What role should movement play among older adults who now find it difficult, even painful, to move much at all?

You need not go through some sort of inventive process to bring these philosophic questions into being any more than Hillary needed to invent Mount Everest. You come

upon them, sometimes stumble upon them, in the course of your daily activity. On occasion, it seems, they even find you. You are studying, teaching, coaching, running a fitness center. You cannot afford, at that moment, to take time out to consider a philosophic issue. Yet it is there, nagging at you, asking you to give it some attention, challenging you to come up with an answer. You get hooked, stop your work, and start scaling some philosophic problem's formidable cliffs.

Not all people are interested in climbing Mount Everest, and certainly not all people are interested in devoting great amounts of time and energy to answering philosophic questions. But you must notice one important difference between these cases. It is quite possible that the circumstances of your life will keep you from developing a fascination with mountain climbing. You might have been born and raised on the plains; you might have had overly protective parents who discouraged you from doing dangerous things; you might be a coward by nature; you might have inherited genes that better equip you for floating in a hot tub than climbing a mountain. In short, you may have no reason to challenge Everest and no interest in doing so.

In contrast, philosophic questions are everywhere, and they are accessible to beginners and experts alike. Your birthplace, your job, your place of retirement, your body type—none of these factors distance you from philosophic issues. And while your upbringing and genetic inheritance can influence your interest in philosophical matters, as well as your ability to do philosophy, they do not normally have the power to eliminate philosophic curiosity and ability altogether. If you satisfy some threshold criteria for what it is to be conscious (awake) and human (capable of dealing with ideas), you are at risk of finding or being found by philosophic questions.

Philosophic questions lie everywhere.

It is only the degree to which philosophic problems are noticed and the tools of philosophy used that differ from person to person. Some of you find your profession rich with theoretical dilemmas, value questions, and moral problems, and you can hardly keep yourself from tackling them. Others know that these issues are there but find them uninteresting, insignificant, or frightening. Thus, you get sidetracked by them less frequently.

Where do you fall in this range of philosophic wonder, curiosity, and sensitivity? Are you more a participant or a bystander? Are you more a lusty mountain climber or one who stays on the plains? Do you enjoy journeying on philosophic trails, or would you rather be somewhere else?

PHILOSOPHIC EXERCISE

At this moment, you embody a certain readiness to find or receive philosophic questions and to want to deal with them. This might be called your Philosophic Readiness Quotient, or PRQ. It is possible for you to get a rough measure of your own PRQ by completing the accompanying Philosophic Readiness Inventory. Writing your answers on a separate piece of paper, respond to each statement using the number that corresponds to your degree of agreement or disagreement. *It is important that you complete the inventory before reading any further because the discussion that follows would bias you and make it difficult for you to produce a meaningful score.*

The Philosophic Readiness Inventory is designed to measure three readiness factors: philosophic curiosity, confidence, and commitment. Your total score is an overall measure of the extent to which you embody these three traits. In other words, your PRQ should indicate the extent to which you are ready to find or receive philosophic questions and engage them. Each subscore should give you a sharper image of precisely where your readiness is higher or lower. Subscores can

Philosophic Readiness Inventory

Rating Scale:

Strongly Agree						Strongly Disagree
1	2	3	4	5	6	7

Set 1

1. I have frequently wondered about the meaning of life, about why I am here.
2. Whether or not I am a member of a religious organization, I regard myself as a spiritual person.
3. It is interesting that people around the world are dedicated, sometimes to the point of giving their lives, to very different values, religious traditions, and types of political leaders.
4. I will probably not understand even half of all there is to know about the meaning of human existence.
5. Compared to others, I think of myself as more introspective, more reflective.
6. There have been a number of occasions on which I have simply marveled over the fact that I am alive.
7. I often find myself pondering questions of ethics, of what is right and wrong.
8. There is much more to life than surviving or "making it," and I think from time to time about what that might be.
9. I believe that there is something very powerful (almost mysterious) about sport, dance, exercise, play, or human movement.
10. I think of my life more as an adventure story than a routine journey.

Set 2

1. I am confident that philosophy is *not* just a matter of talking in circles.
2. I think that the products of religious traditions (such as the Ten Commandments) contain some wisdom.
3. It is possible to distinguish good from bad sportsmanship while leaving very few gray areas of uncertainty.
4. When I get into philosophic arguments, I am confident that I will be able to get others to see the strength of my point of view and come to agree with me.
5. While philosophers may spend a great deal of time sharing mere opinions, they can and should do more than that.
6. Philosophers can uncover the truth with at least as much confidence as scientists do.

(continued)

Philosophic Readiness Inventory (*continued*)

Rating Scale:

Strongly Agree						Strongly Disagree
1	2	3	4	5	6	7

---

7. While there may be more than one valid position on the value of exercise, not every philosophic conclusion on this issue is equally valid.

8. I believe that I can usually ignore my biases when reflecting on values.

9. I am convinced that there are many logical arguments that force me to agree with their conclusions.

10. Everything in life is not relative. I am confident that philosophy and/or religion can uncover solid and enduring values.

Set 3

1. Common sense cannot get me very far. I need a good education to reach my potential.

2. Much of the hope of the world rests with academic study and research.

3. A good general education in college is needed in order to have a better quality life.

4. Intellectuals should be highly respected and listened to.

5. A skilled football quarterback who is also a student of the game is preferable to one who is equally skilled but who learns only by playing experience.

6. Human beings are far superior to lower animals primarily because people can reflect on life and communicate through language.

7. Elementary teachers are underpaid and given too little respect in our society.

8. The rapid development of the discipline of physical education (including physiology, psychology of exercise, sociology of sport) over the past 30 years has been very good for the profession.

9. Experience is important but, without additional ideas and understanding, can be dangerous.

10. Good coaches, teachers, trainers, and sport businesspeople are not born. They are created, in part, through hard work and a good, scientifically sound education.

Add up the responses from each set for a subtotal, then add up the subtotals for a total PRQ. Compare your subtotals and total with the norms listed at the end of this chapter. Save your test paper, since you will be asked to complete the inventory again toward the end of the book and compare your two sets of scores.

---

be used to identify areas that need attention should you wish to raise your PRQ. Or they can be used simply to illuminate why you feel the way you do about philosophy.

If the philosophic process begins by asking questions with the intent to deal with them in some serious way, then curiosity, confidence, and commitment are all important indicators of the likelihood, frequency, and intensity of your getting started. Curiosity is the hook; it allows philosophic issues to look interesting, provocative, challenging, fun. Confidence is the sustainer; it suggests that partial or complete answers to philosophic puzzles are possible. It gets you seriously engaged and keeps you going when the first blush of intrigue may have worn off. Commitment is the justifier; it reflects your judgment that the whole process not only leads somewhere, but somewhere important—that philosophic answers can be valuable in their own right and that they can make a difference in the world.

Curiosity

Some of you as youngsters, or as parents reading to youngsters, encountered a storybook monkey named Curious George (Rey, 1952). This mischievous little primate was always getting into trouble because, try as he might, he could not say no to the many invitations he received to explore, experiment, dillydally, experience the world, or, in short, play. For instance, one day when Curious George was riding his bicycle by a pond en route to delivering his newspapers, it occurred to him that he could turn his papers into boats and float them on the water. True to his character, he could not resist this temptation. The boats were made, and the papers, needless to say, were not delivered.

Subscore 1 should give you some indication of your inherent interest in philosophic questions, of the degree to which you like to play with ideas, of your philosophic curiosity. This measure has to do with your tendencies to wonder, question, and ponder. It also tells about your capacity to be amazed, intrigued, even perplexed by the life you have and world in which you find yourself.

Confidence

All of you undoubtedly have at least some interest in philosophic issues. But whether your curiosity quotient (subscore 1) is high, low, or somewhere in between, you will also have a certain degree of confidence that this interest will lead somewhere. Most philosophers, of course, are looking for what might be called truth, or at least vague or partial truths. If you believe that thinking, reflecting, speculating, and using logic can achieve such ends, your confidence factor should be high. On the other hand if you, much like Professor Jones at the beginning of the chapter, have suspicions that things that cannot be physically measured really do not exist or that philosophers do little more than share opinions, your confidence score will undoubtedly be low.

As the sustainer, confidence provides you with the faith that your reflections may lead to some answers. With such a prospect in mind, you are likely to keep thinking, try out new ideas, study old or new religions, or talk seriously with fellow students about the meaning of life. On the other hand, if you have a high curiosity score but lack confidence in the philosophic process, it is unlikely that you will spend much time in philosophic reflection or debate. You will see philosophic questions as interesting, perhaps even important, but the prospects for finding any answers slim or nonexistent.

Commitment

The third factor in the inventory is commitment—specifically, commitment to the notion that philosophic truths or answers are valuable. It is possible, for example, to be full of wonder regarding philosophic questions (subscore 1) and confident that philosophic processes can lead to at least partial truths (subscore 2), but still uncertain that these answers have anything to do with your life in the real world. A low commitment subscore would indicate that you harbor suspicions about the worth of values and other ideas. You may not appreciate knolwedge for its own sake, or see any practical uses for philosophy, or both. You may think that theory is fine, as far as it goes, but think that it really does not go very far at all. You may put more faith in common sense, real-world experience, and everyday skills than in principles, notions, and theoretical possibilities.

In contrast, a high total for subscore 3 would indicate a commitment to philosophic conclusions as genuine knowledge and to philosophic truths as potential guides for your life on this planet. You may see this knowledge as valuable in its own right, whether or not you put it to use. Or you may reflect on purposes for some behavior, on your moral obligations, or on the values of one lifestyle in contrast to another before getting into action. That is, you use the results of your reflections in guiding your actions.

Interpreting Your PRQ

High or low total scores or subscores should not be a cause for personal congratulations or blame. This is because you probably had relatively little control over the development of these three attitudes or tendencies. They were cultivated by your parents, brothers, sisters, friends, teachers, and spiritual leaders; they were transmitted by television, newspapers, billboards, school textbooks— by everything that impinged on you from the beginning of your life until today. For all you know, some of these tendencies may even be genetically influenced. Regardless, you did not simply choose to be philosophically curious or disinterested, confident or skeptical,

and committed to the value of ideas and theories or not. This does not mean that these attitudes cannot be modified. In fact, becoming aware of them can be a first step in making changes. But, as with all deeply ingrained traits or tendencies, they are not recast quickly or easily.

Whatever your own status may be at this time, I am convinced that generous amounts of philosophic curiosity, confidence in the philosophic process, and commitment to the importance of philosophic insight are important both personally and professionally. If you too believe this and your PRQ was relatively high, then you are undoubtedly ready to begin the journey awaiting you in this book.

On the other hand, if your PRQ was relatively low, I hope that it will not stay there for long. I believe that something in these pages will catch your attention and bother you. Maybe it will be the disturbing image of a career without direction, or differences in your work when it is devoted to values like excellence or play rather than physical fitness and survival, or the way that human development can be arrested when bodies are treated like machines and movement like an impersonal mechanical process, or the provocative puzzles related to fair play and the importance of winning. You may wake up some night and realize that you cannot escape philosophic questions, or deny that there are reliably better and worse answers to them, or ignore their concrete implications for day-to-day living and a satisfying career.

Whatever you learned from taking the PRI, you should now have three answers ready for the question posed at the beginning of this section, namely, Why should a person even ask philosophic questions? You can say, "Because I am *curious*; because I wonder; because I need to stop my hectic pace of life sometimes and decide if all of this makes any sense; because I want to make sure that my personal and professional lives are headed somewhere; because playing with ideas is fun for its own sake."

You can also say, "Because I want answers to my questions and am *confident* that I can find some; because I think that the methods of philosophy actually work; because I believe that my reflections will help me uncover the truth or at least some partial truths."

And finally, you can say, "Because I am *committed* to the importance of philosophic insight; because I believe that philosophic conclusions count as significant knowledge in their own right; because I think that philosophic answers can and should make a difference in my personal and professional lives."

How Are Philosophic Questions Different From Other Questions?

Some people believe that philosophic questions are easy to spot. Perhaps then, you will have no difficulty in identifying which of the following questions are philosophic in nature:

- What is play?
- Is it morally acceptable to bend the rules of a game?
- Was that last 3-m dive beautiful?
- Why are athletes so often considered to be dumb jocks?
- Should physical education be required in the public schools? In our colleges and universities?

If you answered that all five are, or could be, philosophic questions, you are right. If you think that all five need not be philosophic questions, you are right again. This is so, because virtually any and all questions that people can think of offer some possibilities for philosophic analysis. But the opposite is also true. Virtually any and all questions can be approached from nonphilosophic directions.

The issue, then, becomes not so much one of finding unique questions that can be

viewed from a philosophic perspective but of locating the philosophic standpoint in contrast to others. For the five questions just listed, at least partial answers may come from perspectives taken by historians, physiologists, sociologists, and many others. But scholars in these three areas adopt a different standpoint than the one taken by philosophers. They look for answers in different places.

PHILOSOPHIC EXERCISE

Examine Table 1.1 and see if you can identify a common thread that runs through the data used by history, physiology, and sociology. Is the nature of the things they examine the same in any way? Try to determine if this thread is present in philosophy. Then answer the question, Where do philosophers look for answers in contrast to historians, physiologists, and sociologists?

Even though it would seem that questions having to do with the nature of reality (no. 1 in Table 1.1), ethics (no. 2), aesthetics (no. 3), the theory of knowledge (no. 4), and value theory (no. 5) would have little to do with history, physiology, and sociology, scholars from these fields can and do shed light on these topics. For example, can historians, using only their own tools, or sociologists, thinking only as sociologists, answer a question on aesthetics? Can they say with any authority whether or not that last dive was beautiful? They probably cannot. But they can shed light on the current philosophical understanding of beauty by investigating what was regarded as beautiful in previous eras (a historical analysis) or by examining actual attitudes toward beauty in contemporary society (a sociological study).

(Handwritten annotations: "EMPIRICAL TURN" above Physiology/Sociology columns; "PHILOSOPHIC TURN" above Philosophy column.)

Table 1.1 Examples of Multiple Perspectives

Question	History	Physiology	Sociology	Philosophy
1. What is play?	Can we find examples of play in ancient cultures?	Does play perform some function in maintaining physiological arousal?	What roles does play perform in different social organizations?	What are the essential characteristics of play? How is it different than work?
2. Is rule bending morally acceptable?	Did the Homeric Greeks bend game rules, and did they regard it as morally wrong to do so?	Is there any physiological response when players bend rules? Does the heart rate, for example, increase?	What are the norms in our society regarding rule-bending?	What arguments can be given to show that rule bending is morally wrong or right?
3. Was that last 3-m dive beautiful?	Have all cultures been impressed with beauty? Have conceptions of beauty changed?	Is there any way to quantify beauty? What were the anatomical and physiological components of that last dive?	Does our society value beauty? Are we socialized to see and appreciate beauty in diving?	What are the criteria of beauty, and did that last dive satisfy them?
4. Why are athletes so often considered dumb jocks?	Are there any historical occurrences or influences that would help us account for this current attitude?	Are there physiological indicators of intelligence and, if so, how do athletes compare with the general population?	What roles do athletes play in society, and do these roles typically include high intellectual expectations?	Are there different types of knowledge and, if so, how valuable is each type? Would the kinds of things athletes typically know count as impressive knowledge?
5. Should physical education be required in public schools?	What historical precedents might help us understand the merits and demerits of required physical education?	Are there such significant health benefits from physical education that it would be wise to require it in the schools?	Does the behavior of groups of people change in required settings in contrast to elective environments?	What is the value of physical education? Does this value justify the loss of freedom under a requirement?

To take another example, physiologists, using only the tools of physiology, cannot determine whether rule bending is morally acceptable or not. But they can provide facts about certain physiological responses to (and possibly also precursors of) rule bending. By measuring physiological responses, they may be able to indicate whether individuals perceive rule bending as morally improper cheating, on the one hand, or morally acceptable strategy, on the other. Lie detector procedures are based on the understanding that intentional lying is typically accompanied by identifiable and measurable physiological responses.

What then makes a question fair game for historians, physiologists, and sociologists in contrast to philosophers? How can a single question be turned in a historical, physiological, or sociological direction in contrast to a philosophic one? What is the common thread that runs through all of these nonphilosophic methods, a thread that is not present in philosophy?

✳The Empirical Turn

Historians, physiologists, sociologists, as well as psychologists, anthropologists, biologists, and other scientists take what might be called the **empirical turn**. They look for physical or factual evidence. They try to measure or interpret things that can be seen, heard, felt, tasted, or smelled. They analyze documents, electrical impulses, chemical reactions, spoken or written testimony, observed behavior, and the like. When asked to justify a conclusion or finding, they refer to measurable reactions, witnessed responses, or actual words on real parchments.

Just like philosophers, these scientists and scholars rely on meanings and obviously cannot avoid using concepts and ideas in their scientific work. Nevertheless, when it comes to answering questions, when it comes to looking for clues and evidence, they take the empirical turn. They look for something that can be found and measured by their senses, either directly (as when they find and read a primary source in history) or indirectly (as when they note an imperceptible physiological response by recording numbers from a digital counter).

To put this empirical commitment another way, a historian of sport, if asked whether the ancient Greeks engaged in much play, would not be likely to respond, "Let me apply only the laws of logic to that question, and I'll get back to you." A physiologist, if asked whether required physical education does children much good, would not be likely to respond, "Let me merely reflect on that for a few weeks." Or a sociologist, if asked whether athletes in our culture are generally thought to be dumb jocks, would not be likely to respond, "Let me just play with some ideas on this." The three would need to return to their material—primary historical sources, blood chemicals or pulse rates, or the reported attitudes of a number of subjects, respectively.

These examples are not meant to imply that scholars in each field must or even normally do stay strictly in their own areas. Many historians and physiologists, for example, find that they must also think philosophically in order to complete their research. Nor are the examples even meant to imply that these disciplines are healthy or useful constructs. It is undoubtedly important to seek answers to questions from many different directions at once. It is undoubtedly important that professionals in the exercise sciences and physical education be historians, physiologists, sociologists, philosophers, and other sorts of thinkers, at the same time. The point here is that there are a multitude of different and valid approaches to achieving understanding, illumination, and the truth.

✳The Philosophic Turn

Philosophers do not take the empirical turn. Rather, they look inward to find their data.

They reflect. They abstract. They describe, measure, and judge concepts. They employ the laws of logic. As philosophers, they want to clarify ideas, the nature of things, relationships, values, characteristics, and ways of knowing—not the actual weight of molecules, not the specific content of historical documents, not the physical characteristics of electrical impulses, not the fact that certain groups of people really had certain ideas at some time.

It is very important to note that this **philosophic turn** does not mean that philosophers cannot or do not concern themselves with physical reality or real-world experience. On the contrary, most of the material on which philosophers work is the stuff of human beings' day-to-day life—both physical reality (like chairs) and nonphysical things (like hope and friendship). But when an item like a chair is examined philosophically, it is not the actual presence of its color, weight, or chemical composition that is usually of concern. Rather, philosophers would want to know its nature conceptually or in principle, perhaps how chairs differ essentially from other objects. Or they might want to know how they perceive chairs and with what kind of assurance they know that they are there. In other words, they use the tools of reflection and logic, not those of actual perception and measurement.

It is also very important to note that this inward turn taken by philosophers does not mean that their methodology is not scientific, if scientific means careful, systematic, objective, and well grounded. Many philosophers in the past and some still today consider themselves to be scientists and their methods to be as rigorous as those of the physical sciences. As you will see later in this chapter, there are times when philosophic conclusions reach or approach the certainty of the laws of physics, for example.

Philosophers, in short, believe that ideas are important objects—that they can be held, turned around, looked at from different angles, measured reflectively, and shared with others. Because many scientists, working strictly as scientists, do not take ideas as data or count them as evidence, philosophers believe that empirical science cannot produce adequate descriptions of human life and behavior. Philosophers believe they have a partly distinctive realm in which to operate and one that needs and deserves attention.

This distinctive and important realm can be clarified by looking at the question about the ethics of rule bending. Philosophers would focus on the idea or conceptual side of this issue. They would ask themselves questions like the following: What is it to bend a rule rather than break one? Is there some distinction in principle that can be applied here so people know exactly what they are talking about? For example, is faking a foul in basketball by pretending to be knocked down an instance of rule breaking, rule bending, or neither? On what criteria will philosophers decide if this behavior or some other questionable action is morally defensible? On the criterion of keeping promises? On preventing harm? On playing fairly? On promoting the greatest happiness? On something else? How then does rule bending stack up on these measures? Is it morally acceptable behavior? Should coaches be advised to use and condone it or not?

These are complex and probing questions. Persuasive answers to them may not be easy to find.

Lingering Doubts

If these questions frighten you, on the one hand, or raise old skeptical feelings about the impossibility of finding any real answers, on the other, your fears and doubts may not be entirely misplaced, nor are they unusual. The culture in which you live does not promote good philosophic training, nor does it generally teach you to trust your powers of

What criteria should we use to decide if certain sport behaviors are morally defensible?

reflection. If you are like many individuals today, you are probably far more comfortable retreating to something you can really sink your teeth into, something you can actually see or feel.

But infinite amounts of empirical observation still are not sufficient. Consider that:

• You can study all the historical cultures of the world and examine the extent to which they bent game rules. This may tell you a great deal about these cultures, and you may even learn if they felt such activity was morally right. But this does not directly address the question of whether or not rule bending should be accepted.

• You can study all the physiological conditions and responses associated with rule bending for years on end. This may tell you a great deal about why people behave in this way and how they react after doing so. It may tell you much about nervous responses and how these are affected by this questionable behavior. But this does not directly address the question of whether or not rule bending should be condoned.

• You can study all of the groups and subgroups of people you can find to determine their behaviors, motives, perceptions, and values. This may tell you a great deal about why rule bending is so widely practiced, about why so few people think of it as morally wrong, about how peers pressure one another into rule-bending behavior. But this does not directly address the question of whether or not rule bending should be regarded as morally acceptable.

Consequently, in attempting to subdue this question about rule bending, no one can avoid traveling in the company of ideas.

This does not mean, however, that philosophers retreat to some clean world of the mind where all distinctions have sharp lines between them, where all values neatly rank themselves, and where all *should*s and *shouldn't*s are clearly listed. To a degree, at least, the realm of ideas is continuous with empirical reality, with nature. Your ideas are affected by the number of brain cells you have and the chemicals that are contained in them. Your ideas are influenced by your parents, teachers, friends, by your religious background, by where and when you were born, and so on. When you retreat, as it were, into the world of reflection, you retreat to an uncertain arena where you will carry on a battle for objectivity. You must fight to distinguish old biases and unexamined religious beliefs, for instance, from genuine insights.

What Is the Range of Philosophic Questions?

In the course of this book, you will be looking at several different types of philosophic questions in relationship to sport, exercise science, and physical education. It will be useful to define these questions and to look at examples of each that are related to different claims about reality.

1. Questions Having to Do With the Nature of Things. This is an area of philosophy traditionally called **metaphysics**. It is concerned with what things and actions are and how they are similar to or dissimilar from one another. It is descriptive. It lays out the qualities, characteristics, features, or aspects of physical things like chairs, nonphysical things like hope, speculative things like heaven, and all forms of action like running and believing.

What *is* this? How is it different from that? A child confronts metaphysical questions every day.

Sample metaphysical claim: Dancers are more creative than athletes.

Related metaphysical questions: What is the nature of sport? What is the nature of dance? What are the characteristics of creativity? Do the structures of sport and dance prohibit, merely allow for, actually promote, or truly require creativity? Assuming that creativity is at least minimally compatible both with sport competition and dance performances, how are creative acts similar and dissimilar in these two activities?

2. Questions Having to Do With the Value of Things. This is an area of philosophy usually labeled **axiology**. It attempts to uncover reasons for calling certain things, actions, or states of affairs good. Rather than being concerned with what is (the nature of things), it focuses on what should be. Rather than looking at the qualities and characteristics of certain actions, it asks how people should act. It looks at specific values such as excellence and truth and broad values such as the composition of the good life.

Sample axiological claim: Youth league sports are good for children.

Related axiological questions: What specific values are available in competitive situations? In what ways are these values good or healthy? Is competition itself a positive value? Is attempting to defeat a person in a game the same thing as attempting to harm him or her? What are the relationships between competition, on the one hand, and such values as love, justice, fairness, friendship, honesty, and enjoyment, on the other? Might sport be valuable in different ways for children than for adults? What might these different ways be?

3. Questions Having to Do With Good Behavior. This area is often called **ethics**. It is closely related to axiology and is very much concerned with what is good in life, but it focuses on how people affect people for better or worse. It looks both at how individuals should treat one another and how they should treat themselves.

Sample ethical claim: It is morally wrong to take anabolic steroids to enhance performance.

Related ethical questions: On what grounds is it wrong? Because it is unfair? Illegal? Dangerous to one's health? Coercive? Unnatural? Opposed to the spirit of play? What if such drug taking were legalized, and what if users were consenting adults who were made aware of its potentially harmful side effects? Would it still be wrong to take the drug to enhance performance, and, if so, why?

4. Questions Having to Do With What People Know. This branch of philosophy is called **epistemology**. It is about the theory of knowledge—about what human beings know, how they know it, and with what assurance they hold different beliefs or have different insights. It looks at very specific issues of understanding, such as the knowledge that may be present in young children's reflexes, as well as larger problems, such as doubts about people's ability to know anything at all.

Sample epistemological claim: In order to be a good coach, teacher, or trainer, a person must have first been a good athlete, dancer, or performer.

Related epistemological questions: What is the relationship between playing basketball, for example, and teaching it? Are playing skills, traits, and tendencies the same things as teaching skills, traits, and tendencies? What kinds of knowledge or insights might be available to a former athlete, dancer, or exerciser that would not be available to the coach, teacher, or trainer who did not have a performance background? If there are any such unique perspectives and understandings, how important are these to good teaching, coaching, or training?

5. Questions Having to Do With What Is Beautiful. This is the area of **aesthetics**. Like axiology, it is concerned with what is good. But aesthetics focuses specifically on matters of sensual, artistic good—on what is beautiful or pleasing to the eyes, ears, palate, or sense of touch; on what is balanced, harmonious, expressive; and so on.

Sample aesthetic claim: Figure skating today is not as beautiful as it once was because skaters, coaches, and judges are placing ever increasing emphasis on athleticism.

Related aesthetic questions: What exactly is athleticism? Are the requirements of athleticism (such as the display of strength in multiple rotation jumps) necessarily in opposition to the requirements of beauty? Are challenges presented by aesthetics as demanding as the challenges presented by athletic displays of speed, power, and jumping ability? Is there an ideal balance to be struck between these two emphases in figure skating? If so, what would it be?

PHILOSOPHIC EXERCISE

To make certain that you have a sense for the range and philosophic character of the five issues listed, you should now attempt to make at least one additional claim under each of them and list questions appropriate for each. If necessary, return to my samples on the previous pages to help you establish a pattern for writing claims and questions.

SUMMARY BREAK

There are three reasons for asking philosophic questions.

1. They are interesting and arouse curiosity.
2. Real progress can be made in answering them. Thus, they generate confidence in philosophic methods.
3. Answers to these questions can be informative in their own right and useful for making decisions and guiding one's life. Thus, they produce commitment to the philosophic process.

Virtually every question can be a philosophic question. Likewise, many questions can be dealt with historically, physiologically, sociologically, mathematically, chemically, genetically, in religious terms, and so on. Philosophers tackle questions differently because they refuse to take the empirical turn. Their data, their objects of inquiry, are typically under a reflective microscope, not one that sits in a physiology laboratory.

Philosophic questions may be metaphysical (concerning the nature of reality), axiological (concerning values and what should be), ethical (concerning good behavior), epistemological (concerning knowledge), and aesthetic (concerning beauty).

Developing Skill in Pursuing Philosophic Answers

Having learned to ask philosophic questions, we now turn to the next step in the philosophic process, the search for answers. Here too you will need to focus on certain skills and practice them.

How Do You Begin?

Philosophers, just like any scientists, must have some data to work on. It has already been noted that philosophers do this primarily through acts of reflection. That is, they recollect or picture something and, in a sense, hold it there, turn it around, and look it over.

Thus, you need an issue, a problem, some question to work on. You could select one from any of the five areas of philosophy discussed earlier, and it would probably serve you well in allowing you to practice your reflective skills. For our purposes here, we will begin with an axiological issue: What is at the heart of good sportsmanship?

Because we are taking our cue from eight words arranged in an English sentence, we would be wise to make sure that we are all thinking about the same thing. If there is to be any realistic hope for consensus, it is essential that all of us put the same item under scrutiny. To do this, we will need to clarify several key words or groups of words. You may have already identified three of the most important and potentially ambiguous words or phrases to be *at the heart*, *good*, and *sportsmanship*.

At the heart means essential, central, of the utmost importance. In other words, in looking at good sportsmanship, we will be attempting to find one basic characteristic or, at most, a small number of features that best distinguish it from other things—like poor sportsmanship, for instance. If we are successful in finding one or more things "at the heart" of good sportsmanship, we would expect to see that characteristic or those few features in all, or virtually all, examples of good sportsmanship—in ethical sandlot football, ethical Olympic tennis, ethical major league baseball, and so forth. And conversely, because we are looking for essential characteristics of good sportsmanship, we will ignore those items that may occasionally be present in some sport settings but need not be there.

Good means everything in a range from morally obligatory to praiseworthy behavior. That is, we will be looking for characteristics of positive behavior, behavior that would warrant approval, whether this is a duty (an occasion for expected moral behavior) or an optional action (an opportunity for unexpected or noble moral behavior).

Finally, I define *sportsmanship* as moral behavior in sport, where *moral* is an ethically neutral term (there is both good and bad sportsmanship), where *sport* is limited to physically oriented competitive games, and where sports*man*ship means moral behavior of persons, not just males. Sportsmanship, in short, has to do not with what is but with what ought to be regarding the behavior of both genders in vigorous competitive games. And this is not the *ought* of strategy or biomechanics (you ought to hold your racket higher if you want to generate more power) but rather that of ethics (you ought to follow the rules in tennis because you promised your opponent that you would do so).

More space could be used to clarify our question, but by now you should be reasonably confident that you have a clear object for analysis. In short, you now understand that we are looking for one essential feature (or a small number of features) of morally right ways of participating in physically oriented competitive games. (Of course, we could have chosen to look at something else, like gambling, and could have manipulated the language to label morally right behavior in gambling "sportsmanship." Although this might be an unusual use of the English language, what matters is that we can distinguish one thing from another and can keep an item under our reflective gaze as we analyze it.) Now we can start looking for answers.

How Should You Proceed With the Analysis?

Just as there are many ways to hit a forehand successfully in tennis, there are a number of procedures that work in philosophy. And just as fine tennis players do not worry about what technique they happen to be using any given moment, your philosophic thinking should develop to a point where it is done naturally and automatically. Nevertheless, there are a number of proven techniques that philosophers over the centuries have used. I will introduce three of the most fundamental procedures here. While I begin with inductive reasoning and follow with intuitive and deductive procedures, these three methodologies may be used singly or in any order.

Inductive Reasoning

Inductive reasoning is based on our ability to move from the small to the large, the specific to the general, from concrete examples to abstract understandings. If we were analyzing oranges, we might want to line up four or five types of oranges in front of us and try to identify general characteristics that accurately describe all of them in spite of their individual differences. We might want to say something about their shape, color, and structure—qualities that distinguish them, in general, from other objects like potatoes, bananas, and baseballs.

To answer our own question, begin by gathering examples of good sportsmanship. Your goal will be to identify common threads or general principles that accurately describe all the specific examples of good behavior in competitive games that you have collected, in spite of their individual differences. It does not matter if the examples that you gather are faithful representations of events that happened in actual games, because you are not doing sport history or sociology. What matters is that your examples of sportsmanship are genuine, noncontroversial examples of good moral behavior. Remember, your goal is to identify the essence of good moral behavior in sport. Nothing is gained by gambling on a questionable example, and obviously your conclusions would be skewed if you looked at examples of behavior that did not depict good sportsmanship. In short, your list of examples should be clean or non-controversial.

How can you be expected to develop a list of examples of sportsmanship before you understand what is at the heart of this very concept? Actually it is not very difficult at all. In coming up with examples of good sportsmanship, you are trusting your implicit ability to make simple identifications, even though you may not yet be able to describe good sportsmanship's significant features. You deal with most of your world in this way. For instance, you can probably tell play from work, pleasure from discomfort, and love from hatred in your daily life, but yet you may not be able to clearly define them or write essays about their unique characteristics. You can go to the grocery store and find tomatoes even though you have never considered how tomatoes differ essentially from bananas and broccoli. Consequently, you should be able to pick out examples of good sportsmanship even before you can say much about it or describe philosophically how good and poor sportsmanship are different.

A list of examples of good sportsmanship might look something like this:

1. A football player, after knocking down his opponent with a legal but forceful block, extends a hand and asks the opponent (out of genuine concern for his well-being) if he is OK.

2. A baseball coach insists that his pitchers not scuff, cut, or apply any foreign substance to baseballs even though he knows that doctoring the balls will increase his pitchers' effectiveness and that pitchers from some of the other teams in the league frequently break these rules.

3. A basketball coach attempts to make sure that all visiting teams are treated with the utmost respect and are extended all the necessary courtesies, from the physical facilities utilized before and after the game to

hometown fan behavior during the game. She realizes that she will enjoy some home court advantage in spite of the most respectful treatment of the visiting team, but she feels obligated not to exaggerate that advantage by treating opponents in anything less than a hospitable way.

4. In an unofficiated high school tennis match, Player A hits an unreturnable drive that lands a full 3 inches behind Opponent B's baseline. Player B, blinded momentarily by the sun, calls the shot "in." However, A is not willing to accept a point she did not earn. She informs B of the error and, with B's concurrence, corrects the score.

5. A soccer coach knows that a rule designed to prevent stalling by a winning team near the end of a game is unenforceable. Even so, he instructs his players not to use the stalling tactics that are nonetheless employed illegally by other teams.

A longer list of good sportsmanlike conduct could be developed and might even be more useful than this short collection of examples. However, this group of five cases of morally good behavior should be sufficient. What is important here is that you have an uncontroversial set of positive moral behaviors.

PHILOSOPHIC EXERCISE

Because you are looking for one essential characteristic of good sportsmanship, or a small number of central features, you must attempt to abstract one or a few features common to all of these examples of moral behavior. You must ask yourself, Are there any common threads that run through all of these cases of good sportsmanship, and, if so, what are they?

If no answers to the Philosophic Exercise jump out at you immediately, try a few possibilities with me:

- A central characteristic of good sportsmanship is the correction of all wrong calls in a game, assuming that they are clearly observed and are correctable.

This is not a good choice, for it is a featured concern only in the tennis example (4). Because the other examples also show good sportsmanship in spite of the fact that they do not involve the correction of all observed and correctable calls in a game, this characteristic is probably not essential to the presence of good sportsmanship. Moreover, because there may not even be opportunities to correct calls in some unofficiated games, this action is probably too specific. We need to look further for a more comprehensive thread that unites the examples.

- A central characteristic of good sportsmanship is concern for the safety and physical well-being of players, including one's opponents.

This seems to be present in examples 1 and 3. The football player exhibits a genuine concern for the physical condition of his opponent after a forceful collision, and the basketball coach wants to assure that visiting opponents are treated as guests. We could argue that the people involved in the other examples also care about the physical well-being of teammates and opponents, even though it was not this issue that put them on our list. At least there is nothing to suggest that they are indifferent to problems of physical injury. Furthermore, almost every sport we can think of probably includes at least some possibility of physical harm.

The only problem is that such concerns may be too broad. Attention to health and safety is an obligation in virtually everything

we do, both at work and at play. Caring physically for ourselves and our neighbors, therefore, may not tell us much about the essence of ethics in sport. It would be helpful to find something that is both common to all of our examples of competitive activity but also more specific to competitive games.

- Because sport is a rule-governed and rule-created activity, a central characteristic of good sportsmanship is a commitment to play strictly by the rules of the game.

This would appear to be the best conclusion so far. The coach who refuses to let his pitchers illegally doctor baseballs, the tennis player who cannot accept an illegally won point, and the soccer coach who would not take advantage of an unenforceable rule all show an uncompromising commitment to play by the rules.

Examples 1 and 3 do not say anything about following rules per se. However, they do not contradict our tentative conclusion about faithfully following the rules. There is nothing in these accounts that would suggest that the football player and basketball coach disregard game rules when the game is on.

In any case, a commitment to play strictly by game rules remains our best conclusion so far. Even if there are better conclusions than this one, rule adherence should strike us as a feature that is much more central to any conception of good sportsmanship than the more specific and occasionally present feature of correcting erroneous calls and the exceedingly broad issue of promoting physical well-being. This may be because rules have a special or privileged logical relationship to games and game playing. If that is so, it is not surprising that morally right behavior in competitive games is inextricably bound up with some notion of following the rules.

This counts as philosophic progress even if it was a modest gain. With some confidence now, you can state that a commitment to play strictly by the rules of the game is an essential feature of good sportsmanship. This was present in all of our examples of good ethical behavior during play, and you would expect to find it in examples that we have not reviewed.

Intuitive Reasoning

Rather than relying on our ability to induce general principles from a number of specific examples as was done with inductive reasoning, **intuitive reasoning** is based on our ability to see something directly and describe what we see. Thus, we do not have to gather multiple examples of our object of interest. For our question, all that is needed is a single example of good behavior in sport. We can then go to work on that, by varying it and looking for essential features.

This is a very powerful method that can help you understand, for example, what might be called the building blocks of notions like good sportsmanship. The principle of the operation is fairly simple. You imagine an example of good behavior in sport and then play with it, vary it, change it in some way. If a critical building block is removed as a result of a variation, you will know it because the whole building called sportsmanship will fall. Sportsmanship, in the absence of this building block, will no longer be thinkable or intelligible. On the other hand, if a building block that is not critical to the integrity of sportsmanship is removed, you will know this too because sportsmanship will still be there.

PHILOSOPHIC EXERCISE

You can employ intuitive reasoning to make further progress on the earlier conclusion that good sportsmanship requires a strict adherence to the rules of the game. For purposes of analysis, place a game of basketball in front of your reflective gaze and vary it. You may want to walk through this next reflective exercise with me. (It is also summarized in Table 1.2.) Then you can try the process on your own with an image from another sport.

Let us picture a basketball player following the official NCAA rules religiously. He guards correctly, uses legal equipment, does not attempt to deceive officials into making incorrect calls, and so on. Except for occasional accidental fouls that all basketball players make, this individual plays by the rule book. He will look for and take no competitive advantage that is not clearly permitted in the rules.

Table 1.2   Intuiting Good Sportsmanship

Variation	Judgment
1. You are picturing a basketball player following the rules—shooting, passing, dribbling	Sportsmanship is still present here
2. You are picturing a basketball player finding a loop-hole in the rules and taking advantage of it	It is not clear that sportsmanship remains
3. You are picturing a player breaking the rules for purposes of promoting safety or justice	Sportsmanship is still present here

Conclusion: Good sportsmanship does not appear to be guaranteed simply by rule adherence, and poor sportsmanship is not guaranteed simply by rule violations.

Can good sportsmanship disappear even when players are following the rules?

As we reflect on this rule-abiding behavior in basketball do we also see the uninterrupted presence of good sportsmanship? Does the structure or building called good sportsmanship still stand? We will probably conclude that it does. These variations, all of which leave sportsmanlike behavior intact, would appear to support our earlier conclusion that strict adherence to the written rules lies at (or near) the heart of good sportsmanship. But have we done a sufficient number of variations to be reasonably sure about this?

Probably not. We need to vary our subject matter some more, reflect on other types of legal behavior in basketball, and see if good sportsmanship may actually (and surprisingly) disappear. We need to probe for actions that are allowed but yet are morally questionable or improper, if indeed any exist.

As we continue with our reflections, we now picture our basketball player finding a loophole in the rules. This is behavior that is perfectly and clearly legal. But it also may be in violation of the intent of the rules. It may be a behavior that the rule makers knew about but forgot to prohibit or one that they simply never considered when writing the rules.

Such incidents are not difficult to bring to mind. A famous example of loophole finding occurred in a college basketball game a number of years ago. At that time the rules for foul shooting required that the free thrower not step on or in front of the free-throw line before the ball had passed through the cylinder. There happened to be a very large center who was a notoriously poor foul shooter—that is, until he figured out a new method for shooting free throws. He would stand with the ball near mid-court, run toward the foul line, leap from the floor behind the line, fly through the air, and stuff the ball through the basket. Indeed, the shot was perfectly legal. The shooter had not stepped in front of the line before his free throw had passed through the cyclinder. The rule on foul shooting was revised the next season specifically to prohibit this form of free-throw shooting, one that the rule makers had never anticipated and, of course, had never wanted to condone.

We must ask, in the presence of this rule-following behavior does good sportsmanship nevertheless disappear? Have we taken away some important foundation stone of moral behavior in sport? If good sportsmanship disappears or at least grows dimmer, then it may be that we have intuited that there is something more fundamental to good sportsmanship than mere rule keeping. You and I may not be sure yet what that is, but we know it is there because we lost sportsmanship, or at least came to doubt its presence, while reflecting on a perfectly legal, though loophole-oriented, activity. We may want to conclude that playing strictly by the written rules is not sufficient for meeting the requirements of good sportsmanship. We may think, in other words, that there is no one-to-one correlation between playing by the rules and being a good sport. But we are not sure.

More variations may be needed. In order to test our tentative conclusion, why not look for the reverse situation? Rather than searching for examples of rule following that show poor sportsmanship, we might look for cases of rule breaking that are consistent with good sportsmanship. In other words, we will try to find an instance of blatant rule breaking that allows us to intuit that good sportsmanship is still intact.

We can picture a situation in basketball in which a player illegally grabs an opponent, but does so for the purpose of keeping the opponent from falling into the stands and injuring himself. Or we can picture a situation in which officials relax the rule on traveling because a certain gymnasium floor is smooth and glassy. Players on both teams travel on numerous occasions. However, in order to keep the game moving and not penalize players for something that is beyond their control, only the most blatant instances are called. Or to take an even more extreme

variation, we can imagine that an official has made an obviously wrong call late in a game that is tied. Players and coaches on both teams saw what really happened. Yet, the ball is to go unjustly to one of the teams. A player on this team, not wanting to win on such a call, decides to travel intentionally as soon as he receives the inbounds pass. He reasons that this will return the ball to the team that deserved it in the first place.

Perhaps you will conclude that, in spite of these rule-breaking variations, sportsmanship stayed intact throughout. It could even be that such rule breaking is associated with very high and optional standards of sportsmanship. In any case, your suspicions about the lack of a one-to-one correlation between rule following and good sportsmanship, on the one hand, and rule breaking and poor sportsmanship, on the other, seem to be on target.

We should be fairly confident, then, that there is something more fundamental than playing by existing rules to explain one of the central features of good sportsmanship. We may not yet know what that is, for our variations on rule following and breaking have only pointed out that good sportsmanship does not appear to be guaranteed simply by rule adherence, nor does bad sportsmanship seem to be guaranteed simply by rule violations.

Again, you have made some progress. Your understanding of sportsmanship is more sophisticated and, hopefully, more accurate. Normally, you might want to say, in conclusion, that good sportsmanship requires that one follow the printed rules, but there appear to be exceptions to this—where people should follow rules that do not exist, on the one hand, and should violate rules that do exist, on the other.

What principle or building block will explain both this normal sportsmanlike behavior and these exceptions? You would probably need to do some more variations to find out, but there is no space here to pursue this question any further. The analysis that has been provided should be sufficient to show how this method of taking a single example, varying it, and intuiting conclusions works.

Deductive Reasoning

Rather than beginning with specific examples and inducing broader principles (inductive reasoning), or taking a single example and attempting to intuit the truth directly (intuitive reasoning), **deductive reasoning** requires that you begin with one or more broad claims and then look for specific facts that logically follow from them. It is possible to begin with a fact (some proposition whose truth has been demonstrated) or a hypothesis (some proposition whose truth is still in question) and attempt to see what follows. Derivations from facts often take the form, "Because this is the case, then such-and-such must be true." Derivations from hypotheses often take the form, "If this is the case, then such-and-such must be true." For our question, we would begin with facts or hypotheses about good sportsmanship and attempt to derive further information.

PHILOSOPHIC EXERCISE

You can pursue your earlier analyses about rule-governed behavior and the nature of sportsmanship in the following way: (1) If it is true that playing only by the written rules does not necessarily satisfy the requirements of morally good behavior in physically oriented competitive games, and (2) if it is true that violating some written rules under certain circumstances can satisfy the requirements of morally good behavior in these

settings, then what follows? Check my example in Table 1.3 (next page) and see if you can add any more of your own.

To make sure that the reasoning in the table is tight, we would need to define more clearly several terms in the premises—words like *playing by*, *violating*, *satisfy*, and *requirements*. Any new words in the conclusions would also have to be clarified. For instance, the terms *go beyond* and *simple allegiance* in the third conclusion require this treatment. Nevertheless, it is possible that these three deductive conclusions are fully justified by the two premises with which we began. Once again, this counts as progress in understanding what is at the heart of good sportsmanship.

How Do You Know That You Have Reached a Valid Conclusion?

Physiologists and other empirical scientists speak of degrees of confidence in their answers, and philosophers do too. Some scientific findings are virtually inescapable. Statistical procedures employed in empirical methodologies indicate in these cases that it is extremely unlikely that the outcome could have been produced by chance events. As you will see, there is an analog to this in philosophy. There are conclusions that are virtually inescapable. For example, our deductive conclusion that anyone wanting to fully satisfy the requirements of good sportsmanship would have to go beyond a simple allegiance to the written rules *must* be true if our two premises are valid. This conclusion follows logically and necessarily from the premises.

Nevertheless, in both empirical science and philosophy, there are far more cases in which conclusions must be held tentatively. And it

Table 1.3   Good Sportsmanship Through Deduction

Premise: If it is true that . . .	Conclusions: Then it must follow that . . .
Playing only by the written rules does not necessarily satisfy the requirements of sportsmanship and violating some written rules in certain circumstances can satisfy the requirements of sportsmanship.	Anyone playing entirely by the written rules may or may not be satisfying the requirements of good sportsmanship. Anyone violating one or more of the written rules may or may not be satisfying the requirements of good sportsmanship. Anyone wanting to fully satisfy the requirements of good sportsmanship would have to go beyond simple allegiance to the written rules.

is rare, if ever, that absolute certainty is achieved.

Pitfalls of Inductive Reasoning

In the first exercise for inductive reasoning, we took five examples of good sportsmanship and attempted to find a general characteristic or thread that ran through all of them. Our conclusion, or at least the one that we found to be the strongest of the three we considered, was that sportsmanship requires a commitment to play strictly by the rules of the game.

However, we further analyzed this conclusion and found it to be lacking. Based on this hindsight, we should have originally placed only a low degree of confidence in this earlier finding. Do you recall how you felt when you came upon this conclusion about playing strictly by the rules? Did it strike you as being *the* answer to the puzzle about sportsmanship?

Several important sources for error can be identified in this type of philosophic reasoning. First, questions can be raised about the examples of sportsmanship that got onto the list that I supplied. Are they all examples of sportsmanship? Are they all examples of the

same kind of sportsmanship? Of course, if this list of particulars from which we induced a broader conclusion is flawed in any way, our conclusions are likely to reflect this.

Second, this list of examples is very short. Would we have seen something else had we found 10, 20, or 30 examples of sportsmanship? And even if we had taken the time to develop a list of 30 examples, could we ever be absolutely sure that the next example we encounter would not force us to modify our conclusion? Probably not. We must assume that our list accurately represents all past, present, and future instances of good sportsmanship.

In short, inductive reasoning operates under twin uncertainties:

1. Examples may be biased or simply wrong. That is, they may not be examples of the thing in question.
2. The list of examples may be misleadingly incomplete. One additional item might force a very different conclusion.

However, for all of the uncertainties raised by this method and in spite of the inaccurate conclusion that it produced on this occasion, our reflections here were not a waste of time.

They alerted us to the issue of rule adherence. They put us on a trail that later led to a more accurate and illuminating conclusion. In addition, the answer produced by this method was not far off the mark. Sportsmanship, after all, has *something* to do with a commitment to play strictly by the rules of the game, even though it turned out to be more than this.

Pitfalls of Intuitive Reasoning

Here we took a single example of participation in basketball and reflectively varied it, observing whether good sportsmanship remained or disappeared. Our hope was to find central building blocks of sportsmanship. Our assumption was that if, through our variations, we removed a critical foundation stone to sportsmanship, good sportsmanship would fall. We found that, when we looked at certain variations of playing strictly by the written rules (the strange but legal foul shot), sportsmanship disappeared or at least grew dimmer. We were compelled to conclude that adherence to written rules does not necessarily satisfy the requirements of sportsmanship. How much confidence should we place in this apparent insight?

Is it possible that any disappearance of sportsmanship during our variations was due to some biases held prior to the analysis, perhaps to some beliefs promoted by our parents or a coach about just how far athletes should go in stretching the rules? Certainly, this could have happened. That is why it was important to certify these results by trying other variations. In fact, we did follow-up variations where a certain kind of rule breaking (grabbing an opponent to promote safety, modifying rules about traveling when playing on a slippery basketball floor, and breaking a rule to promote fairness) did not eliminate the presence of sportsmanship. This should have helped to certify our earlier conclusion about the disjunction between following the written rules and the requirements of good sportsmanship.

As a check, it would also be useful to ask others to think up their own examples and counterexamples, to see if they come to the same or similar results. Most importantly, it is critical to continue with the variations and resultant descriptions until something significant is laid bare.

You and I did not get that far. Although we discovered that something closer to the heart of sportsmanship lay hidden behind merely following the written rules and avoiding their violation, we did not put our finger on what that "something" is. If we had come up with more variations, we might have obtained clearer, more significant results, and confidence in our conclusions about relationships between rule adherence and sportsmanship would probably have increased. We might even have reached the point where we would claim that certain specific relationships are necessary ones, that we had discovered at least one firm truth about good sportsmanship.

Pitfalls of Deductive Reasoning

We began here with some givens or premises that I supplied and then attempted to deduce conclusions. I supplied three examples. If my reasoning was accurate, and assuming that I had sufficiently tied down the meanings of all critical terms, these sample conclusions were necessary. They were wholly warranted or required by the information given in the premises. Consequently, we should have a great deal of confidence in these conclusions. Something that is logically required must be that way, both today and tomorrow, for all people, whether we want to believe it or not.

Nevertheless, we must still remain cautious, for deductive conclusions are helpful only if our premises are sound. Factual, reliable premises are not always easy to come by. In addition, even when our premises are valid, we may still make errors of deduction.

We need to have others certify our deductions to see if they truly make as much sense as we originally thought they did.

Review

Philosophy is the art and science of wondering about reality, posing questions related to that wonder, and pursuing answers to those questions reflectively. Philosophic questions are everywhere and are virtually impossible to avoid altogether. Almost any question can be turned in philosophic and nonphilosophic directions, and philosophers attempt to answer questions reflectively—without taking the empirical turn. There are several different types of philosophic questions, which variously address the nature of things, value, good behavior, knowledge, and beauty. The tendency to ask and pursue philosophic questions is related to one's philosophic curiosity, confidence, and commitment—measured in this chapter by the Philosophic Readiness Inventory.

Skill is involved in finding answers to philosophic questions. First, it is important to define the object to be analyzed. Analysis can proceed on a given question using a variety of methods, including those that are inductive, intuitive, and deductive in nature. Each one can be employed successfully and can produce conclusions deserving varying degrees of confidence.

Looking Ahead

In chapter 2 you will ask questions about the nature of human beings and use your reflective skills to draw conclusions about what people are and what they are not. You will review the idea that a human being is a composite of mind and body and that physical education should focus its energies on the physical part of persons. In chapter 3 you will review a contrasting claim that a human being is a whole individual and that physical education should focus its energies on whole persons. All of this preliminary hiking is necessary to allow you to travel through the more difficult terrain of Part II, where you will encounter different interpretations of the good life and how sport, exercise science, and physical education can contribute to it. There you will be reflecting on how the activity-related professions can best strengthen the fabric of our society and improve the lives of individual people. Of course, you cannot do this until you know what it is to be a person.

Checking Your Understanding

1. Can you describe your own readiness to do philosophy in terms of curiosity, confidence, and commitment? On the basis of your own personal experiences and background, can you explain your scores on the Philosophic Readiness Inventory?
2. Take a general question such as, What is the value of sport? and describe how a philosopher, historian, sociologist, and physiologist might go about answering it. In general, what is the difference between the way philosophers answer their questions and the way scholars in these other fields answer theirs?
3. Describe the range of philosophic questions. For example, take a topic like modern dance and formulate at least one question about it from each of the five areas of philosophy.
4. Explain why it is important to begin a philosophic analysis with definitions,

clarifications, and descriptions of what is being analyzed.

5. Describe the three philosophic methods used in this chapter and explain how they differ from one another. Use them on a new philosophic question such as, What is the meaning of "winning"?

6. Identify at least one strength and one weakness of each of the three methods. Which one do you like best, and why?

Key Terms

Philosophy, p. 4

Philosophic process, p. 4

Empirical turn, p. 13

Philosophic turn, p. 14

Metaphysics, p. 16

Axiology, p. 16

Ethics, p. 16

Epistemology, p. 17

Aesthetics, p. 17

Inductive reasoning, p. 19

Intuitive reasoning, p. 22

Deductive reasoning, p. 25

Further Reading

For a comprehensive overview of the traditional field of philosophy in relationship to sport, exercise science, and physical education, see Osterhoudt (1991). For the best anthologies that address the five types of philosophic questions identified in this chapter, see Morgan and Meier (1988) and Vanderwerken and Wertz (1985). For a helpful discussion of doing philosophy, see Harper (1985).

Norms for the Philosophic Readiness Inventory

Category	Low	Middle	High
Set 1 Philosophic curiosity	33-70	24-32	10-23
Set 2 Philosophic confidence	35-70	26-34	10-25
Set 3 Philosophic commitment	32-70	23-31	10-22
Total PRQ	100-210	73-99	30-72

Chapter 2

Dualism: Bodies Separated From Persons

Irene Cramer is a personal fitness trainer in New York City. She works for a company that has contracts with various large hotels. Guests at these hotels who want the services of a personal trainer call Irene's company to set up appointments for a fitness assessment or guided workouts. Irene likes her job. Because her hours are flexible, she has time to spend with her husband and children. She loves the city, and she enjoys the variety of people she meets. Often former clients specifically ask for Irene when they return to town on business.

Irene, however, has a long-standing problem with herself, one that continues to nag her as she now approaches middle age. She frequently deals with her own body as a thing to be evaluated, manipulated, changed, and evaluated again. She thinks of her body as a machine—one that is in constant need of repair or improvement. She works on her own body very much like she works professionally on improving the appearance and fitness of others. Irene is never satisfied with her appearance. Though she is fit and not overweight, she frequently finds fault with the way she looks or feels. "How odd!" she muses. "Here I am, a 35-year-old fitness trainer in good health and reasonably good shape, and I am not comfortable with my body. Life would go so much easier if I could forget my body and just live!"

Why do people like Irene separate themselves from their bodies, perhaps even to the point of opposing them? Are there any good psychological or philosophical reasons for separating persons from their bodies? Is it good, for example, to treat bodies simply as machines?

Your philosophic travels in the last chapter provided you with some skills that will be needed in the analysis ahead. Inductive, intuitive, and deductive reasoning skills will all be required if you are to successfully address the topic at hand. Here you will begin to search for answers to the question, What is a person?

IN THIS CHAPTER, YOU WILL

- **learn about four images of human nature that separate bodies from persons;**

- **consider both the attractiveness and shortcomings of these images;**

- **review the harmful effects of dualistic thinking on sport, exercise science, and physical education; and**

- **take your first steps in answering the question, What is a person?**

The primary issue at stake in this chapter is how we look at our bodies and how this affects us as athletes, coaches, and physical educators. We live in a culture that makes it difficult for us to deal with our bodies in an unconcerned, natural way. On the one hand, we tend to give them too much attention and credit. We worry about our weight; we stand looking at ourselves in mirrors; we are uneasy when we know that others are looking at us; we spend hours choosing the right clothes to wear or cosmetics to put on.

On the other hand, we give our bodies too little attention and credit. Physical education is usually one of the first subjects to be cut from public schools during difficult financial times. We tend to think of our minds as being more important than our bodies. We honor the intellectual professions and often look down on those who must labor with their hands. Sometimes we even dislike the way we look or feel and set up a kind of internal battle between our selves and our bodies.

Are minds more important than bodies?

Are "intellectual" professions more important than movement-based professions?

Does physical education have a stake in this issue of how persons are related to their bodies?

What difference does it make if minds and bodies are separate and independent parts of persons or if minds are more valuable than bodies?

What Is a Person?

You already know the logical reason for attempting to answer questions on the nature of persons. If you are to judge later how sport, exercise science, and physical education can best help people, you must first know what a person is. Even though we are still in the process here of trying to better achieve such an understanding, a partial definition can be offered now. A **person** is an individual, a self, an "I." Persons have unique histories, they live in the present, and they project themselves into the future. They act and are acted upon. Persons are aware of their own existence; they are capable of understanding ideas and relationships between ideas. In short, persons are self-conscious, intelligent beings. **Personhood** is the state or condition of living and experiencing these qualities. To achieve personhood is to have gained an identity, have a personal history that affects one's present and future, generate ideas and be affected by them, be aware of one's existence, and display intelligence.

Bodies are flesh, bones, blood vessels, hands and feet, the cells in our brains, and so on. Bodies are the site of our sense perceptions—our hearing, smelling, touching, seeing, and tasting. Bodies are always located somewhere, and they always exist at a certain time. Finally, bodies are capable, in principle, of moving

or being stationary. **Embodiment** describes one fundamental condition of personhood, namely, that humans are always located somewhere and sometime and that human consciousness is never free from the influence of body constraints like chemicals and the number of brain cells in one's head.

Bodies Separated From Persons

The **separation of bodies from persons** is not to be taken literally. We have no authoritative evidence to suggest that persons, or selves, exist apart from their bodies or that bodies enjoy a human existence after the persons who were supposedly housed in them have departed. Rather, the image of separation is to be taken metaphorically. This metaphor is useful here because it produces a picture of independence, self-sufficiency, and self-determination—in short, an image of the sorts of separate lives that, supposedly, selves and bodies enjoy.

The metaphor of separation raises important questions about the degree of independence, self-sufficiency, and self-determination that persons have apart from their physicalness. For example, can a person think, set a life course, and decide on value priorities largely free of any influence from the stomach, arms, legs, and feet? Can a person develop in full and healthy ways with minimal attention or credit given to physical influences? These are strange and perplexing questions, but they are also very important ones.

The Significance of the Issue

Problems of separating bodies from persons are, for obvious reasons, unavoidably problems for the professions associated with sport, exercise science, and physical education. In fact, I cannot find an issue that is any more critical to the future and longevity of the field than this one. Attitudes or understandings that separate bodies from personhood, or drive a wedge between minds and bodies, or devalue the significance of embodied activity are direct threats to the welfare of the movement-oriented professions. If personhood is only distantly related to embodiment, then the body can be treated as one object among others, as a thing that has no privileged position or priority. If bodies are separate from minds, if physical doing is separate from thinking, then education can be organized accordingly, and the majority of the educational effort can be devoted to the intellectual half of human development. And, if the body is a separate entity that is less important than the mind, then body-related professions will forever receive, and perhaps deserve, second-class status.

These are bedrock, foundational concerns of the profession. When embodiment is seen to be central to human development—indeed, to what it is to be human—then physical education and related professions will reside on a level playing field with the other educational arts and sciences and with any number of other people-related professions. When embodiment and thoughtfulness are understood to be inseparable aspects of human life, the professions that emphasize movement activities will stand shoulder to shoulder with those that focus on writing, counting, computing, engineering, philosophizing, or any other human project.

Is there any reason to be concerned about this? Consider the following. If educators have badly misunderstood the nature of persons, then they probably have been miseducating individuals just as badly. If they have seriously underplayed the importance of embodiment in human development (e.g., if people are thought to explore their world primarily in sedentary ways like reading books rather than touching, feeling, walking

and hiking, or if individuals are thought to express themselves primarily through words and sentences rather than also through gesturing, dancing, or moving creatively in sport), then educators have probably produced a quality of living that is far less than it could have been. But has such a monumental mistake been made? And, if so, where did we and our predecessors go wrong? It could be that they have mistaken human bodies as machines to which people are somehow connected.

The Body as a Machine

There is no question that the human body is like a machine. The body performs a variety of functions. It pumps blood, regulates its own temperature, metabolizes fuel, and moves. Like a machine, it falls into disrepair and requires periodic maintenance. As do all machines, it conforms to a number of laws—the laws of chemistry, physics, biology, and so on. In some ways, the human body is also a complex, motorized, active, and reactive system of levers. Why does one body work better than another? Why is one athlete superior to another? Answers lie, at least in part, in the lawlike generalizations that result in one body-machine being more efficient or effective than another. Partial answers lie at each level of inquiry—from chemistry to genetics, from physics to physiology, from mathematics to psychology.

Moreover, treating the human body as a complex machine has worked. It has allowed physical educators and exercise scientists to gain a great deal of important scientific information about people—about how they might live longer and healthier lives; about how they might become better athletes, exercisers, dancers, or just day-to-day movers; and about how they might learn faster. Thus, there is some justification for the sort of language used by

The movements of physical beings cannot be fully understood if they are looked upon as mere "machinework."

many scientists when speaking of the human anatomy—language like *circuitry* (for the nervous system), *plumbing* (for the vascular system), *upstream* and *downstream* (for vascular location), *pump* (for the heart), *computer* (for the brain), and *underpinnings* or *pins* (for the legs).

Yet, for all of its accuracy and power, this image of the human body merely as a machine, even a remarkably complex machine, is unfortunate. First of all, it is not sufficient. Bodies are not, it seems, simply machines, at least not ones whose functions are largely linear and predictable. That is, physical being and movement in live humans cannot be fully understood by applying classical assumptions and principles of "machineness" to them. Something else is needed, and both philosophers and empirical scientists are beginning to close in on what that something else is.

Four Images of Body–Person Separation

The separation or distancing of people from their physical nature has been predominantly the consequence of a philosophic school of thought called **dualism**. Under dualism, people are thought to be composed of two very different things, usually called mind or soul, on the one hand, and body, on the other. Typically, the person, or self, is more closely associated with the mental or thinking half of the individual. The body, while important, has less to do with who the person is or what he or she can become.

You may not be familiar with the names of the four dualisms I describe in the sections that follow, but you should already be very familiar with their characteristics and effects.

All of them are still alive and well—even though their philosophic founders died many years ago and the height of their popularity is long past. The four dualisms I refer to are object, value, behavior, and language dualism. A summary of their characteristics is shown in Table 2.1.

The Body: Different From the Mind (Object Dualism)

Object dualism suggests that people are composed of two radically different things or objects—namely, mind and body (Descartes, 1641/1960). The mind is not the physical brain. Rather it is nonphysical, and it produces nonphysical thoughts or ideas. The body, on the other hand, is physical. Like rocks and baseball bats, it is extended in space. Consequently, a person is a curious composite of one element that takes up space (the body) and another that is not physical in any sense (the mind). These two elements can somehow interact, for the mind can "tell" the leg, for example, to kick a football and the leg usually obeys. The body, in turn, can affect the mind. This happens, for instance, when the body is injured. The mind, for a period of time, is preoccupied with thoughts of pain and of tending to the injured body part.

The consequence of this line of thinking is a two-part person, where each part is radically distinct from the other. There is the body, which is essentially a machine. Like all machines, it follows the laws of matter. Then there is the mind, whose nature it is to think. It follows the laws of reasoning.

The Attraction of Object Dualism

Object dualism has an element of truth to it. There is a sense in which bodies are like machines. Your body must obey the same laws that affect tables, chairs, and automobiles. And like these other material objects, your body is extended in space. Additionally, there is a sense in which thinking is utterly nonphysical. How much does an idea weigh? How could anyone ever slice a theoretical principle in half with a knife? What color and shape does love have? There are no answers to these questions if they are taken literally rather than figuratively.

Thinking seems to follow different laws than those that govern simple physical matter. Human consciousness, for example, is able to negotiate the following logical terrain:

1. All great athletes wear Chuck Taylor Converse Allstar sneakers.
2. Susan is a great athlete.
3. Therefore, Susan wears Chuck Taylor Converse Allstar sneakers.

Rocks, baseball bats, and human bodies, on the other hand, know nothing of these laws of logic. They do not move for logic. They just sit there until a physical force with sufficient mass and velocity impacts them.

The way we have been raised to talk about ourselves adds to the attractiveness of this form of dualism. We commonly speak about minds and bodies as if they enjoyed separate, largely independent lives. Perhaps you have asked a friend the day after a strenuous game, "How does the old 'bod' feel today?" Or maybe you have said to yourself, "I know how to swing a golf club, but I just can't make my body do it." Or, "I don't know where my mind is today, but I simply cannot concentrate on this algebra." Or, "I am about to lose my mind."

While some of these common statements may be meant figuratively, there is little question that we are comfortable when talking about our mental and physical parts as if they were separate and largely independent of one another. Our language, in part, has influenced the way we think about ourselves. Our

Table 2.1 Four Forms of Dualism

Name	Fundamental assertion	Sample of effect on profession	Result
1. Object dualism	A human being is composed of two things—mind and body	Tendency to believe that we educate or otherwise tend to the body, not the whole person	Deification of the mind
2. Value dualism	Mind, thinking, and mental activities are superior to the body, moving, and physical activities	Tendency to think that genuine or mainstream education is intellectual education; efforts to make ourselves appear scholarly or otherwise intellectual	Deification of intellectual education
3. Behavior dualism	All (physical) doing must be preceded by some thinking	Tendency to compartmentalize thinking; to believe that thinking (if it occurs at all in sport) takes place apart from the action	Deification of thinking over doing
4. Language dualism	Verbal symbols are radically different from and superior to other kinds of symbols	Tendency to overlook activity as a significant form of meaningful expression and communication	Deification of words, verbal langange

language has undoubtedly biased us toward accepting two-part persons when, in fact, no such beings exist.

Weaknesses of Object Dualism

There are many problems with this brand of dualism, so many in fact that this position now enjoys very little support (Meier, 1975; Schrag, 1972). Criticisms have come from many quarters, and it is important for you to see why several of them are so powerful.

Criticism.   Mind and body are abstractions. As abstractions, they do not helpfully describe the actual whole, thinking-embodied person (Schrag, 1972). A person is more than the sum of his or her (abstract) parts. Evidence for this position:

• No description of machinelike qualities, however sophisticated and complex, will ever produce an accurate account of a human being. It will produce only a description of more and more complex machines. Laws of physics and mathematics cannot account for the marvelous workings of consciousness (Penrose, 1989).

• No description of logical qualities, however down-to-earth and simple, will ever produce an accurate account of a human being. It will produce only a description of less and less complex rules of logic.

• Mind (thinking) is never found apart from bodies. Body (being in time and space) is never found apart from mind (purposes, goals, coordination), except perhaps at death. Thus, to talk of them as if they could be separated is, at minimum, misleading.

• It is not clear what pure mind and pure body would be as regards the live human being. Human thoughts, purposes, and perceptions always show traces of body (where people were born, what they have experienced, what their chemical makeup is, and

so on). Physical nature and functions, on the other hand, always show traces of mind. Even autonomic functions and simple reflexes are coordinated and end-directed (Dewey, 1970).

• Mind and body do not seem to act on one another externally, as indeed they would if they were radically distinct entities. It is not accurate to say that a freestanding, independent mind tells the body what to do, or that a freestanding, independent body responds that it will or will not obey. Rather, when individuals think of purposes (like kicking goals in soccer) and supposedly tell their bodies what to do, they already are their bodies. That is, their thoughts are already affected by their bodiness. For example, people have a certain number of brain cells that allow them to come up with fairly complex purposes. They have had specific experiences that influence what purposes they will devise. Their body size and skill levels automatically make some purposes realistic and interesting, and others foolhardy and irrelevant. Thus, there seems to be no entirely independent or outside-of-body action by mind on body.

The reverse is also true. There is no outside-of-body action by body on mind. When the body responds to an intention to kick a soccer goal, it is already organized, directed, coordinated, educated. Autonomic functions, for example, show organization and coordination. Reflexes also exhibit coordination. Movement habits are the residue of previous experience and education. Thus, when physical actions begin, the body undertaking them is already "minded."

Consequently, in life we cannot find a pure machine-body that responds to the supposed commands of an external mind. Live bodies are already homogenized with "mindness" before they would receive their first command. Physical aspects are already organized, coordinated, habituated, historicized, socially contextualized, "motherized," "fatherized," "midwesternized," and otherwise educated (they are already "minded") before they would receive any order from a supposedly external mind.

Criticism.   It is difficult to understand how two radically distinct entities (mind and body) would, or even could, affect one another. Evidence for this position:

• It is not clear how something that is only physical (body) could affect something that is only mental (mind), and vice versa. How, for example, could a football punter kick an idea downfield? And how, for example, could a mere idea tackle a 230-pound fullback? It would seem that force and mass cannot move ideas. Conversely, it would seem that ideas cannot get in the way of force and mass. How then can dualists explain the obvious interactions between thoughtful and bodily aspects of personhood? How can dualists, as it were, paste people back together again?

• It is not clear where the mind, as utterly nonphysical, would be. In fact, it is not clear that the mind, as entirely nonphysical, could be anywhere. Marbles can be put in a jar, but how could ideas and purposes and values be placed in such a container? Ideas, some would say, are in one's head. But again, as nonphysical, how could they be there or anywhere, for that matter? How then can dualists explain the obvious fact that consciousness is here and now, and that it is related unequivocally to individual bodies, say, ones living in Florida or Alaska, in the 20th century?

Toward the Defeat of Object Dualism

If these arguments have prompted you to reorganize your thinking about personhood and realize that it is inaccurate to imagine persons as composed of two very different parts, you need to translate that understanding into your language (how you talk about human beings and your field) and action (how you treat yourself, your students, athletes, patients, or clients).

PHILOSOPHIC EXERCISE

Review the following statements, and see if you can rephrase them in a way that removes dualistic images and emphasizes the whole person. If you think they are acceptable as written, give at least one reason for this judgment.

1. Teacher justifying required physical education: "Every single student (has) → Is a body."
2. Definition of the educated person: a sound mind in a sound body. Around being/perso
3. The best physical education is an education through the (physical.) - Experience
4. The best physical education is an education of the (physical.) - whole Person
5. Frustrated athlete: "It [the body] won't work today." I'm not
6. Individual to self: "I've got to get the old body in shape."
7. Teacher to reluctant students: "Get your bodies moving!"
8. Coach to hesitant athlete: "You're using your mind too much."
9. Coach to squad: "Winning is 90% mental."
10. Sign in front of local fitness business: The Body Shop

If you are having any trouble in rephrasing or rewriting the statements, you may want to read over the following generalizations on the use of holistic language.

✓ Avoid referring to bodies as something that people have, own, or otherwise bring along with them. When you use such language, this has the effect of distancing you from your physical nature. Things that you have or own can be left behind. But obviously you cannot do that with your physical nature. Thus, you do not just have a body; you *are* your body.

✓ Avoid referring to bodies in impersonal terms. When you refer to your body as "it," for example, this implies that this object is just one thing among many things in the world.

✓ Avoid referring to bodies in instrumental ways. When you say that you are going to work the body, for instance, this implies an external, instrumental relationship between you and your body.

✓ Avoid using the words *mind* and *body*. Because they refer to nonexistent abstractions, it is far better to say, "I am going to exercise" than, "I am going to exercise my body."

✓ Avoid using the words *physical* and *mental*. When you say that you are a physical educator, for example, this could be taken to suggest that there are others who are mental educators. It might be better to say that you are a dance educator or a movement instructor, for dance and movement are activities that people (not bodies) engage in. (You will note that I have not been successful in purging this text of these words, though I have made some attempts to minimize their use.)

PHILOSOPHIC EXERCISE

Review the following situations and behaviors to see if you can modify them in ways that are less dualistic. Should you think that no changes are needed, defend your position.

1. You walk into the fitness center in which you work to meet a new group of adults who have signed up for an aerobic-dance class. Your eyes are drawn to this one male body that is remarkably out of shape and overweight. You immediately begin to think of weight reduction and fitness techniques that might be used on this extreme case.

2. You sell sporting goods and make it a practice not to delve into the personal recreational preferences and lifestyles of your customers. You are extremely knowledgeable about the equipment in your shop, and you are more than willing to tell shoppers about the advantages and disadvantages of the items that you sell. But you leave it entirely to your customers to make decisions about what supplies and equipment are right for them.

3. You are a dance instructor in a large high school and are in the process of developing a unit plan. You want to educate your students as whole persons. Thus, you develop two columns of objectives, one called cognitive goals, the other, organic goals. You plan to devote half your time and energy to each.

In working out answers, you may want to consider some of the following behavioral generalizations for combating object dualism:

✓ Meet students or clients as the unique people that they are. Even though you are being professionally trained to look at bodies for health problems or examine actions for potential improvements, you must never miss the person who is the body or who expresses herself or himself in movement (see Hellison, 1973). You should not think of yourself as a technician who is a master at fixing bodies or movements. Rather, you should think of yourself as a professional who has been trained and educated to help people, particularly in relationship to their movement lives.

✓ Get to know the person before you prescribe. You do not have the luxury of objectifying a body or a movement and, on that basis alone, devising a prescription. Otherwise your recommendations might be right for the abstract machine-body, but wrong for the individual. What will you find when you get to know the person? You will encounter a unique history of experiences, hopes, fears, values, and perceptions. Perhaps you will meet a character, an identity, a bit of personal style. Regardless, the distinct person you encounter should at least influence the content of your prescription.

✓ Don't pretend that you can manipulate bodies—work on them, train them, educate them—without affecting the whole person. As Williams (1964) was fond of saying, "The hand is as much mind as body" (p. 248). Or in another place: "You cannot do that [train bodies in isolation from the person]. Every time you lift a weight you affect the whole man, not just a muscle" (1948, p. 246). Heart rates do not get produced in a vacuum. They come with pain, and accomplishment, and interest, and boredom, and love, and hope, and virtually any other affect that can be thought of. They come attached to human purposes and embedded in human stories. They are related to what people have been, what they are now, and what they hope to become.

✓ Don't attempt to give support to the whole-person concept through any acts of "balancing the pieces," of providing, for example, an equal number of mental and physical objectives for a lesson. While this is well intentioned, it

It's easy to miss the human stories that come with achievement.

nevertheless gives subtle support to a dualistic notion of the human being. It may get you thinking in terms of mental versus physical rather than of the person as a whole.

✓ Build a curriculum that cuts across mental-physical distinctions. A curriculum built around movement activities that affect the whole person is superior to a curriculum that contains supposed cognitive activities apart from supposed physical involvement. Everything that is done in gymnasiums, on athletic fields, or at dance facilities—whether it involves sitting and talking or moving and exercising—involves insight *and* chemicals, understanding *and* bulk, feeling *and* levers. The insight is different because of the chemicals; the chemicals are different because of the insight.

The Body: Guided by the Mind (Value Dualism)

Under **value dualism**, human beings are again composed of two parts—mind and body. But the emphasis here is on their relative ranking and importance. Of the two, the mind is superior. It directs, controls, and supervises the body. The body is distanced from the thinking person because it is less capable.

Many of the writings of Plato (1951) exemplify what I am calling value dualism. In terms of the mental-physical opposition under discussion here, Plato placed mind over body, thought over emotion, reflection over sense perception, and knowledge over sensuous pleasure. Specifically, mind (or soul, as Plato called it) and mentalistic functions are superior to body because they attain more impressive ends (they are more capable) and because they themselves do not

stand in need of guidance or control (they are more independent). While Plato believed that a satisfying lifestyle included some degree of balance among activities directed toward physical maintenance, pleasure, reflection, empirical observation, and other factors, he maintained that human beings are at their best when they are in contemplative repose, when they are reflecting on some truth. In fact, Plato suggested that there is a world of Ideal Forms (an Ideal Chair, an Ideal Swing in baseball, Ideal Love, an Ideal Goal in field hockey) that can be encountered only through imagination and reflection.

Three strains of Platonic dualism are of specific interest because they have direct implications for the supposed inferiority of the body. First, reflection is deemed to be more powerful than sense perception; imagining the Perfect Dive is recommended over attempting to see one. This is because sense perceptions can be mistaken and because real tables and chairs and swimming dives are never absolutely perfect.

Second, Plato felt that the body was the third and weakest member of the person. Because of its appetites, passions, and cravings, the body for Plato is unruly and untrustworthy. It requires guidance from reason (the first element of the person) through the spirit (the second element).

The third argument was perhaps the strongest denigration of the body. Plato believed in the immortality of the soul. The soul, he argued, is unlimited, indivisible, unchanging, and permanent. The body, in contrast, is limited, divisible, changing, and temporary.

The Attraction of Value Dualism

This brand of dualism is still attractive today for a number of reasons. There are elements of truth in this position, and the contemplative life devoted to the acquisition of solid wisdom or an athletic life guided by reason and devoted to excellence (Weiss, 1969) has a kind of dignity and nobility to it.

There is little question that sense perceptions are untrustworthy. Our seeing, hearing, touching, smelling, and tasting can, on any given occasion, give us false information. For example, playing center field, we see the batter take a mighty swing, hear a loud crack of the ball against the bat, and see the ball start on a trajectory that would take it over our head. We begin to run back to make the catch, but we have been deceived. The ball actually struck the end of the bat, and it turns out to be a short blooper that falls in front of us. On the other hand, logic (and possibly some other types of reflective thinking) would seem to be more reliable. Consider the proposition that all footballs have shape and weight. Even though we have not observed all footballs in existence, this idea would seem to be necessarily true. The force of the logic would indicate that there is no deception here.

Plato's reservations about passions and appetites also have an element of truth to them. While we are not as prudish as some of our ancestors have been regarding sex and other pleasures of the flesh, we also understand that an unbridled pursuit of sensuous enjoyment can produce an unbalanced life, if not worse. Passions and appetites can be exceedingly forceful. They may urge us to do things that we really do not want to do. A grumbling stomach may distract us when we are trying to study. Sexual passions of the moment may lead us to take risks that are unwise.

Finally, Plato's descriptions of the body as a physical object are reasonably accurate. Bodies (in fact, all physical things) are limited, divisible, changing, and temporary.

More important, however, than the partial accuracy with which Plato described problems with sense perception, the dangers of unbridled passion, and the limitations of physical objects is the attractiveness of the ends to which he felt human beings ought to devote themselves. He argued that human

beings should commit themselves to certainty, permanence, and excellence. Unfortunately, the achievement of all three objectives, he thought, is won more often in spite of being embodied than because of it.

Certainty is a seductive value. We normally do not like being cast adrift in a world of doubt where this or that might be true, where we are not sure of anything. Many of you want your professors to tell you what is right. Citizens look to their leaders to give them the truth. We get frustrated when we hear anyone claim that there really are no right and wrong answers.

The drive for permanence is probably as forceful as the need for certainty. The realization that we are temporary creatures is unsettling. The fact that we are small, insignificant, and vulnerable specks in the universe is not particularly comforting. The human tendency is to fight against this impermanence. We want to leave our mark on the world; we want to do at least one significant thing before we die; we want to pass on our heritage to our children and our children's children; we want to be remembered.

Finally, who among us is against excellence? We are generally not happy when labeled average, mediocre, or even normal. In achievement-oriented cultures there is a sense in which people are not pleased with being like everyone else. We want to achieve distinction through something we ourselves have accomplished.

For all three values, the body presents problems. As noted, our physical senses play tricks on us and keep us from being absolutely certain about much of anything. Our bodies age and die; they remind us daily of our frailty and impermanence. And our passions and the limitations imposed on us by our bodies prevent us from achieving excellence very often, if ever.

Weaknesses of Value Dualism

Value dualism shows many of the same weaknesses as object dualism, for at least in the case of Plato, his value dualism rests on a clear separation of mind from body. Those criticisms leveled at Descartes that can also be directed toward Plato need not be repeated here. It is possible, however, to build upon them by identifying additional problems with the dualistic tendency to place mind over body, reason over sensation.

Criticism. There is no separate and independently existing world of permanent Ideal Forms. Evidence for this position:

• How could the existence of a world of Ideal Forms ever be demonstrated? When you and I sit in our easy chairs and reflect, for example, on the Ideal Jump Shot, does a single, clear, unmistakable vision pop into our heads? Can you and I later talk about the exact same picture we had of this motor skill? And if it turns out that we had somewhat different visions of what an ideal jump shot is, which, if either one of us, made contact with this supposed world of Ideal Forms?

• A world of Ideal Forms is not needed to explain common experiences. You and I can make conceptual distinctions, for example, between baseball and basketball without suggesting that there is, or must be, a shadow world of Ideal Baseball and Ideal Basketball behind them. Our partial and imperfect sense perceptual experiences with these two activities allow us to say, for example, that one of them is inherently time limited (a clock determines the duration of the contest in basketball) and one is not. (A baseball game, in principle, could last indefinitely.) We abstracted these ideas from real-world experience, not from a reflective vision of Ideal Sport Types.

Is there such a thing as the ideal jump shot?

• It could be that any insistence on a world of Ideal Forms is little more than a commentary on human cowardice. We may become depressed, frightened, or nauseated if we had to admit that human existence leads nowhere and has no firm values on which to rest. Thus, the notion that there is some world of Ideal Reality out there could be nothing more than a convenient invention or a statement of blind faith about how we would like things to be.

• A sufficiently distant historical view of the evolution of humankind might show that ideas and patterns of thinking are anything but fixed once and for all. Rather they change and evolve just like the rest of nature. It is understandable that people might not notice this change, for it occurs slowly over hundreds of years. Nevertheless, any belief that reality is unchanging could be misplaced.

Criticism. It is not accurate to say that bodily sensations or sense perceptions are, by nature, highly vulnerable to errors and that reflection and contemplation are, by nature, largely immune to mistakes. Evidence for this position:

• It is not difficult to find examples of a sense perception that was accurate or contemplation that went astray. In fact, it would seem that most sense perceptual identifications are later confirmed as having been accurate. (We see what we think is a baseball bat across the diamond. Later, when we approach it and pick it up, we conclude that indeed it is a baseball bat.) Conversely, it is not difficult to find examples of reflective "truths" that turned out to be less solid than once thought. Everyone knows that the logical opposite of love, for example, is hate or hatred. But is it? Could it not be successfully argued, as indeed Buber (1958, 1965) has done, that indifference is the best antonym for love and that, in important ways, love and hatred are actually very much like one

another. For example, they both acknowledge the existence and individuality of another person. On the other hand, if we are indifferent, we may not even notice that a person is there.

• It is not clear that contemplation has any sort of pure access to truth. Why must it be supposed, for example, that reflection is immune to contamination from physiology, language, and day-to-day socialization? If you and I are entirely organic, if there is no spiritual ghost hidden in our bodies, then does it not make more sense to believe that our thinking is an integral part of our biological, English-language lives than something from another world? There is also a good deal of genetic, sociological, and psychological evidence that supports this view that even human thinking is affected by a multitude of chemical, biological, linguistic, and cultural influences—that is, by both nature and nurture.

• It may be more accurate, therefore, to think of reflection as continuous with sense perception, as influenced by the same sorts of roadblocks to accuracy and objectivity, though perhaps in different degrees. This would allow for an account of what seem to be different amounts of uncertainty that go with various types of sense perception (e.g., seeing something nearby in a well-lighted room as opposed to looking at an object across a field at dusk) and reflection (e.g., following a simple line of logic as opposed to speculating on something like the meaning of life). You would then see that you need not be skeptical of all judgments based primarily on your senses; nor would you be trusting of all conclusions reached through reflection.

Criticism. It is not clear why sensuous feelings and desires need to be regarded as inferior, neither is it obvious that something called the mind or soul is in a superior position of control. Evidence for this position:

• Puritanical or body-denying attitudes are logically unnecessary—even if there is a world of Ideal Forms and even if our senses are somewhat unreliable. If, for example, there is an Ideal Chocolate Ice Cream Cone in Plato's shadow world, why would I have to adopt an ascetic attitude and deny myself the pleasure of eating one in this world of real, imperfect chocolate ice cream cones? In other words, even if Plato is right about the existence of some nonphysical world of Ideal Reality and even if he is right about the limitations of sense perception, none of the following seem to be required:

- That great amounts of time be spent reflecting and contemplating and very little time be invested in looking, smelling, walking, and running. We could even argue that rich sensuous experiences in dance and sport could reflect ideal control and serve as an important resource for later reflections (Weiss, 1969).

- That sensuous pleasures (e.g., satisfactions from having your back rubbed or hitting a golf ball on the "sweet spot" of the driver) be regarded as inherently subhuman or animalistic and inferior to nonsensuous activity. We could even argue that humans are able to transform base, survival, irrational, or passionate behavior into civilized activity while it remains nonetheless sensuous. Humans, for example, can turn "feeding" into "dining" by adding candlelight, love, conversation, and meaning to the good taste of the food.

- That impulses be singled out as inherently dangerous, as aspects of personhood that have to be subdued or controlled. We could even argue that some thoughts or ideas are more harmfully controlling than so-called bodily desires. A notion of fear can paralyze a person—keep him from venturing outdoors, or prevent her from answering the phone. A twisted concept of justice can turn a person into a dangerous criminal. Why then designate the body or our sensuous desires as the source of harmful or bad behavior?

In short, it is possible to be a Platonist and still be a full participant in the activities of this world, including sport, dance, exercise, play, and games. This is so because even athletes can attempt to approximate an ideal or perfect movement, because even dancers can transform "animal movements" into expressive human gestures, and because even the "bodily" urges of a person who exercises are no more dangerous or controlling than "mental" notions of fear and twisted concepts of justice.

• Because a body-denying attitude is not required by Plato's belief in a world of Ideal Forms, it must have come from somewhere else. That other place could be religion. Perhaps Plato holds a religious commitment or bias in favor of the spiritual over the worldly and has repackaged it as if it were a philosophic truth.

• It is possible that the picture of human beings as rational animals, as individuals who must forever live under the guiding light of pure reason, is too narrow or limiting. The existence of something called pure reason is itself uncertain, and any reduction of personhood to its thoughtful aspect would seem to ignore or discount much day-to-day experience as embodied, moving, in-the-flesh individuals.

• The decision to place mind over body tends to ignore qualitative variations that exist in the realms of principle and theory, on the one hand, and sense perception and appetite, on the other. That is, such a supposed distinction may deflect attention from a far more important one, namely, what makes reflective-tending activities good or bad, true or false, excellent or mediocre, and what makes body- or sense-oriented activities praiseworthy or not? Could it be that impressive intelligence can be found in kicking around ideas *and* soccer balls? More on this will have to be saved for chapter 3.

Toward the Defeat of Value Dualism

I trust that you have taken another step in reorganizing your thinking about personhood and have come to realize that people are not composed of two or more parts, where one of the parts (mind) is independent of and superior to the other (body). If so, you again need to translate this into your language and professional actions.

PHILOSOPHIC EXERCISE

I have listed 10 statements that reflect some variety of value dualism. See if you can rewrite them to better reflect a neutral attitude on the worth of people's thoughtful and sensual aspects. If you think any statements already show this neutrality, give reasons for your judgments.

1. A frustrated athlete after an unsuccessful performance: "I have to learn to trust my mind."
2. My goal in sport is to perform the perfect dive.
3. The key to being successful in activity is to think more and react less.
4. My biggest enemy in sport is my emotions.
5. It doesn't matter how it feels; what matters is whether or not I got it right!
6. If it doesn't hurt, it can't be doing any good. (No pain, no gain.)
7. A personal fitness instructor to student: "Work harder, work harder."
8. I want to become the ideal shortstop.
9. All too often my senses deceive my mind.
10. "When the One Great Scorer comes to write against your name—/He marks—not that you won or lost—but how you played the game." (Grantland Rice)

In attempting to rewrite these statements you may want to refer to the following generalizations that can be made regarding talk about the value of ideas and sense perceptions and the worth of corporeal and thoughtful aspects of personhood:

✓ Avoid talking as if there is something out there (mind, Ideal Forms, ideas) that guides you or controls your sensuous impulses. This is not a call to stop thinking or reflecting, but to realize that any meditation or contemplation undertaken already includes your embodiment—your feeling, touching, and seeing experiences, your family background, your geographical roots, even the amount of electrical activity in your head.

✓ Avoid talking as if there are two worlds rather than one—a supposed real world of perfection or Ideal Forms and another world of day-to-day experience, an unreal world of partial experiences, imperfect pictures, and mere appearances. You might say, for example, that your goal in tennis is to take *a* perfect swing rather than *the* perfect swing—or better yet, take an excellent swing.

✓ Avoid talking of emotions or sense perceptions as the sole or prime source of athletic problems. No athlete's enemy is his emotions, for example. His enemy is bad or ill-timed emotions. Conversely, no athlete's friend is his ideas. Only good or appropriate ideas are friends.

Think of feeling, emotion, and sense perception as sources of truth themselves.

Athletes get things right, for example, by sensing appropriate actions. Your descriptions of successful sport or dance movements should reflect this.

✓ Language should allow you to separate the physical and reflective tendencies of impulses and pleasures from their value or worth. (This involves tone of voice as well as the words chosen. The couplet *physical pleasures* can be spoken with a sneering or regal tone of voice, an intonation that communicates volumes about biases of the speaker against all things earthly, animalistic, or physical. Everyone has heard it used when some people talk of lowly *physical* education, or *PE*.)

✓ Speak of movement activities in terms of fun, enjoyment, and play—not in spite of the fact that they are "physical" and sensuous, but *because* they are so! Workouts should more often become "playouts."

PHILOSOPHIC EXERCISE

Certain situations and behaviors need to be changed to overcome value dualism. Review the three examples here to see what you might do differently. If you find nothing objectionable relative to value dualism, explain why the practice is acceptable.

1. A certain physical education teacher is devoted to excellence, even perfection, and he has a number of boys in a mixed badminton class who are particularly gifted. He thinks that with a little more work they will be able to perform the drop shot with ideal form and accuracy. He spends a considerable amount of time with these boys, largely ignoring the girls and other boys in the class.

2. A coach of a high school football team runs his preseason program as if it were a military boot camp. The enemy is lack of discipline—shown by poor health habits, eating the wrong foods, staying out late at night, giving in to sexual interests, and neglecting unruly bodies that need to be pounded into shape, trained, and brought under conscious control. "This is war!" he shouts.

3. Irene Cramer, the woman you met in the example at the beginning of the chapter, was never satisfied with the way she looked. She never measured up to the ideal. She forever evaluated herself in the mirror against some standard that she had no hope of satisfying. Consequently, she did not much like her body; she did not much like herself.

In working on your answers, you may want to check the following behavioral rules for combating value dualism:

✓ Use the standards of excellence more to invite, intrigue, and inspire than frustrate and condemn. There is usually nothing wrong with an ambitious goal that challenges and excites.

✓ Be careful of ideal standards that are narrow and discriminatory. It is important that high goals are not just muscular or tall or Caucasian or male goals. You should be able to find aspects of excellence in the movement domain that almost any student, given dedicated practice, can achieve.

✓ Don't let yourself become guilty of what I call the ultimate irony in our field, that is, to be a coach or movement professional who distrusts the body or otherwise treats it as the enemy. You are the people, if there is anybody in society, who should celebrate wholeness and brandish human intelligence in lusty, athletic, and modern-dancing ways. You should make sure that athletics, dance, exercise, and sport are fun; tell others that they are fun; and once and for all identify sensory pleasure as one of the key values of your domain.

✓ Complement or replace the pursuit of sterile ideals—like the perfect movement—with more human objectives, for example, with personal goals, personal meaning, and personal stories.

✓ Stop thinking of success as a product of the mental and error the result of the physical. Right and wrong cut across all behavior from the more reflective and logical to the more active and sense-perceptual.

✓ Don't let mere physical games and play be a source of embarrassment. You should not fall into the apologetic trap of suggesting that your students and clients typically get more than it would appear that they are receiving. You should not organize your programs to indicate that what appears to be mere physical exercise, only a game, or simply play, is actually more than that because it leads to other good things. These activities themselves are valuable and wonderful!

The Body: Involved in Doing, Not Thinking (Behavior Dualism)

An outgrowth of object and value dualisms is something that might be called **behavior dualism**. This unfortunate schism does not speak primarily to the question of how humans are put together (the concern that led some to object-dualism answers) nor to the question of which part or parts of the

human being or types of understanding are more valuable (the concern that led some to value-dualistic answers). This dualism came about when people tried to answer the question, How is skillful human behavior to be explained?

Behavior dualists believe that in every example of skillful activity, whether it be hitting a baseball, solving a math problem, or accomplishing a pirouette, two things (not one) are going on. These two things have been called variously theory and practice, thinking and doing, or reflecting and acting. When a person successfully kicks a soccer goal, for instance, that behavior, some claim, actually involves two activities. There is the mental planning, map drawing, and strategy setting. And there is the physical running, faking, positioning, and kicking.

It is easy to see how this separation of behavior came about. It is a logical consequence of the picture of the human body as a machine. Machines cannot act on their own. Even complex computers are not self-sufficient. All machines need an operator, a programmer, someone who gets the machine doing the right thing. This would be no less true for human bodies. People dare not suppose that their bodies accidentally do the right thing, for the consistency of their actions and steady improvements rule out purely fortuitous causes. Individuals dare not suppose that their bodies magically do the right thing, for that is no answer at all. The obvious and necessary answer is that there must be a "pilot for the ship," a "ghost in the machine." There must be something that coordinates and directs the body in skillful actions. That something is mind, and its activity is thinking.

It is no problem, these dualists say, that personal experiences of play rarely involve separate moments of theorizing and doing. And it is no problem that spectators of skillful behavior do not see two things going on, but only one—skillful performance. These dualists say that there must be thinking and doing, a bit of theory followed by a bit of practice. How else can people explain the obvious goal-directedness, coordination, and insight of the behaviors that they experience as participants and see as spectators?

The Attraction of Behavior Dualism

Anytime we begin with a picture of the human body as a machine, we are largely committed to some form of behavior dualism. The more distant from personhood the body is considered to be—the more it is an object out there, the more it is seen as an entity that simply obeys various mechanical laws—the more it will stand in need of some operator. Behavior dualism will seem to be uncontroversial, obvious, even necessary. But the seductiveness of behavior dualism goes beyond this. None of us, I would guess, want to be regarded as simply impulsive, reactive, spontaneous, or mercurial, and least of all are we comfortable with an image of ourselves as aimless or purposeless. We do not want to be thought of as mindless doers or dumb jocks. If we want to rescue our human dignity (or so we may believe), we should be thinkers, too. Thus, our various doings must be preceded by a little theory. What would otherwise be mindless running and jumping is organized beforehand, we could say, by no small amount of high-level thinking.

There seems to be an element of truth here. Surely, when we play sports, we do not stop thinking. For example, we concentrate on our project or on the visual field in front of us. Because concentrating is itself a form of thinking, it may be true that we are doing two things out on the athletic field. We are thinking about kicking soccer goals, for instance, and are actually trying to kick them. There are sports, like golf, that seem to suggest that there is a necessary sequential relationship between thinking and doing. It would seem important for at least some thinking to come first, for otherwise it could not inform our doing. In golf, we survey the landscape, figure the distance to the hole, look for dangers (like out of bounds areas), choose the right club and then, and only then, take a swing. Surely that is an example of thinking and then doing. Perhaps all sports behavior is like this even though it is harder to notice it in high speed, reactive sports like basketball and football.

Weaknesses of Behavior Dualism

There are a number of forceful criticisms that can be leveled at this variety of dualism. In this sense it is much like its two relatives, object and value dualism. Behavior dualism is no longer an academically respectable position, but it still retains an inordinate amount of influence in popular culture. Some of the arguments that led to what has been at least a weakening of behavior dualism are listed here.

Criticism. Thinking versus doing is a false dichotomy (Ryle, 1949). Evidence for this position:

• Thinking is itself a form of doing that can be done well or poorly. That is, thinking is itself a skill. Consequently, there is no dichotomy at all. In attempting to separate thinking from doing, all that has been accomplished is the separation of one type of doing from another.

• If thinking is itself a form of doing, and if all doing requires previous thinking, then what informs it? This leads to an infinite regress, one in which each doing requires a preceding thinking, where that thinking turns out to be yet another form of doing that requires previous thinking, and so on.

Criticism. Human behavior involves no independent "pilot" that would steer a ship and no separate ship that would need this help. Evidence for this position:

• The whole notion of two things going on in skillful behavior is based on a faulty notion of human beings. The body as machine is an erroneous abstraction, as is any notion of an independent thinker that pilots this supposed ship or machine.

- Performers have no experience during skillful activity of two separate things going on, of listening to some inner voice that gives a bit of theory and then responding. Rather, you and I receive invitations intuitively from the sense perceptual world, and accept or reject them. We see the right thing to do and do it. We move in certain ways and not in others because the former ways feel right while the latter do not. We do not normally have time to run propositions through our heads and subsequently act on them. (If we were to try this, we would usually find ourselves in great trouble, particularly in high speed, reactive sports like basketball, water-skiing, and soccer.)

- Skillful performances are characterized more by forgetting the body than remembering and directing it. When we are right or in the zone, we typically have no experience of thinking about our bodies or directing them. It is usually when skills break down, on the other hand, that we start objectifying a movement pattern, running performance tips through our heads, and talking to ourselves.

Criticism.   There is no need to appeal to separate acts of thinking to account for intelligent behavior. Evidence for this position:

- It could be that athletes and dancers are directed more by feeling and intuition than facts or propositions. And it could be that these feelings and intuitions are, in their own way, just as shrewd, insightful, and true as propositions or facts are in their realm. In other words, it could be that skillful activity involves a unique sort of intellectual activity, one that does not utilize or produce propositions, facts, or statements (Polanyi, 1958, 1966; Polanyi & Prosch, 1975; Ryle, 1949).

We achieve our best performances when we forget the body and do not try to direct our movements.

This would be a kind of thinking and knowing that is homogenous with skillful doing. It occurs in the process of that doing, not before the activity begins. This knowledge informs us, as it were, from the inside of our actions. It shows up as felt yeses and nos rather than truths that we reflected on, transferred to paper, or used in a chalk talk. Many great athletes, after all, are not very good theoreticians of their sport. They cannot say nearly as much as they can do (Polanyi, 1966).

• If the previous notion is correct, then skillful performance can be accounted for without appealing to a separate, truth-generating entity that works beforehand to guide some supposedly helpless machine that is about to be turned on. Intelligence works to help us identify creative and right choices at the sport scene. When we sense that it is right to drive to the basketball hoop this way and not that way, we are doing one thing, not two. We are acting insightfully all as a unit. We are recognizing, intuiting, feeling, moving. As we change location in time and space, our intelligence, operating through right and wrong feels rides "on" our shirtsleeves, "in" our left kneecap, "as" our feet and the rest of our body. When we make a smart skip pass, it does not mean that we first chanced upon a proposition about good passes and then acted on it. We simply saw or sensed an opportunity and seized it. In many cases, it is very difficult to say (factually) what happened.

Toward the Defeat of Behavior Dualism

If you have taken the third step in reorganizing your thinking about personhood by realizing that performers are not doing two things in skillful performances, it is important that you find ways to act on that new understanding. First, notice how people support this harmful dualism by the way they talk about skill. Then, look at other behavioral changes that might be needed.

PHILOSOPHIC EXERCISE

See if you can change the wording of the following 10 statements to eliminate the theory-practice dualism that may be implicit or explicit in them. If you find the wording unobjectionable, explain why the statement does not imply any improper dualistic perspective.

1. A coach to his staff: "We need to recruit athletes who can think."
2. An athlete explaining his home run to reporters after a game: "As the pitch was coming, I remembered what the coach had told me about this guy's fastball and how I would have to open my hips in order to get around on it."
3. Golf is a thinking person's game. There is a lot of theory that goes into top-level play.
4. Think first! Play second!
5. Once you start to play the game, quit thinking.
6. A coach to her athlete: "I don't want you to think. I want you to react."
7. The term *dumb jocks*.
8. The term *cerebral player*.
9. Coach to player who made a mistake: "You moved without thinking."
10. Coach to staff: "I want a player who can think on his feet."

You may want to review a few generalizations about the way you should and should not discuss activity skills. Here are some generalizations for avoiding the thinking-doing dichotomy:

✔ Be aware of the fact that the words *thinking* and *thought* are dangerously ambiguous. Although they can certainly be applied to the process of playing skillfully itself, they most often and for most people carry connotations of quiet reflection and the production of propositions and truths. Consequently, when you say that you want performers who can think, it is not clear what you are proposing. And because thinking is normally associated with reflective, fact-generating mental activity, this term in effect reinforces and promotes the erroneous perception that skillful behavior involves two activities (thinking and doing), not one.

✓ Be judicious in using the couplets *motor skill* and *physical skill*. They carry connotations of machinelike activity and efficiency. Moreover, motors must await instructions from a control center. Any movement that is physical would seem to need guidance from some source that is mental. Thus, as much as possible, you should avoid describing skills as motor or physical in nature.

✓ Talk of yourself and your subject matter in ways that cut across the thinking-doing dichotomy. It is better, for example, to say that you teach sport or dance than to indicate that you teach physical activity.

✓ Don't talk as if thinking must, or even usually does, precede doing. Even though it may make athletes and dancers sound more thoughtful or rational, you should not invent intellectually initiated sequences that do not exist or talk about them just because they sound good. Remember, performing as exercisers, athletes, and dancers includes thinking; it does not suggest that helpful thinking must have occurred beforehand. To paraphrase Descartes, you should not say, "I am hitting a softball. Therefore, I must have done a bit of previous theorizing." But you can say, "I

am hitting a baseball. Therefore, I must *be* thinking."

✓ When you speak of human intelligence, don't automatically equate it with reflective, proposition-forming, verbal, mathematical, artistic, inductive, deductive, or any other singular sort of cleverness. The human capacity for insight has many different facets. It must not be suggested in language that human success or excellence can be traced back to a single sort of thinking or insight (Gardner, 1985). Great sport performances are not "great propositions in a uniform." They probably have very little to do with reflective ideas or facts at all, at least for the athlete him or herself. They imply another sort of brilliance or intelligence—not the kind that gets measured by standard IQ tests, but the kind that produces wonderfully graceful, meaningful, effortless, inventive, and creative actions on ballfields and in gymnasiums, exercise facilities, and dance studios. This is another idea that we will have to pursue in chapter 3.

PHILOSOPHIC EXERCISE

Professional actions need to accompany the new ways of talking about sport, exercise science, and physical education. Review the following situations and behaviors to see if you can modify them in ways that combat behavior dualism. If you feel that they are entirely compatible with a holistic vision of human beings, describe why that is so.

1. A conscientious physical education teacher is always careful to explain the principles behind each skill before her students are allowed to practice them.

Typically, she will spend 15 minutes of each 35-minute period giving such explanations. She believes that students who understand strategic and scientific ideas related to their movements will be able to perform them better.

2. A dancer is not progressing as fast as he would like. He spends hours each day practicing his technique, but he remains tentative and his movements are too disconnected. He thinks about each sequence and about how he can make them more of one piece. He watches videotapes of himself and can see the lack of flow in his performances. He thinks he knows how to correct the problem, but his ideas rarely work.

3. A certain YMCA instructor is a superb skill teacher. She guides her students through movement activities with the proper cues, the right feedback, and success-producing sequences. Whatever the activity, her students learn to play well in an unusually short time. But she is also a stickler for cognitive outcomes. After a good degree of skill has been gained, she asks her students what they have learned about the strategies and principles of playing that game. She is often frustrated by how little they can say. She wonders if they have really learned anything.

4. Sam is proud of the fact that he always grades his physical education classes on their knowledge as well as their skill. He takes time to teach and test both. Yet he is concerned that he does not have enough time to do either one as well as he would like. Nevertheless he will not give up either one. While, in his heart, he feels more committed to his skills objectives, he likes the academic respect he thinks he has gained by giving theory tests.

Some general guidelines that will help neutralize behavior dualism are listed here:

✓ In skill and activity settings, where improvement in performance is your primary objective, the presence and visibility of theory should be carefully monitored and limited. In the first place, the relationship of theory to practice is an uncertain one. The comprehension of good theory does not always lead to good performance. In fact, too much thinking (even correct thinking) about an activity can lead to awkward, tentative movements—a kind of paralysis by analysis, as it is commonly identified. Secondly, if you were consistently to begin skill lessons with a bit of theory, students and clients could draw the erroneous conclusion that good practice is dependent on good theory, or that good theory must precede good practice.

✓ In activity settings where skill development is the primary objective, spend a minimum of time talking; focus on showing, guiding, pointing, watching, demonstrating, acting out, and enjoying.

✓ In the curriculum and in your teaching, honor skill for its own sake. Your actions should reflect a conviction that good skill itself is a way of knowing and a foundation for learning more. Skill does not need theory to give it value or educational importance. Thus, should academic achievement awards be given for excellent performances in sport, exercise, and dance? If creative, insightful doing is itself a form of good thinking and knowing, then the answer should be yes! There is no need for pencil and paper tests to add academic achievement to physical education or to prove that learning has occurred. The qualities of the performance itself give sufficient evidence for both.

✓ In education, there should be a support system for movement skill development, just as there is for skill development in math and English. That is, there should be an instructional presence from remedial or lower special education levels through honors work. The educational rules (e.g., grading policies) that apply to this curriculum and teaching should be the rules that pertain to skill teaching in whatever subject matter and throughout the school system or university. Educational turf then should be staked out in part on the nature and educational significance of skill teaching per se. You should not be forced to elevate yourself by pretending that you are really about theory nor should you lose stature by admitting that skill development is not based directly on learners comprehending good theory about their activity.

✓ Don't feel defensive about your limited opportunities to supplement skill learning with theoretical background. In the best of all possible worlds, one with infinite resources and time, you would undoubtedly want your students not only to be highly skilled in various movement activities but also to understand the principles that underlie those intelligent doings. The understanding of theory, if nothing else, would give students greater independence and sophistication, allowing them to modify future practices on their own. But with classes that are too large and time that is too short, you simply cannot do it all. You have to set priorities. If the top priority is skill teaching—particularly the teaching of such things as games, sports, exercises, and dance—there will be little time to devote to students' understanding of the many physiological, psychological, biomechanical, motor-learning, sociological, and philosophical theories and facts that stand behind them.

If this sounds like anti-intellectual heresy, remember that similar decisions have been made by others in academe. Many skill-oriented English-composition teachers have little time to debate

Don't be a victim of theory overload. Movement skills are best learned by moving.

different theories of sentence structure or paragraph formation. Likewise, biology laboratory teachers have almost no time to lay out different theories of inductive reasoning in science. Why then should you feel uneasy about your limited ability to pump more theory into your skill-teaching settings? Skill development has been allowed, and should be allowed, to stand on its own at all levels of learning—in lower, middle, and higher education.

✓ Don't be guilty of promoting a bait-and-switch curriculum. That is, students should not be attracted with the promise of play and skill development and then be fed a steady diet of facts and principles. If you want to have significant theory components in your courses or in your sports medicine prescriptions, this should be noted up front (a little truth in advertising).

✓ Sport, exercise science, and physical education should align themselves more with the performing arts than with any of the academic sciences. This acknowledges the fact that all educational fields teach skills (remember, all forms of reasoning themselves are skills), but that skill interests in sport, exercise, and dance parallel those of the fine or performing arts in many important ways. All the spatial and temporal concerns of timing, shape, pattern, force, direction, speed, accuracy, location, volume, touch, syncopation, and so on fall across music, art, sculpting, painting, mime, theater, dance, sport, and exercise. So do particular concerns with footwork and handwork, with seeing, hearing, feeling, smelling, and touching.

✓ Relish your distinctiveness, celebrate your unique contributions to humanity's skillful activity, accentuate your differences from other fields. If it were true

that theory must precede practice, and if it were true that practice is somehow beholden to theory, performers could not revel in their distinctive artistry. Great performances in basketball, astounding movements in field hockey, unbelievable sensitivity to the terrain in a bicycle race, and marvelously unpredictable creativity in dance would all be anticlimatic. The really important things would have happened earlier—when the theorizing was going on in performers' heads.

✓ Acknowledge the importance of a healthy reciprocal relationship between theory and practice. Theory can inform your practice, and likewise, practice can inform your work on theory. Knowledge about biomechanics can lead to performance modifications, and experience in competition can provide clues about the need for and direction of additional research in biomechanics. Thus, while theory and practice can stand on their own, they also reside in this reciprocal and potentially mutually beneficial relationship.

The Body: A Processor of Nonverbal Symbols (Language Dualism)

Language dualism is concerned with the place and significance of verbal symbols in relation to other conventions for expression and communication. Typically, and probably rightfully so, the development of language is regarded as a significant step, sometimes even *the* significant step, in the evolution of lower forms of animal life to the level of human existence.

When looking for contrasts between animal and human life, language jumps out as an obvious difference. Apes, for example, can move well, even more skillfully than humans in some ways. They can respond to signals. They can solve simple problems. They apparently are capable of some degree of affection. But apes have not developed, nor can they use, complex languages. They have only minimal capacity to express their ideas (whatever ideas they indeed have) and have few conventions or symbols by which they can further their primitive understandings.

While all this may seem somewhat uncontroversial, some rather extreme claims have been made about the distinctiveness and power of verbal symbol systems in contrast to other human conventions—say, dance or, more broadly, symbolic movement. Language dualism shows up in such claims as the following:

1. The evolution from forms of animal life to human existence is signaled and furthered by the rise of verbal language (but not the appearance of symbolic forms of movement).
2. The human capacity to think in abstract ways is revealed and developed through the use of verbal language (but not symbolic forms of movement).
3. The human capacity to learn and understand is dependent on verbal language (but not symbolic forms of movement).

This is not the place to contest directly the claim that people are able to think only or primarily through words and sentences (see Willard, 1973). This is, however, a very significant issue for those in the arts, sport, exercise science, and physical education. If this position could be defeated—if it could be demonstrated that people think quite well without using words and sentences—it would go even further than the analysis here to show both verbalization as overrated and the verbal-nonverbal distinction as of less importance than many currently think.

The position that opposes language dualism, and one that will be defended here, is this: Whatever the powers of verbal symbols—powers to shape thinking itself, powers to permit easy communication, powers to record ideas and abstractions as well as point to things like tables and chairs, or powers to help people uncover yet additional thoughts—these strengths are not different in kind than those produced by the nonverbal conventions of movement, gesture, mime, posture, and stance with which sport, exercise science, and physical education professionals work. Any claims to the effect that verbal language is highly significant and profoundly influential while nonverbal language is not are open to many criticisms.

The Attraction of Language Dualism

There is no question that language is powerful. What individuals *say* is undoubtedly influenced by their culture's vocabulary and sentence structures. For example, our word *love* has too much work to do in the English language. I love ice cream cones, my dog, my children, and my wife—but not in the same way, and definitely not in that order. Yet, one word, *love*, is forced into duty to communicate four distinct ideas. Had I grown up in a Greek culture, I could say four different things because that language has a word to go with each one of these notions of love.

It is also undoubtedly true that language influences, at least to a degree, the way people think. It has been shown that people in some cultures have difficulty in understanding certain concepts. Rather than attributing this to a culturewide absence of gray matter, this is probably a result of verbal training. It could be, for example, that if there were no word for some abstract idea or if there were no sentence structure that would allow people to express this idea, children would grow up without an ability to generate this idea on their own or perhaps even to understand this

Movement: An alternative way to "talk."

notion if it were given to them by someone else.

Thus, language dualism is at least partly true. Verbal language is remarkably powerful, and it may have had much to do with the ascendency of human consciousness from various subhuman predecessors. But, of course, from this fact it does not necessarily follow that nonverbal language is weak or insignificant. Nor does it follow that nonverbal language did not have as much or even more to do with human evolution.

The picture of verbalization as far more significant than nonverbal thinking and symbolic activity is particularly seductive because words are the favored medium of exchange in North American culture and, to a greater or lesser extent, in all human cultures. Language is featured, highlighted, the focus of attention in formal and informal education. While there is some interest in when baby takes her first steps, there is frequently more interest in whether baby is talking yet.

Verbal expressions of intelligence are often equated with intelligence per se. For example, the verbally oriented Scholastic Aptitude Test (SAT) and Graduate Record Examination (GRE) are commonly thought to give a fairly comprehensive picture of human intellectual ability.

When verbally articulate people are encountered, high degrees of intelligence are often attributed to them automatically and subconsciously. In North America we are taught to think that individuals who write books or who can speak eloquently and confidently before large audiences must be intelligent. Likewise, we tend to believe that individuals who use big words must have high IQs. It is telling that we do not make the same kinds of judgments about athletes whose movements are dramatically creative or dancers whose choreography is exceptionally meaningful or even pianists whose interpretations of a given piece of music are brilliant. We are typically not nearly as impressed with nonverbal expressions of insight, meaning, and understanding as we are with words and sentences that express some knowledge.

Verbalization is also attractive because of its convenience and versatility. We generally can produce words and sentences with less energy than sport, dance, mime, or even simple gestures. We have dictionaries in virtually every home. If we forget the meaning of a word, we can easily consult this handy resource and be reminded of its definition. If words are not doing the work we expect of them, they can be modified by putting them in a different context, changing the meter, volume, or emphasis in a spoken sentence, or even by inventing new words.

Written language is easy and inexpensive to produce and reproduce. We find that things on which to make language marks (like rocks, tree trunks, and paper) are everywhere, and things by which to make those marks (coal, lead, chalk, and ink, if not laser printers) are also widely available and inexpensive. The muscular skills needed to speak, write longhand, or type at a typewriter or word processor keyboard are relatively easy to learn. We do not have to be blessed with outstanding motor skills, or be youthful, or even in good shape in order to make the proper sounds for oral expressions or the physical marks of a written language. Little wonder then that we rely so heavily on the spoken and written word to further understanding and to record and communicate ideas. Little wonder that we tend to overlook the real and potential value of nonverbal language.

Weaknesses of Language Dualism

This variety of dualism is more subtle than the others, though many scholars today agree that the symbolic process in humans, whatever form it takes, is distinctively human and

is for that reason significant (Cassirer, 1944; Metheny, 1965, 1968). From this perspective, oral and written language is seen as overrated and nonverbal language or symbolic forms tend to be overlooked and undervalued. Some arguments that can be used to undercut verbal–nonverbal dualism are these:

Criticism. The appearance of language in both verbal and nonverbal forms rests on the same evolutionary advance of human beings over lower forms of animal life. Evidence for this position:

• The conclusion that verbalization (formal spoken and written language) is the key to the distinctiveness of human existence is inaccurate. Our capacity to abstract, to take multiple perspectives on both physical objects and nonphysical ideas, to get some distance between ourselves and the world out there, may be this key (Cassirer, 1944), and verbalization may be only one indicator among others that this has indeed occurred. The emergence of human life, specifically the development of multiple ways of dealing with the world and thereby gaining distance from it, the formalization of a world out there, produced a need for stand-ins for experiences—a need for language, for symbols, both verbal and nonverbal. Given this explanation of the evolution of human consciousness, it is not clear why verbal symbols would, in principle, hold any privileged position.

• If this is true, then a litmus test for the effectiveness of a language would be its capacity to represent this increased complexity. While we know that written and spoken languages are usually efficient and cost effective, we also know that other conventions can do the same work. Practically speaking, words and sentences are very handy. But in principle they have no sacred or advantaged status. A hand gesture can say something through connotation (suggested or implied meaning) and denotation (direct or meant content) just as a sentence can. In principle, then, it is no more uniquely human for verbal language to advance, capture, record, or communicate diverse meanings than it is for dance movements, mime, paintings, music, or sporting acts to do so. What is critical for any and all conventional recordings of abstractions is that they can perform the task of representing something else.

Criticism.   It is possible that the cultural visibility and popularity of verbal language has been taken to signify superiority. Evidence for this position:

• In much of the western world, we have been trained to express ourselves verbally. We work on verbal language skills virtually from birth to death. Abilities to read, write, speak, and have command of a reasonably extensive vocabulary are at the very center of what this culture calls education. We encounter countless courses and subjects in preschools, grade schools, colleges, and universities that directly or indirectly reinforce the message that verbal language skills are the hallmark of the educated person.

The development of our gestural, musical, and other movement-oriented languages, on the other hand, are largely left to chance. In America, we rarely hear anyone complain, "You write nicely, but your abilities to gesture, mime, and dance are lousy." When someone says, "How sad it is that Joe cannot read," it is a safe bet that this person is not complaining about Joe's inability to decipher music, dance, or art symbols.

Very few of us have been trained in nonverbal communication, and apart from the arts and physical education, few courses have anything to do with nonverbal languages. Even in fields like sport, exercise science, and physical education, where nonverbal skills are taught, many students are encouraged to move simply for recreational or fitness purposes. They are not taught to regard their movement skills as a vehicle for exploration and communication. Thus, with the massive socialization that favors verbal languages, it is little wonder that most of us see words as different than and superior to other kinds of symbols.

• It is difficult to read the marks of any symbolic process unless we are well trained in the traditions of that particular convention, whether it be baseball, dance, music, poetry, or prose. Because much of the educational process in much of the world is designed to enhance our verbal abilities, it is only natural then that most of us are more comfortable with spoken and written language than with other means of communication or expression.

Criticism.   If the creation of art is one of the highest or most impressive accomplishments of human existence (Polanyi & Prosch, 1975), nonverbal expression, ironically, may hold some advantages over verbal symbolization. Evidence for this position:

• There may be as many nonverbal art forms as verbal ones, or even more. These forms, taken as a whole, may have as large a cultural impact as their verbal counterparts, or perhaps even a larger one. Among some segments of society that are not verbally oriented, movement and fine arts would appear to be particularly influential. Popular, nonverbal art is everywhere. There is dance, sport, exercise, music, painting, elements of acting, mime, quilt making, basket making, and all sorts of other manually oriented crafts.

• Verbal languages are limited in at least two senses. First, vocabularies and thus the ideas that can be expressed by them are finite. There may be subtle qualities or features of something that we wish to communicate, for instance, but there are no words for us to use. The sheer number of distinctions we notice outdistances the size of our vocabularies and our skills to put words together. We have an insight, but verbal languages leave us with

Movement can express ideas when words cannot.

nothing to say. Second, complex relationships among things in the world are often difficult to capture and communicate in sentences. We may sense connections and even compatibilities between love and hate, rules and freedom, habits and creativity but find it difficult to put aspects of these relationships into straightforward words or sentences. Poetry may help, but dance, music, mime, and other communicative forms may be more useful.

In short, possibilities for coherent, insightful human expression are not exhausted with prose verbalization. In fact, this form of communication has severe limitations when it comes to artistic levels of expression. There are times when words fail us, and many of those times could be ones during which we are doing some of our most advanced and impressive thinking. We are forced to dance it out, act it out, sculpt or paint it out, even to sport it out! For instance, we may have a flash of insight about the effortlessness that can accompany some remarkably difficult strength routine in gymnastics. If we tried to communicate this mystery in prose we might use oxymoron descriptors like *effortless effort* or *easy difficulties*. These words make it sound as if we experienced a contradiction, and in a way we did. We discovered that two apparent opposites actually go together in some way. We know that *effortless effort* makes sense even though we have to struggle to see it. But if we are lucky (and skillful), we can more or less capture it and express it in sport, in dance, perhaps in poetry—in whatever symbol system we have at our command.

Toward the Defeat of Language Dualism

If you agree that your culture has tended to honor verbalization beyond its merits and, correspondingly, to undervalue or ignore nonverbal forms of expression, you should begin to rethink what you typically say and do. You need to be certain that your insights result in modified behavior wherever and whenever changes are needed.

PHILOSOPHIC EXERCISE

Review the following statements and see if you can reword them to reflect a more balanced attitude toward different forms of communication and expression. If you believe that they are satisfactory as they stand, explain why they are acceptable.

1. If you don't think clearly, you will never be able to write well.
2. I can't tell you how much this award means to me.
3. I am going to coach this team by the book.
4. I keep hearing the coach's words, over and over again.
5. The power of language is great.
6. Coach to player: "What are you trying to tell me? Put it into words, will you?"
7. If you cannot write it down, you don't know it.
8. Good writers think well; good dancers move well.
9. "The pen is mightier than the sword." (Bulmer-Lytton)
10. There was never a truer word spoken.

Here are several generalizations that can be made about how sport, exercise, and dance professionals should talk about verbal and nonverbal language:

✓ Take care to use the word *language* in a way that includes both its verbal and nonverbal forms. Too often when *language* is employed, people have in mind only the written or spoken word. It may be necessary, depending on context, to specify verbal and nonverbal languages when speaking of communication forms.

✓ Talk about human movement in the context of language and its functions. (Metheny [1965, 1968] used everyday words like "meaning," "connotation," "denotation," and the coined terms, "kinestruct," "kinescept," and "kinesymbol.") Other language-oriented terms would include *expression, sense, vocabulary, semantics, syntax, context, diction, tone, clarity, ambiguity, statement, message,* and *symbol.* While each of these terms is generally associated with verbal communication, each still makes sense in nonverbal expression. A nonverbal vocabulary, for example, might include a number of distinct gestures, images, movements, and sounds. To study nonverbal syntax might be to look at the arrangement of movements and their relationships to one another. Nonverbal semantics might be concerned with the meanings of gestures, dances, mime, and so on.

✓ Remember that not only dance but also sport and exercise have expressive aspects to them. This is not to say that the central purpose of sporting and exercising is to say something, to make truthful or insightful statements, or to record understandings. Nevertheless, whenever performers swing a bat or lift a barbell they inevitably express something. They say something about who they are, what they know, and what they are trying to accomplish. While they may not be artists, they may nonetheless generate highly creative, insightful, and memorable statements.

Consequently, you should apply the language-oriented terms noted above to sport and exercise more frequently than they currently are. This is not to neglect dance, but only to say that you probably are already far more comfortable thinking in terms of nonverbal symbol systems in relationship to dance than you are to sport and exercise. And if dance is not given its due for its capabilities as a nonverbal language, this is doubly or triply so for sport and exercise.

PHILOSOPHIC EXERCISE

Take a look at the following behaviors and situations for modifications that would combat language dualism. If you think that they already do so, simply provide a rationale for your position.

1. A public school system in a large American city has a physical education curriculum that includes a large number of different movement activities, including dance, sport, and exercise. Typically, a unit in which a single activity is taught lasts only two weeks. Then the class moves on to another activity for another two weeks. Some students complain that they never get good enough at any skill to really enjoy it.

2. A fitness instructor requires her clients to keep a diary and to write down every significant experience in her program. She often reminds them, "It doesn't count if it's not written down."

3. A male physical education instructor is not a particularly strong supporter of dance. He tells his male colleagues that dance is for women. He thinks that the need to express feelings is somehow feminine. He tells his male athletes that sport is very simple. It is about winning and losing—period!

4. A western town's recreation program is based on two solid principles: the promotion of lifetime activities and the development of personal health and fitness. Every activity that is considered for inclusion in the town's programs is put up against these two criteria. The head of this recreation program believes his services to be consistent and forward looking.

In developing your action strategies for the situations described in the philosophic exercice, you may want to review the following suggestions:

✓ Place a renewed emphasis on the quality or depth of skill acquisition so that at least one form of nonverbal expression can be used well. Too often instructors frustrate their students by giving them two weeks of one activity, one week of another, and so on. No wonder that they cannot express themselves effectively at the end of these short introductions. No wonder that they cannot say much through their primitive, awkward, and often self-conscious movements. No wonder they are left with an unsavory taste in their mouths after experiencing PE.

✓ Develop curricula and programs with a firmer commitment to movement as a form of human expression. Traditionally, this orientation has been reflected in varying degrees at elementary school levels, particularly in what has been called movement education. And traditionally, this uneven attention falls away quickly as students advance toward culturally popular games and fitness activities. For boys and men in particular, the expressive side of movement has been sorely neglected. However, as high-level athletic programs pick up momentum for girls and women, this neglect threatens to be the norm for all.

✓ Recognize and cultivate close curricular and professional ties with other fields that emphasize nonverbal expression on the one hand (fields like art, music, and theater) and those most responsible for teaching languages on the other (English, speech communication, reading, and foreign languages). You need to recognize that, to a degree, you share common interests and purposes with the other symbolic activity and language disciplines.

✓ Make expression a theme, an objective, an issue for discussion, analysis, and other sorts of attention. Typically, and especially with high school or young adult students or clients, an exclusive emphasis is placed on what is accomplished or made, not what is felt or meant. The latter issues need to be put on the table and dealt with in terms of movement skills.

✓ Highlight and better utilize your most effective expressive movement forms. Some general possibilities come to mind. More dance, less exercise. More folk and modern dance, less aerobic dance. More inventive and creative sport actions, less predictable or routine competitive activity. More experimentation in exercise, less rote behavior. More culturally meaningful content, less imported, scientific, or ideal content.

Review

This chapter is focused on the question, What is a person? This is an important issue because descriptions of personhood that distance the body from human existence are, in general, hostile to the movement professions.

It must be addressed early in the development of any philosophy of sport because the way in which activity is seen to help people depends, in part, on what people are.

Four old (but still lively) brands of dualism separate physical reality from persons. Object, value, behavior, and language dualisms are still attractive, even if they are no longer defensible and can be defeated with various criticisms. Ways in which you speak and act may need to be changed if the effects of dualistic thinking are to be reduced or eliminated.

Criticisms of dualism produce descriptions of what a human being is not. A person is not a thing called "mind" somehow and somewhat connected to a thing called "body"; or a being in which a powerful, insightful, and eternal mind directs and outlasts a dependent body; or a being for whom every action is preceded by a bit of theorizing; or an individual who has achieved human stature because he or she can use verbal symbols rather than nonverbal ones.

This discussion of dualism shows why Irene Cramer's attitudes and behaviors (in the example at the beginning of the chapter) are unfortunate. She too frequently objectified her body and too harshly judged it against some ideal standard she held for it. She fought with her body and was unable to enjoy and celebrate her physicalness. Her situation is sadly ironic. As a fitness instructor and one who should exhibit the best in consciousness-embodied wholeness, she failed to integrate her body and movement activities into the complete, capable, and happy person she might have become.

Looking Ahead

In chapter 3, you will review the claim that a person is a whole being. You will use some of the lessons learned from the mistakes of the dualists in developing a new horizontal image of human existence. You will also continue to search for practical implications of holism for physical education.

Checking Your Understanding

1. Why is it important to answer the question, What is a person? before examining ways in which sport, exercise science, and physical education are valuable?
2. In general, why is mind-body dualism so harmful for physical education?
3. Describe each of the four forms of dualism covered in this chapter and provide at least one reason for its attractiveness and one criticism that shows its weakness.
4. For each of the four forms of dualism, provide at least one recommendation for changing the way physical educators should speak and another recommendation about how they should act.

Key Terms

Person, p. 33
Personhood, p. 33
Body, p. 33

Embodiment, p. 33
Separation (bodies from persons), p. 33
Dualism, p. 35
Object dualism, p. 36
Value dualism, p. 42
Behavior dualism, p. 49
Language dualism, p. 56

Further Reading

A number of good articles on dualism are included in Morgan and Meier (1988). See Hanna (1970) for a readable introduction to nondualistic thinking. A classic anthology by Spicker (1970) includes many early essays that attacked dualistic interpretations of human beings and their behavior.

Chapter 3

Holism: Bodies United With Persons

John Farley is a biology major at a well-known university, enrolled in the pre-med program. To date, halfway through his sophomore year, he's doing well, pulling mostly A's, with a B every now and then. When John started his pre-med studies he planned to be a cardiologist. His parents were delighted with that decision and are not at all reluctant to mention to their friends that their son is studying to be a doctor. John knows that they are very proud of him and are excited about his choice of a career.

The only problem is that John is doubting that he has made the right decision. He has difficulty picturing himself working day after day with heart patients in a hospital or clinic. He thinks that he wants a more active life, and he believes that he would be happier and more effective if he worked with young and generally healthy people in a nonmedical setting. John was a very successful high school athlete, and he well remembers (since he has no time for playing now) how much he loved to compete and work out. John is thinking of changing his major to exercise science and heading toward a career as a trainer or an exercise specialist in an athletic setting. But he is worried about telling his parents about this.

John knows that the exercise science major used to be called physical education. Aware of the stereotypes of brainless athletes and tired old coaches, he can imagine his parents' reaction when he tells them about his new plans. He would let them know that the exercise science curriculum is virtually identical to his premedical studies. He would explain that exercise science is actually one of the most demanding academic majors at his school. He would remind them that athletic trainers work with bodies just like doctors do and that both help promote biological health and well-being.

Yet he knows they won't be convinced. Somehow working in medicine sounds so intellectual, so easy to talk about. Working in the sport and exercise professions sounds so muscular, so difficult to dress up in impressive language.

Why is one body-related profession so highly respected and the other often given relatively little status? Why is John inclined to defend his decision on the grounds that physical education is academically demanding? If John wanted instead to defend his decision on the grounds that physical activity involves the whole person and is in its own way intellectually demanding, how would be go about it?

In chapter 2 you investigated the nature of persons. You reviewed four dualistic interpretations that proved to be incomplete and inaccurate as well as harmful for our field. By identifying what does not work in describing a person, you gained important clues about directions you could take in this chapter. Here you will complete the preliminary work for your philosophic travels by attempting to describe a human being as a whole person and to determine the accuracy of this picture.

IN THIS CHAPTER, YOU WILL

- look at the significance of holism;
- review four early expressions of holism;
- encounter a fifth and more modern description of persons; and
- examine implications of this description for sport, exercise science, and physical education.

The vision of persons as whole psycho/physical beings was gained many years ago, and at least four generations of exercise scientists and physical educators have been raised on a doctrine of **holism**. They were taught that

1. the physical aspect of persons is inextricably united with and influenced by every thought that people have;
2. the thoughtful aspect of human existence is inextricably united with and influenced by body composition, health, and movement; and
3. the whole person is greater than the sum of his or her parts.

The only problem is that the doctrine didn't take. As you saw in chapter 2, it did not turn our culture, language, and practices in physical education on their heads. The vision of integrated persons reflecting intelligence in everything from their chemistry to their movement, and showing traces of embodiment in everything from their attitudes to their values, was supposed to cause an earthquake (Griffith, 1970). Instead it caused barely a tremor. Holism was to change drastically and dramatically the way we think about people—how we educate them, treat them medically, provide for their welfare, promote their religious growth, recreate them—but it has not! Thus, we are left with many remnants of dualism in a world that professes to believe in the whole person. And we are left with many questions:

Why are academic majors typically held in high esteem but performance programs like music and physical education held in lower regard? Why can you major in performance in a field like art but not in physical education?

Are there multiple types of intelligence? Have you ever noticed how some things come easy for you, while others are very difficult? Have you ever thought that you are smart and not so smart at the same time?

Have you ever tried to defend your career choice to another person? To yourself?

The Significance of Holism

In the last chapter we saw how the distance between persons and their bodies is related to the centrality of physical education in schools and the importance of other movement-related professions in society. We said that the greater this distance, the less important our contributions. As those who tend to the inferior physical aspects of the person, we would be the handmaidens of those who did real education.

Thus, we must draw out the implications of holism for our professional activities and duties. We must be able to see clearly why and how people are whole and to tell others clearly and convincingly why this is so.

If we cannot do this, we may well be limited to relatively menial jobs in education, sport medicine, and elsewhere. Management, therapeutic, recreational, and communications assistants, staff members, paraprofessionals, technicians—that is what we and all other activity professionals will be if object, value, behavior, and language dualisms continue to hold sway. That is why we need to be sure about holism and find a way to describe it to others clearly and forcefully.

However, we do not have the luxury of dismissing dualism as some curious item in philosophy's antique shop. John Farley, our premed student at the beginning of the chapter, was an unfortunate heir of thinkers like

Descartes and Plato even though they lived hundreds of years ago. He was experiencing the effects of dualistic thinking even though he probably was not aware of it. The biases that his parents and society held against physical games and other supposedly non-intellectual movement activities were based on unexamined beliefs about people and which of their parts and activities are more important. Thus, while John, you, and I might wish to reject this inheritance, it comes without our asking for it and against our will. We have little choice but to work at combating it.

Early Expressions of Holism

Since the beginning of the 20th century, our profession has attempted to describe people in nondualistic terms. Here are four of the most popular phrases used for this purpose. You may already be familiar with one or more of them.

1. *A sound mind in a sound body (Mens sana in corpore sano*—Juvenal). A person is a whole being composed of two closely related elements—mind and body. A healthy mind resides in and therefore is, at least in part, dependent on the presence of a healthy body. Conversely, a sound body is, in part, produced under the guidance of a good mind.

2. *A unity of mind, body, and spirit* (the YMCA Triangle—Gulick). A person is a whole being who has three aspects. No one part should be excessively elevated over, or given attention to the exclusion of, the other two. The human being should be symmetrical and balanced.

3. *Education through the physical* (Williams, 1965). A person is a whole being, and the profession should take advantage of this fact by teaching social and moral lessons through sport, dance, and exercise activities.

4. *Education of the physical* (McCloy, 1966). A person is a whole being, but the profession should still focus on the individual's physical aspects. Physical education should aim primarily at organic outcomes like cardiovascular fitness, greater strength, and improved flexibility, even though attitudes and ideas will also be affected.

PHILOSOPHIC EXERCISE

Are any of these traditions defensible today? Which one of the four do you prefer, and can you provide any arguments for your choice? Based on what you learned in chapter 2, which one makes the most accurate claim about embodiment and its relationship to personhood? Are any of them entirely satisfactory? If you happen to be strongly opposed to all four, write another description. (A sound person? Education as the physical? A psychophysical unity?) Once again, provide a minimum of one argument to defend your decision.

Merits and Shortcomings of These Descriptions

The four early descriptions of whole persons were all well intentioned, and all contributed to an appreciation of the integrated nature of human beings. Nevertheless, each also has its shortcomings.

1. *A sound mind in a sound body*

According to this statement, physical education is important because good thinking (a sound mind) is dependent on organic health (a sound body). Thus, education should be balanced; the physical should not be neglected for the mental. In fact, the human being is so fully integrated that complete human development is possible only if the whole psychophysical organism is educated and otherwise tended to. *This marked an advance from the belief of some dualists that the mind operated with a high degree of independence from the body and even enjoyed an existence of its own.*

Nevertheless, there are many problems with this spatial metaphor, which suggests that something called mind is *in* something else called body, rather like a marble in a glass jar. You already know that this leads to an unanswerable question. How can something that is not physical (an idea) be in something else that is physical (one's body or head)?

Also, the very identification of mind and body as human components provides a dualistic framework for understanding persons. It may imply that the body serves the lesser function in this arrangement. Its health is important as a means to another end—good thinking—not as an end in itself. Notice that Juvenal left the statement one-sided: "A sound mind in a sound body." He could have added, "and a sound body around a sound mind," but he did not.

2. *A unity of mind, body, and spirit*

According to the old YMCA triangle, physical education is valuable because the physical side of persons is one of three closely related aspects of human beings. In order for people to reach their potential, their education and training must be balanced. No single type of learning should be elevated above the other two. The triangle also eliminates the bothersome spatial metaphor of something in something else, of a healthy mind in a healthy body. And, on some views, there is nothing wrong with adding a religious dimension to personhood. It makes some sense to talk about sound and unsound religious habits or beliefs just as it does, at least roughly, to speak of good and poor mental and physical health. *This signaled an advance for physical education because physical aspects of human existence were given a position of equality with spiritual and intellectual elements.*

Yet there remains the image of the person composed of three corners that are somehow unified to make a single triangle. Moving around the triangle, the mind corner fades into the body corner, which, in turn, fades into the spirit corner, which returns to the mind corner. Ultimately, the problems with this image of personhood are much the same as those of the mind-in-the-body metaphor. If there are no pure corners of a triangle (called mind, body, and soul), there can be no triangle made up of them. And even if there were such corners lying around someplace, how are they related to one another? What happens at those places in the triangle where one corner fades into the others? How can a nonphysical corner (mind or soul), for example, fade into a physical one (body)?

This image also may be misleading by suggesting that mind or intelligence is a single, uniform thing. It could be that we have multiple intelligences rather than a unidimensional object called mind. We will examine this idea later in the chapter.

3. *Education through the physical*

For Williams (1965), the author of this phrase, physical education is important because dance, games, exercise, and play are marvelous laboratories for learning. If people are whole beings, teachers cannot isolate and work on any pure physical element. When one moves physically, Williams believed, the whole person is affected. Thus, through the physical (e.g., by means of participation in various games, play, and dance), the student could, and almost invariably would, learn other things. By manipulating these

When one moves, the whole person is affected.

movement laboratories skillfully, teachers could assure that these other things that students learned were also good things— predominantly for Williams, socially useful outcomes like the habits, skills, and knowledge related to good citizenship. *This marked an important advance because physical education gained a more central place in education. Physical activities were not aimed at merely mechanical, biological outcomes, but were extended to important social and psychological objectives.*

Yet, Williams's language, too, is unfortunately dualistic. His phrase points to something called "the physical," and he leaves us with an image of well-intentioned teachers using this physical part of persons as an avenue to get at other more important ends. There is an implicit value dualism here, one that gives the physical the status of a mere means.

4. *Education of the physical*

Charles McCloy (1966), the author of this phrase, believed that physical education is valuable because organic contributions to overall human development and happiness are pervasive and significant. The whole person is completely biological and thoroughly influenced in every aspect of life by such biological qualities as strength, flexibility, motor skill, and overall health. Thus, his education *of* the physical was not a territorial claim about a part of the human being that is separate from some mental aspect. Rather it was a nondualistic claim about how our physical nature and characteristics affect our personalities, attitudes, goals, values, and our work and play. *This was an advance for physical education because some dualists felt that physical training, growth, and development were peripheral to the achievement of human potential. They believed that physical well-being was an optional pathway to human success and happiness.*

Yet McCloy's language has as much a dualistic ring to it as does Williams's phrase. The term *of the physical* conjures up pictures of physical educators working on the bodies of their students, much as mechanics work on cars that need repair and preventive maintenance. We are left wondering if there are other teachers "of the mental." And as was the case with Williams, McCloy's description suggests that physical education provides a means to other more important ends. The phrase may suggest that education of the physical is a necessary precondition for an effective education of the mental.

A Vertical Interpretation of Persons

While these expressions of holism promoted important advances for our field, they failed to produce an earthquake of new thinking, speaking, and acting. They produced only a tremor because they still accepted a fundamentally dualistic image of human existence. I call this image a vertical interpretation of persons. It is one that has mind over body, thinking over doing, and verbalization over nonverbal expression.

In the vertical image of persons in Figure 3.1, the human being is still composed of two parts—a mental and a physical part. The superiority of the mental half is symbolized by placing it above the physical aspect.

Mind and body are now understood to be closely related. They intimately affect one another. Thus only a dotted line separates the two. In other words, there is no gulf between mind and body. A sound mind essentially requires a sound body. And the playing of physically active games pretty much guarantees that attitudes and ideas will be affected. Yet the dotted line remains because these four interpretations still rely on notions of mind and body, and they often depict the body in the role of a means to mental ends.

The arrows symbolize the two-way relationship that exists between mind and body

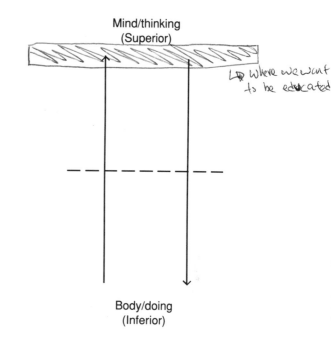

Figure 3.1.   Vertical image of persons.

in this vertical, holistic model. The upward pointing arrow makes Juvenal's point that physical health affects mental functioning; Williams's point that participation in physical games affects the whole person—including his or her personality, hopes, and ideals; and McCloy's point that physical strength, flexibility, cardiovascular fitness, and other parameters of physical health play an important role in the achievement of human potential. The downward pointing arrow makes the complementary claims: that mental health affects physical functioning; that theoretical understanding and attitudes affect the whole person—including posture, skill, and physical health; and that knowledge plays an important role in the achievement of overall human potential.

Nevertheless, with the dotted line in existence and with mind on top, this vision of human life may send the message that a reflective life, all else being equal, is better than a physically active one.

A New Vision: Five Holistic Principles

We need a new and improved vision, one that does more than replace a gulf between mind and body with a dotted line. We need to get rid of the line altogether. In fact, we need to stop thinking of human beings in terms of two parts and stop placing something called mind over something else called body. From our previous analyses, we can now state five principles that will guide us in drawing a more accurate picture of persons.

1. *Such a picture will have to show that physical influences are always at work in shaping all that we are and do.* It will have to acknowledge the fact that we are totally chemical and physical, and that—because we are embodied—we are totally historical and always act from a perspective in time and space. This chemistry and this embodied perspective affect our every behavior, no matter how reflective and sedentary it may be. Genetic inheritance does matter; where and when we were born does matter; whether we experienced love or rejection as a child born to specific parents in a specific home does matter; whether we had a fine coach who inspired us when we were ninth graders does matter.

2. *Such a picture will have to show that the influences of consciousness are always at work.* We are influenced by our personality, driven by our ideas, deflected by our perceptions, modified by our recognitions. This is true no matter how movement oriented our activity, even if it is only a reflex action, and no matter where we look, even at our chemistry. Ideas do matter; they make people change their

behavior, do one thing and not another. Ideas, for example, cause human beings to dedicate themselves to various causes, even to give up their lives heroically. Attitudes may partly determine how long we will live.

3. *Such a picture will have to show that these workings have no complete independence from one another.* It will have to take the interpretation of consciousness and embodiment seriously. These are internally, not externally related. Neither one can be reduced to the other—ideas to physical states, or physical states to ideas. Because these two realities are homogenized in personhood, neither one retains a separate abstract character. The footprints of chemicals can be found in human ideas. For instance, optimism and pessimism may be caused, in part, by our chemistry. The footprints of ideas can be found in human chemistry. For example, nervous ideas can cause an increased acidity in our stomachs.

4. *Such a picture will have to depict different levels of behavioral intelligence.* It will have to take seriously the fact that some actions are highly insightful, adaptable, and complex while others are largely blind, inflexible, and simple. Solving a complex equation is very different from scribbling simple arthmetic. Making a creative move to the basket is very different from lining up a 1-foot putt.

5. *Such a picture will have to depict different types of activity.* It will have to take seriously the fact that some behaviors are carried out largely in muscle and motor ways while others take place reflectively, often with little or no movement involved. Kicking a ball and thinking about kicking a ball both involve some skillful doing, but one is motor-active while the other is thought oriented, sedentary, and thus largely motor-passive.

Impressive Intelligence: Two Pictures

The fourth requirement indicates that we have to remember that our actions show

$$VCO_2 STPD, L \cdot min^{-1} = (F_ECO_2X$$

$$=(0.0390 \times 125.13)-$$

Impressive intelligence in advanced skills: sedentary . . .

greater and lesser degrees of intelligence or insight. The two pictures here show high degrees of insight—that is, behavior that requires an impressive level of intelligence. Notice that one individual is involved in motor-oriented activity and the other in reflective-tending behavior.

Could it be that there are criteria other than "physical" and "mental" that determine the level of intelligence utilized and expressed? Could it be that tossing a ball around and tossing around some ideas could require, in their own ways, comparably impressive displays of intelligence? How would we see that? Are there characteristics of impressive intelligence that may be present whether one is dealing with balls or ideas?

Here are some possibilities for what we might see. The actions of both individuals are partly *free and unconstrained*—some in close relationship to things like space, time, and gravity and others in close relationship to numbers, mathematical relationships, words, and sentences. Their behavior is unpredictable. Their freedom gives them options not available to lesser performers. They can go where they might not be expected to go and

. . . and in action.

Table 3.1 Behavioral Characteristics of High and Low Intelligence

Low intelligence and insight	High intelligence and insight
Experiences constraint	Experiences freedom
Actions are repetitive	Actions are unpredictable
Has difficulty adapting to new circumstances	Adapts to new circumstances well/quickly
Relies on past solutions	Is inventive/creative
Behavior is simple	Behavior is complex
Has limited or narrow vision	Uses broad perceptual input
Actions are rigid; resistive to change	Actions are flexible; open to change
Experiences standard, public meaning	Experiences new, personal meaning

do what they might not be expected to do. They are all *inventive and creative*. They are so good at what they do that they can find novel answers to many of their problems. They can adapt to new conditions at a moment's notice. Their actions are *complex*. For example, their skills are based on many different habits that no longer require their attention. Thus, they can do many things at once. Their attention is *expansive and distant*. They can take in a considerable amount of information at one time. Their attention runs past the space right in front of them, past the ball, past the specific numbers being manipulated, past the letters, words, and sentences. These characteristics are highlighted in Table 3.1.

PHILOSOPHIC EXERCISE

Have you seen yourself described here? Do you have things that you do particularly well

that can be accurately described as free or unconstrained, unpredictable, inventive and creative, complex, and expansive? Are some of these things motor oriented? Are others more sedentary and reflection oriented?

List two of your best skill-based activities and describe what you feel like when you are performing wonderfully well. Can you find adjectives other than those that I've used? Do you see that these descriptions apply equally well to sedentary *and* nonsedentary, verbal *and* nonverbal, mental *and* so-called physical activities? This discovery should tell you that these distinctions deserve far less attention than many people are inclined to give them.

Unimpressive Intelligence: Two Pictures

The pictures on page 77 show a low degree of insight—that is, behavior that requires an unimpressive level of intelligence. Once again, one picture shows someone trying to solve a movement-related problem, while the other shows someone engaged in a sedentary act. Thus, what makes these behaviors unimpressive is not that they involve physical activity. The determining factor must be something else.

Here are a few possibilities for what that something else might be. The actions of both individuals are highly *constrained*. They are largely at the mercy of things like gravity, balls, spaces, distances, numbers, letters, or words. They experience very little freedom. Consequently, their actions are *predictable*. They are likely to perform by the book. Because they are overwhelmed by their tasks, they show *little inventiveness or creativity*. They can barely keep track of the basics. Their actions are *simple*. They are in the very early process of building up habits that will allow them to do many things at once. But for now, they must be content with doing one thing

Unimpressive intelligence in beginning skills: sedentary . . .

at a time. And finally, their field of attention is *narrow and close by*—at the space right in front of them, at the ball, at the numbers, or at the letters.

PHILOSOPHIC EXERCISE

Do you also find yourself on this page? Are there things that you are learning (or for which you have little ability) that can be accurately described as lacking freedom, highly predictable, uninventive and uncreative, simple, and narrow? Are some of these things physically active and others more sedentary and reflective?

Identify two of your worst activities. Try to describe these, at least in part, with adjectives that I did not use above. If you find that you can use the same words across the sedentary-nonsedentary divide, this again should tell you that this difference may not be a very important distinction after all.

Let us now attempt to improve upon the vertical image of whole persons by drawing a new diagram—a horizontal picture. We will eliminate things called "mind" and "body," erase the dotted line that separated the physical from the mental, and rewrite the rules for what counts as impressive (intelligent) human behavior.

A Horizontal Interpretation of Persons

The image diagrammed in Figure 3.2 seems to meet the five requirements of holism outlined earlier.

. . . and in action.

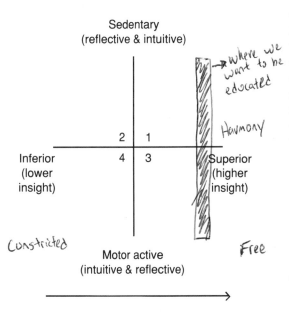

Figure 3.2. Horizontal image of persons.

Notice first that the top and the bottom of the image do not represent mind and body or the mental and physical. Rather they depict two poles for all human behavior. At the top is sedentary activity that includes both reflection (the recollection and use of facts and propositions) and intuition (the use of various intellectual skills—such as computing, writing, deducing, inducing, and imagining). It is called sedentary because, as intellectually active as this behavior is, it can be done in a chair with minimal movement and little reliance on sensory perception. Sedentary activity can be done insightfully and well, and this is symbolized by quadrant 1 in the diagram. It is this behavior that is experienced as free and unconstrained, unpredictable, inventive and creative, and complex. One's attention is not at the numbers, or words, or new ideas—as it is with beginners—but is rather expansive and distant.

Sedentary reflective activity can also be done poorly. This is symbolized by quadrant 2. While behavior here is every bit as sedentary and reflective or intuitive as activity in quadrant 1, and for that reason might be called in our society "intellectual activity," it is nonetheless primitive, rote, reflexive. As indicated previously, it is constrained, predictable, noncreative, simple. One's attention is narrow and close by. It is doing philosophy, math, composition, history . . . whatever, by the numbers in lock-step fashion.

The bottom portion of the image symbolizes the other pole of human behavior—the perceptual and motor active one. Here activity cannot be accomplished in a chair, and it typically relies heavily on sensory perception. This behavior requires thinking every bit as much as the activity at the top of the diagram. However, at this pole of behavior, intuitive skills (knowing how) usually take precedence over reflection. Consequently, the order of thinking activity is reversed at the bottom of the diagram. Intuition is emphasized over reflection. As was the case with sedentary activity, motor active behavior can be done well or poorly—that is, with great insight, creativity, and artistry (symbolized by quadrant 3) or with minimal insight, in rote and predictable fashion, with little or no interpretation and flair (quadrant 4).

Of crucial importance here is the substitution of vertical goals, both personally and in education, with horizontal ones. On this nondualistic version of personhood and human behavior, it is not important to move up the image toward reflection, mind, thinking, or so-called intellectual activity. Nor is it important to avoid behavior near the bottom of the image—the nonverbal and supposedly nonintellectual arts, crafts, and sport skills. What is important is to advance to the right side of the image (symbolized by the arrow aiming in that direction). As whole people, we want and need to act insightfully whether this be in more or less sedentary reflective or intuitive ways or in more or less motor active intuitive or reflective ways. And as whole people, we need to be educated toward the *entire* right side of the image, not predominantly in the direction of quadrant 1, as is too often now the case in dualistic education.

We must now determine if this new horizontal image satisfies the five holistic principles discussed on page 74.

1. It takes physical reality and limited, embodied experience seriously. Human activity in all four quadrants is influenced by chemistry and genes, by physics and physiology. Inferior behavior (quadrants 2 and 4) is dominated by these material influences, and thus is relatively constrained. Superior behavior (quadrants 1 and 3) is influenced by these physical elements but is not dominated by them. Consequently it is relatively unconstrained. But all behavior is influenced by physical reality, whether on the left-hand border of this image or the far right side.

2. It takes consciousness and ideas seriously. Behavior in all four quadrants is influenced by insight and ideas, emotions and perceptions. Superior behavior (quadrants 1 and 3) is dominated by insights, but even inferior behavior (quadrants 2 and 4) shows traces of emotion and ideas. Thus, all human behavior is influenced by the human capacity to think and perceive.

3. It shows that the conscious and physical sides of people and their behavior have no independence. In fact, there is no mind and body in this figure. There are only two poles of behavior—tending to the sedentary and to the motor active; and there are only two poles of quality for those behaviors—tending to the impressive and to the unimpressive. Where is body here? It is everywhere playing different roles and having different degrees of influence. The same can be said for consciousness. Because there is no separate "mind" and "body" in this image, it is impossible for one

to direct the other. Likewise, it is impossible for one to operate apart from the influence of the other (e.g., mind reflecting on ideas without being affected by chemistry and socialization, or body operating simply as a machine). Everything the person is and does is influenced by both ideas and biology.

4. It shows that human behavior, projects, and actions differ in character. Some are sedentary or still in nature. They rely very little, if at all, on actual sense perception, muscle coordination, cardiovascular endurance, and so on. They do rely on memory, imagination, and various reflective skills—whether they be the procedures of writing, doing philosophy, manipulating numbers, or imagining scientific hypotheses. Others are active in nature. They rely very little, if at all, on reflection, proposition formation, the memorization of facts, or other reflective skills. But they do rely on effective sight, motor skill, endurance, and the like. In short, the diagram acknowledges the existence of diverse types of behavior, diverse skills, diverse human practices (MacIntyre, 1984).

5. It shows that both general types of behavior (sedentary and active) can vary in terms of their use of intelligence and insight. There are impressive displays of intelligence that take dance forms and others that take rocket science forms. Likewise there are unimpressive displays of intelligence that go in these two directions. Thus, a spectrum of behavior—from low to high intelligence (left side to right side, respectively)—is included in the picture.

Which part of our new image is the most important? While all five points are significant, I think that the fifth has the greatest implications. This is the claim that most forcefully reorients our thinking from vertical to horizontal. It indicates that intellectual activity and insight fall to the right half of the diagram, not the top. Insight and intellectual power are not limited to reflective/verbal/

sedentary doings (the top half of the diagram). Insight and intellectual power permeate the full range of human behavior from the most sedentary (top of quadrant 1) to the most active (bottom of quadrant 3). Thus, in principle, we can be involved in insightful, right, true, or brilliant acts on our dance floors and in our gymnasiums just as can the philosopher, mathematician, or writer in his or her easy chair. Our intellectual displays merely take a different form.

It turns out, if this new image is accurate, that what is important is not that we use our "mind" more than our "body," or allow the "mental" to direct the "physical," or use words rather than movements, or reflect before we act. What is important is that we are free rather than constrained, creative rather than unimaginative, unpredictable rather than patterned, insightful rather than blind. We have new ground rules for what counts as humanly impressive—and these rules give no advantage, in principle, to the pen over the bat, the word over the gesture, the true proposition over the true movement.

What matters in determining the quality of human behavior is not *that* we are doing a so-called physical activity, but *how* we are doing it. And the same is true for the supposed intellectual side of life. It matters not so much *that* we are doing a reflective-sedentary activity but *how* we are doing it.

PHILOSOPHIC EXERCISE

Pretend that you are a dualist. One day, an unfriendly person approaches you and says, "You are an athlete. Therefore, you must be a dumb jock." Or, "You are a dancer. Therefore you must be nonintellectual." How, as a dualist, would you be inclined to answer?

Now, using our new horizontal image of personhood (where dance, sport, and other movement activities fall across the full range of intellectual involvement), how would you be inclined to answer? What if this individual had never seen you compete or dance? Would she be able, with any assurance, to make that claim about your being nonintellectual? On the other hand, what if she had seen you dance or play and still made the same claim? Would you have reason to take more stock in her judgment?

SUMMARY BREAK

We now have some answers to the question with which we started: What is a person? These answers involved the drawing of a new horizontally oriented image of persons, but we can also put this picture into words.

1. A person is not composed of mind and body but is rather one piece of cloth.

2. This one piece of cloth is a product of multiple levels of influence from simple chemicals to abstract beliefs, from experiences in one family to general attitudes, from being raised in one neighborhood at one time in history to the logical requirements of thought processes.

3. All of these influences affect the whole cloth in varying degrees all of the time.

4. Given this radical wholeness of persons, human potential cannot be reached through any workings of mind over body, mind directing body, or abstract propositions informing mechanical doing. Human potential is reached, at least in part, by acting truthfully or rightly whether in predominantly sedentary/reflective ways, or predominantly active/intuitive ways, or both.

We can no longer be satisfied with old descriptions of holism that hold on to dualistic premises and images. Although early expressions of holism alerted past generations to the integration and interdependence of biology and personality, and of chemistry and thinking, they did not give up a fundamentally vertical, dualistic interpretation of persons.

Three Implications of the New Holism

Our descriptions have some remarkable implications for day-to-day thinking and acting. You may not be ready to accept some of these deductions, and all of us will have political difficulties in selling some of them. But if our new description is on target, some implications for action will appear radical and will inevitably run against the grain of our common practices.

What Counts as Intelligent?

We have redefined the nature of intelligence and the workings of intellectual insight. The old definition of intelligence was uniform and narrow. It had to do with our ability to use numbers and words, follow logic, and understand and remember abstract concepts. Our new definition includes human capabilities to see and act correctly, insightfully, or truthfully. With Gardner (1985) we came upon the likelihood of multiple intelligences—some that work best with words and abstract concepts, some that work best with sense perceptual discriminations; some that work best with logic, some with a sense of direction and spatial location; some that work best with words, some with sounds and rhythms; some reflectively in an easy chair, some intuitively through a magical move on a modern dance stage.

Therefore, no longer can you encounter philosophy, English, or math majors on your campus and assume that they are intellectually advanced simply because they do philosophy, English, and math. For all you know, they may deal with ideas, words, and numbers in the upper left portion of Figure 3.2. Why should you honor rote, unimaginative, predictable philosophy, English, and math just because it is reflective?

No longer can any of your friends or colleagues assume that, just because your cleverness is exercised in a mostly nonverbal, dance/athletic, sense-perceptual world, you are intellectually impoverished. For all they know you could be absolutely brilliant. You may kick, swing, or pirouette in the lower right portion of Figure 3.2. In fact, many of you probably found this field to be attractive because you were already well on your way to that lower right area of creative activity. Why should anyone overlook the intellectual significance of creative, insightful, sensitive, unpredictable movement just because it is movement-active?

If you wanted to demonstrate your special activity IQ, you would not ask others to read what you have written about sport, dance, or exercise or look at the test scores you received in physiology of exercise and motor-learning classes. You would invite them out to the baseball field, into the dance studio, or into the weight room and say quite simply, "Please watch!"

And if somebody asked you if you are intelligent, you would undoubtedly have to answer, "Yes and no." You may have two left feet when it comes to dance but still show a grace and shrewdness on the wrestling mat. You may break out in a cold sweat in the presence of quadratic equations but still make confident, clever discriminations in the world of basketball. Intelligence, in other words, breaks out, shows itself, works, functions—describe it as you wish—in different ways. Table 3.2 lists examples of behaviors showing high and low intelligence.

Table 3.2 Actions/Behaviors Showing High and Low Intelligence

Behaviors requiring comparably low uses of intelligence	Behaviors requiring comparably high uses of intelligence
Scribbling the word *cat*	Writing a prize-winning novel
Recognizing the word *ball*	Reading and comprehending a complex textbook
Adding 1 and 1	Solving an advanced problem in calculus
Expressing blind patriotism	Understanding reasons for the checks and balances of democratic government
Painting by number	Painting the *Mona Lisa*
Playing an easy piano piece mechanically by following the printed music	Playing improvisational piano at an international competition
Looking at one's hand while learning how to release the basketball correctly	Making a creative move to the basket in the NBA

If anyone still is not convinced of our non-dualistic conclusion, ask him or her to make the following comparisons:

Would it be better to experience exhilarating freedom in activity environments or stifling bondage in a reflective setting? (Whatever the setting, the more insightful human being receives a greater number of invitations to act, adds style and flair to routine effectiveness, experiences openness and opportunity.)

Would it be better to be an unpredictable, creative basketball player or a machinelike, unimaginative mathematician? (Whatever the setting, the more insightful human being frequently does the unexpected, treats repetitive situations differently, produces surprises, refuses to be merely a machine.)

Would it be better to behave in complex ways as a masterful athlete or act according to simple scripts as a philosopher? (Whatever the setting, the more insightful human being refuses to write scripts beforehand, does not reduce skills to simplistic formulas, respects a memorable performance as a partly inexplicable result of many thousands of factors.)

Would it be better to act inventively as an Olympic competitor or react involuntarily to some stimulus as a scientist? (Whatever the setting, the more insightful human being is the author of his or her actions, not the victim of a situation.)

Would it be better to surpass good habits as an improvisational soccer player or be chained to habits as a mechanical and awkward psychologist? (The more insightful human being does more things automatically, focuses attention elsewhere, is freed from minor details, has a foundation of good habits and, because of that, can go beyond them.)

Would it be better to be able to play tennis masterfully and artistically or do political science in a stimulus-response, knee-jerk fashion? (Whatever the setting, the more insightful human being is less a soldier who mindlessly reacts to impinging data and more a creative partner who intuits meanings.)

These comparisons should at least raise questions about the privileged status of the so-called intellectual professions. The truth of what was claimed earlier should now be even clearer. It is not so much what you are doing that counts but rather how you are

Some qualities of insight-in-action: free, creative, unpredictable, complex, right.

doing it. People are smart in different ways, and some of those ways focus on the spatio-temporal movement skills with which you and I are immediately involved.

What Happens to the Status of Physical Education?

There would be absolutely no reason for movement professionals to feel defensive, act defensively, or even bother to claim that they are not defensive. Physical educators would no longer need to cloister themselves in schools of health, physical education, and recreation. They would not need to forfeit the high ground of impressive intelligence and smart behavior to others. They would not necessarily have to apologize for the fact that their perceptual and motor acuity may be stronger than their verbal or mathematical intelligence. They would find some comfort and peace in their own pattern of intelligence,

their own form of brilliance. They would be just as happy to be called artistic as brainy. They would be just as happy to have someone comment, "What great movements!" as, "What great sentences!"

Physical educators would be more likely to form close relationships with other academic units in high schools, colleges, and universities—units that utilize the same or similar forms of intelligence and thus have a common ground for mutual respect. As noted in chapter 2, foremost among these would be the arts, where there is a premium on the ability to move sensitively and correctly in time and space—whether at a keyboard with one's hands, an easel with a paintbrush, or on a pair of ice skates with the whole body. But new ties and mutual respect might also develop with the language arts when expression and communication are seen to be whole person activities that might include posture, sport movement, and dance gesture as much as verbal pronouncement. In short, as we came to a less dualistic vision of human life, we should come to a less compartmentalized view of academics and education.

What Happens to the Significance of Performance?

Motor-oriented performance would be on an equal footing with reflective-tending actions. Movement might be accorded respect comparable to that given to various sedentary activities. Curricular decisions and ground rules would, in many cases, change.

For example, if sedentary-tending actions like writing and computing are thought to be basic skills, then motor-oriented activities like dancing and hiking should probably be basic skills too. If cuts in the curriculum are needed for fiscal reasons, these should not fall only or disproportionately on the movement arts. If there are compelling reasons to give academic credit and grades for creative philosophic exploring, then it may be right to award academic credit and grades for creative aquatic exploring. If there are faculty sabbaticals taken for reflecting more intelligently, there should be sabbaticals for moving more intelligently. If students can be kept out of athletics because of low grades in English, then students should also be kept out of English for low grades in physical education. If there are honors courses in math, there should be honors levels of curriculum in movement. If someone must be able to spell and count before he or she is allowed to graduate, then that same person should probably be able to gesture and move with some minimal level of competence before getting a diploma, as well.

Conversely, we might need to change some of our own practices with which, unfortunately, many in our field have become too comfortable. If, for example, it is proper to pass students in movement education because they attend class and take showers, then it may be proper to pass students in philosophy for showing up and keeping a clean notebook. If it

is virtually impossible to receive a grade lower than a B in physical education (let alone fail), then it should probably be impossible to receive anything below a B in Spanish or biology. If it is sound practice to offer mostly beginning-level, remedial sport skills in college, then it is probably right for university departments of chemistry and physics to present mostly a grade school curriculum. If it is possible to be effective in the movement domain by merely rolling out the ball or turning on the music, then it may be a good teaching strategy in civics class to hand out some books and merely tell the students to read. If it is acceptable to give movement students two-week units in folk dance, modern dance, aerobic dance, gymnastics, golf, and weight training, then perhaps it is right for math teachers to give only two weeks of long division, two weeks of multiplication, two weeks of algebra, and two weeks of calculus.

Finally, if skillful movement does not just lead to knowledge but can be itself a legitimate and valuable form of knowing, and if skillful movement does not just rely on previous intelligent behavior but can be itself a form of insightful (if not brilliant) activity, then why not offer bachelor's, master's, and doctoral degrees in performance? Students in our field could make a fundamental choice (as indeed they do now in the arts) to emphasize the practice, the art, and the skill, on the one hand, or the theory, science, and facts and propositions about movement, on the other. Why not require performance faculty to give periodic recitals or demonstrations (as long as their health and age permit)? Why not award tenure and grant promotions to performance faculty, at least in part, on the basis of their growth and development as master performers?

PHILOSOPHIC EXERCISE

Do you think that these analogies are sound? Have I gone too far? Are there any good

Should we think movement skills are as important as academic skills?

reasons for the different standards, different practices, and different degrees of seriousness with which we take our reflective-tending and movement-tending careers and subject matter?

See if you can criticize any of the conclusions I drew or implied in this section. Provide at least one argument for the validity of different standards where you think they may be supportable. Then see if you can add any more implications for behavioral change in line with my own. What about faculty benefits? Student awards and honors? Libraries, study halls, new kinds of IQ tests, different categories for the SAT, names for new masters and doctoral degrees?

A Partial Concession

I may well have been guilty here of drawing some unwarranted deductions from the previously developed description of whole persons. As implied in the philosophic exercise,

there may still be relevant differences between our field and others that would justify double standards. But one of the functions of philosophy is to allow us to break with convention, with standard ways of seeing things, and to follow ideas with at least a little bit of abandon. We may have to pull back to a more conservative position, but we will have given ourselves an opportunity to see the world from a different vantage point based on the force of philosophic reasoning itself.

For instance, the claim about the no-pass, no-play legislation (where high school students are ruled ineligible for athletic participation when their academic grades are too low) was generated philosophically. In a nondualistic world, logic may tell us that sport should no more be thought of as a mere means for English, than English is thought of as a mere means for physical education. But even in a nondualistic world, practical reason tells us that there may be good reasons for using athletics to promote better work in such subjects as math, English, and social studies. It can be argued that an inability to speak and write would do a person more harm than an inability to move well in a game.

Yet consider the philosophic argument. Picture yourself as a high school physical education teacher and coach. Imagine going to an English teachers' department meeting and, with a very serious expression on your face, saying that you are working to get a policy passed whereby no student who is flunking physical education will be allowed to continue with their studies in English. You tell them that this is your Motor Affirmative Action Policy (MAAP, for short).

Movement education has been so neglected for so long, you inform them, that now—until the scales are better balanced—education must compensate in the other direction. Because it is so important that students can see, gesture, play, explore, create, and dance effectively, teachers must threaten them with nonparticipation in English if they do not measure up regarding their movement and sense-perceptual education.

One of your English teaching colleagues might note, "But you cannot threaten them with English; they do not want to be here in the first place. Some students will intentionally flunk physical education just so they can spend more time with you and less with us."

"All the better," you respond. "Until this lack of balance between writing and moving has been redressed, they *should* be spending more time with me."

You thank your colleagues for their understanding and cooperation. You graciously remind them that once some educational balance is achieved, you will no longer need to use English as a means to enhance efforts in movement education and will recommend that the school board rescind MAAP.

Review

The vision of persons as whole beings has been in existence for some time but it has not had the impact that many predicted for it.

Four traditional descriptions of integrated persons allowed physical education to make some progress in arguing for the centrality of activity and movement in human development. Nevertheless, these four visions retained a vertical and somewhat dualistic image of human existence. While they moved us forward, they also held us back.

A new horizontal image of persons is needed in order to satisfy five basic requirements of holism. This image eliminates entities called "mind" and "body," erases any line or gap between supposed physical and mental activity, and redefines what counts as intelligent and insightful behavior. The crucial part of the image is that it depicts free, unpredictable, creative, inventive, sensitive, and insightful behavior as both sedentary/reflective and active/intuitive. There might be different forms of human intelligence that merit comparable recognition, attention, and support. Practical implications of this new description of persons involve at least three areas: what deserves to be called "intelligent," what the status of our profession should be, and what respect performance should enjoy.

John Farley's decision (in the example at the beginning of the chapter) to change from premed to PE was more difficult than it should have been. He was the unfortunate heir of Plato and Descartes, of dualistic ways of interpreting life, of doubts about the significance of activity in sport, dance, games, and play. He was caught in the current confusion about what it is to be intellectual, insightful, or simply smart. Even though he was not planning to major in performance itself (he wanted to be an athletic trainer), his career choice suffered because of its mere association with a nonsedentary and supposedly nonintellectual profession.

Looking Ahead

On the foundation of your familiarity with philosophy and a new answer to the question,

What is a person? you should be ready to begin Part II. There you will examine the current condition of society, identify its most pressing needs, and then philosophically evaluate the merits of four of our field's traditional values: fitness, knowledge, skill, and pleasure. Eventually you will rank these values and decide how sport, exercise science, and physical education can best contribute to the good life.

Checking Your Understanding

1. Why are each of the four early descriptions of persons at least partly holistic, and what progress did they allow our field to make?
2. Why are each of these early descriptions of persons at least partly dualistic, and how did they hold us back?
3. Describe the five essential ingredients of holism in your own words. Which of the five, in your judgment, is the most important, and why?
4. What are the key improvements in the horizontal image of persons over previous pictures that were vertical in nature? Can you identify at least three of them?

5. What are some practical implications of holism in understanding what counts as smart, how the profession is regarded, and how performance is dealt with?

Key Terms

Holism, p. 69

A sound mind in a sound body, p. 70

A unity of mind, body, and spirit, p. 71

Education through the physical, p. 71

Education of the physical, p. 72

Further Reading

Articles by Smith, Steel, and Kretchmar in Vanderwerken and Wertz (1985) provide useful analyses of the workings of intelligence in sport, exercise, and dance. Griffith's discussion of human beings "a-foot" in Spicker (1970), is a classic in this area. Those interested in a nondualistic vision of performance in arts should see Fraleigh (1987), regarding dance, and Sudnow (1978), on jazz piano.

Part II
The Values of Sport, Exercise Science, and Physical Education

It has often been said that sport, exercise, and other activities are good for people. As flattering as this is, we dare not accept such claims on mere faith. We must substantiate such statements to make sure that we can deliver on our promises.

We need to be concerned about a second matter as well: Which values, among those that we can effectively promote are most important? Which good things that we can produce are needed most here and now, in this particular society? Which values are best, in general, for human betterment? These questions about the values of movement activity will be addressed in this part.

Chapter 4

Sport and the Needs of Society

Katie Freedman is a talented 14-year-old basketball player who lives in an upper-class neighborhood near Society Hill. She wants to play Division I college basket-ball and has been attending summer basketball camps since she was eight. Now that she is on an organized school team, she is beginning to get a considerable amount of publicity. She is even receiving letters and phone calls from college coaches. Her parents are excited about her success and boast to their relatives and friends about her early notoriety. Katie's quest for excellence in basketball is picking up momentum. It would be difficult for her to turn back now.

There are moments when her parents worry about where their daughter's basketball life is headed and whether her talents and singular focus on becoming one of the best woman players are actually a mixed blessing. What effect, they wonder, will this have on the rest of her life? Will Katie's dedication to excellence have negative as well as positive outcomes?

Is the current interest in elite level sports healthy? Is it generally in the best interests of very young athletes to focus on one sport in an attempt to achieve excellence, receive a college scholarship, or sign a professional contract? What are the most pressing needs in American society?

In Part I you did some spadework on the nature of human existence. This should place you in a better position to understand what people (specifically, whole people) want and need. This should also place you in a better position to identify what we can offer them. In this part you will examine cultural needs and philosophic values. We begin in this chapter by looking at society and the individuals in it.

IN THIS CHAPTER, YOU WILL

- **examine three reasons why philosophers need to look at society,**

- **analyze several needs of contemporary society, and**

- **review ways in which sport and physical education both contribute to societal ills and provide a resource for cures.**

Philosophic journeys always occur in the context of history and culture. While values have objective characteristics that make them inherently stronger or weaker, the people whose lives could benefit from these values come from very different historic and cultural situations. Values like health, physical fitness, and excellence for example, may be needed more by some than by others. Even good values like these can be overemphasized and cause unintended harm. Establishing value priorities and designing life activities based on them raise a number of questions.

Are you largely the product of your environment? Do you think that you have been programmed or manipulated to value certain things?

Are your attitudes toward competition, physical fitness, masculinity, and femininity, for instance, nothing more than the majority views of your culture? Are these good and defensible attitudes or simply the ones that have rubbed off on you because of your socialization?

Do youth sports teach youngsters the wrong lessons? In retrospect, were your Little League experiences entirely positive ones? Did all of your coaches keep things in their proper perspective?

What functions do sport, dance, and exercise serve in our culture today? Are those functions good ones?

How will historians judge our culture? Will they call this time a golden age or a period of cultural decline?

Will they interpret our society's interest in health, physical appearance, longevity, improved performance, and winning positively or negatively?

Why Look at Society?

In this chapter I will be using the terms **society** and **culture** interchangeably. A society or culture is defined as a sizeable group of people who show a degree of unity over time. This unity is typically based on a shared history, common values, and ongoing practices, and it often promotes the formation of separate governments, distinctive institutions, and special languages or symbol systems. The society or culture given the most attention in this book is the North American culture of the late 20th century, but much of what is said here applies to other western and eastern cultures as well.

What then are the reasons for looking at society or culture? You will recall from chapter 1 that the philosophic method does not rely on an empirical turn. Yet here you are being asked to look empirically, much like a sociologist would, at various facts about society. It is important to understand why a philosopher would do this.

Taking Individuals and Institutions Seriously

If our philosophic reflections are to have any practical applications, we must be certain that they retain at least an element of realism. Our philosophic insights, if they are to work, must be able to affect two influential elements in society—people and institutions. By looking at society, we are reminded that there is an interplay between its institutions (like education, religion, industry, government) and the

individuals in it. Because institutions affect and mold individuals, and because individuals can modify their institutions (Bellah, Madsen, Sullivan, Swidler, & Tipton, 1991; Lenk, 1979), we know that philosophic conclusions should take both individuals and institutions seriously.

Imagine that you developed a wonderful individual philosophy about the amateur ideal for the Olympics. You urge athletes to play only for the love of the competition, to avoid political and economic interference, and to steer clear of excesses related to diet, training, and over-commitment. Your philosophy has some merit to it. It may even inspire some athletes to mend their ways and attempt to recapture the amateur ideal. But this philosophy, as an appeal to individuals alone, would have very little chance to effect much change. Why? Because institutions influence how people think and behave. In this case, certain institutions (such as the International Olympic Committee, the government, and big businesses) have vested interests in the Olympics as they exist today. If these institutions were not urged or forced to change their practices, individuals who believed in the principles of your amateur ideal would not stand much of a chance to realize their dreams for significant change. Thus, for your philosophy to stimulate large-scale reformation, it would have to take institutions and their power seriously. We do too if we are to develop philosophic ideas about sport, fitness, and play that can be put to work.

The opposite error is just as serious. Imagine that you developed an athletic philosophy that excellence is everything and successfully sold this to the sport-related institutions of your society. But this philosophy, as a blueprint for institutions alone, would not necessarily provoke widespread change. Why? Because individuals affect what values institutions embrace. Individuals can be stubborn; they may not accept every value that is put forward by the governments and big businesses of their society. Thus, for your athletic philosophy about excellence to be effective, it would have to take seriously individuals and their independent ability to think and choose. Likewise in this book, our philosophy must appeal to individuals who might adopt it and who might, in turn, affect the institutions around them.

Distinguishing Biases From Insights

Looking at society reminds us that some philosophic "insights" may actually be cultural biases masquerading as insights. We know that even our first thoughts as infants are affected by the culture into which we were born. Thus, what we believe is true in some objective sense may only be a reflection of what we have been programmed by our culture to accept.

Suppose that you genuninely believe that physical fitness is a stronger value than play or fun. How did you come to this conclusion? Do you think that there is objective evidence that would support your position? Or is it possible that you are merely giving voice to a fashionable misconception? Is your conclusion more an insight or a bias?

When we do our philosophic hiking in the next three chapters of Part II, we must continually search for objective evidence and be on the lookout for cultural biases. We must be sure that we do not simply accept our societal norms, our history, or our local indoctrinations as the way things should be. Just because a coach that we admired did something in a certain manner, we should not automatically conclude that it was the right or best way.

Separating Greater From Lesser Needs

A look at society can help us distinguish potential needs from actual ones and, from among the actual needs, those that are serious from those that are less critical. A potential need is something that all human beings require—like health, love, and meaning in their lives. An actual need is something that is missing or deficient here and now, for a specific people at a specific time. In this book, we want to address actual needs. Given limited resources, we do not want to spend time and energy producing goods and services that are good in theory but are not needed in fact.

Imagine once again that you have just concocted an ideal philosophy of health and fitness. Your vision includes a broad range of fitness parameters—from strength to cardiovascular endurance to psychological well-being. Furthermore, your reform program is designed to transform institutions *and* affect individual beliefs. But you have no access to any facts about the condition of this society that you intend to help. You have no idea if it even needs or is ready for the health and fitness ends your program will be promoting. No matter what the merits of your philosophy are, you are in a precarious position. In terms of affecting real people in a real society, all your philosophic work may come to naught.

SUMMARY BREAK

It is important not to confuse sociology with philosophy. Sociologists typically measure real things related to groups of people, institutions, or individuals affected by groups of people. In other words, they take the empirical turn when looking for evidence.

Philosophers make most of their progress reflectively. However, this does not relieve them of the responsibility of developing ideas that are timely and useful. Consequently, it is helpful for philosophers, at least on occasion, to look at society. This can help them make philosophy work by taking both individuals and institutions seriously, by telling cultural biases from philosophic insights, and by separating greater from lesser societal needs.

Three Views of Contemporary Society

During any period of modern history, we could find commentators who described their society largely in positive terms and others who judged that same culture negatively. This is no less true today. Some sociologists think we are doing pretty well; others feel just as strongly that the opposite is true. Such judgments are difficult to make about a culture that is inside and all around each one of us, and even the passage of time rarely provides objective proof or conclusive answers.

It is also difficult to be critical about a life that you may have been socialized to accept as the way things should be. Nevertheless, it is important to muster up some courage in this regard and consider seriously several criticisms that have been leveled at the world into which you were born and that has inevitably affected your sport, dance, and play life.

I have singled out three broad themes for consideration: (1) excessive survivalism, (2) runaway individualism, and (3) oppressive rationalism. Interestingly, all three base values are good things in and of themselves. Certainly the good life includes survival (there is no life, let alone a good one, without it), individuality (we want to be loved and accepted as distinct people; we need to make our own choices and find our own niche in

life), and reason (we do not want to live lives that are misguided or irrational). Problems show up, however, when these three values get out of control, when they are overemphasized, when people put too much faith in them.

Excessive Survivalism

You need to understand **survivalism** broadly in order to appreciate its influence on our society. Three social theorists' perspectives on survivalism are presented in the box on p. 96. It has many faces, including economic, physical, and psychological ones. Many people today have economic survival concerns. Will I get a job? Will I keep my job? How will I make ends meet?

Many individuals also have health concerns. How long will I live? Will I ever get cancer or some other life-threatening disease? How long will I stay youthful? Does my diet contain enough fiber? Do I get enough exercise? Finally, many people are preoccupied with psychological survival questions. Will I live a happy life? How will I make it through this class or this semester? What can I do to avoid boredom and unpleasant thoughts? Can I stand being married? Can I stand not being married?

Why has survival become a dominant value, and why do individuals dedicate their lives too fully to mere existence? The answers are not clear. Some believe that the decline in religious values has left an opening for other values (like survival) to emerge. Some think that because we live in a world where most all values seem to be uncertain and relative, we are forced to rely on only the most obvious human needs and goods. In other words, when we are not sure that higher values (like truth, love, and justice) are real or cannot figure out what they mean in day-to-day life, we revert to lower more fundamental goals—goals like making it economically,

Survivalism: Perspectives of Three Social Theorists

Lasch (1984) believes that Americans are self-preoccupied. He thinks that we use Zen, diet, fitness, television, and human relationship programs to live for the moment, to get through the day and week. He claims that survival is the rallying call of the late 20th century. Individuals are more interested in therapy than religion, "making it" than succeeding, winning than achieving. We would rather survive than be right. The modern equivalent of salvation, says Lasch, is mental health. "Self-preservation has replaced self-improvement as the goal of earthly existence" (p. 53).

Bellah, Madsen, Sullivan, Swidler, & Tipton (1985, 1991) suggest that we live in a therapy-oriented society. They say that many Americans cope more than they play, endure more than dance, avoid psychic pain more than relish meaning, survive more than celebrate. They claim that many of us feel lonely, isolated, and restless. In an effort to get through life, we become too preoccupied with our own feelings and too busy making cost-benefit analyses about best options for our future. Our life, they say, becomes "so ascetic in its demands as to be unendurable" (1985, p. 139).

Much earlier, Arendt (1958) pointed out that, contrary to popular opinion, pleasure is not the primary goal that most people pursue. Rather it is survival. "We deal here with life philosophy in its most vulgar and least critical form. In the last resort, it is always life itself which is the supreme standard to which everything else is referred. . . ." (p. 311)

psychologically, and biologically. Still others think that America's involvement in the Vietnam War, economic stagnation, and the near exhaustion of many natural resources have caused many people, particularly those in North America, to become defensive and to lose no small degree of national hope. In response, it is said, individuals aim at immediate gratification in the form of psychological and economic survival rather than more lofty, deferred, long-range goals.

Survivalism in Physical Education

If this analysis is right, we should be able to see elements of excess survivalism in physical education. Many of the following suggestions are very speculative and do not apply

to every person, physical education program, or subculture in North America, let alone around the world. Nevertheless, they may still have sufficient accuracy as generalizations to warrant our attention and concern.

An Inordinate Focus on Health

Our profession is vigorously promoting physical fitness and health. These two "buttons" are pushed vigorously and repeatedly whenever we try to defend ourselves to school boards, tax payers, legislators, clients, and others who have an interest in our services. Physical fitness and health sell in a society that is preoccupied with appearance, youthfulness, and survival.

Look at a recent issue of any of our professional publications. What themes are most

A meaningful form of play? Or more a modern way to escape, cope, and survive?

often represented in the articles and advertisements? If you read the same materials I do, you will no doubt reply, health and physical fitness. And look at our most visible national promotions such as Jump Rope for Heart, Physical Best, and the President's Council on Physical Fitness. They take advantage of what currently resonates in our culture.

Workouts as a Psychological Fix

We commonly hear people today say that they *have* to get in their workout. They habitually exercise to feel good, divert their attention from their school or office work, experience an endorphin high, or simply to get through the day. Exercise becomes a psychological coping strategy for withstanding the stresses of day-to-day life.

As a psychological fix, exercise need not be interesting, creative, uplifting, particularly meaningful, or even fun. It simply needs to work. This presents individuals with different criteria for selecting activities. Efficiency, impact, effectiveness, cost, and availability replace potential, complexity, rich meaning. An exercise that quickly, thoroughly, and reliably quiets unsettling thoughts and provides later feelings of pleasant exhaustion is a good activity. The presence or absence of other qualities is largely irrelevant.

Recreating to "Recharge the Batteries"

Recreation and lifetime sports are promoted and valued by many as means for "recharging their batteries." After an exhausting week of work, human beings need to get away from it all and exercise or play. After months of dulling labor, people need a break, a vacation, a period of sustained recreation. This respite prevents burnout and gets people ready to tackle their jobs with renewed energy and interest. Recreation then becomes a crucial cog in the wheel of economic success and survival. The cycle of work/recreation/more work leads to greater productivity and financial well-being.

This use of recreation as a means for economic survival is different from exercise as a psychological fix because it functions best when it is fun and at least moderately interesting. Weekend activities and vacations need to be different from work, something to look forward to, something to relish. (People sometimes like their recreational activities so much that they try to jam too much of them into a short period of time and end up more exhausted than when they began.) But these regenerating activities need not be much more than fun and pleasurably diverting in order to perform their recreative function. As a means to greater work productivity, they need not take on a life of their own and serve as an important source of human development. As with the use of exercise as a psychological fix, they need not be a source for creativity, personal development, and rich meaning. They merely need to divert attention from work and replenish work energy.

Winning as a Necessity

Many individuals who play sports in our culture or who cheer for favorite teams have been socialized to regard winning as a life-and-death matter. Part of making it in our culture is being a winner—either directly as an athlete, businessperson, or worker or vicariously as the fan of a successful team or a citizen of a successful country. Our language is full of remarkable claims about the importance of winning: "Nobody ever remembers who finished second." "Losing is worse than death because you have to live with it." "Winning isn't everything; it's the only thing."

While many of our physical education and athletic programs are grounded on more moderate philosophies of winning, the strength of this survival value probably reaches into even the best situations and affects even the most enlightened coaches. Everybody wants to be a winner, even (for some) if they have not improved one iota and even if their performances are anything but excellent or artistic. Victories seem to be important even if they have to be gained by bending the rules and playing weak opponents. Symbolically and psychologically, if not actually, to survive in our culture is to be a winner. Sport and athletics offer some of the best stages society has for rehearsing, reenforcing, and acting out this survival commitment.

PHILOSOPHIC EXERCISE

If excessive survivalism has damaged sport, exercise science, and physical education, it is important to identify ways to reduce its presence and influence. Some of this analysis will occur in later chapters, but here you are encouraged to form some initial hypotheses about what can be done about this problem.

1. How might health and physical fitness be retained as valid objectives of physical education but given less emphasis?
2. Can health and fitness be taught in a context of human values rather than the more sterile context of biological survival? If so, how might this be done?
3. How might workouts be transformed into uplifting experiences, rather than temporary fixes?
4. How should workout activities be selected if they are to provide values that go beyond providing a psychological salve, or allowing one's batteries to recharge?

5. For you, what exercise activity is best biologically? Is the same activity the best for you as a human being?

6. What theme might replace the one of being a winner-survivor? Can we emphasize the quality of participation apart from its role in producing winners and apart from its function in promoting ego survival?

Runaway Individualism

Individualism, like survival, is generally regarded to be a good thing. The American heritage, in part, focuses on the rights and opportunities of individuals. Individualism has two facets (Bellah et al., 1985). *Utilitarian individualism* expresses the principle that we should all have a chance to get ahead on our own. *Expressive individualism* speaks to the idea that we all have a right to free expression and self-definition. These concepts are embraced as self-evident truths, not only by Americans but by many people around the world.

The problem with individualism comes when it gets out of control, when individual rights, interests, and activities dominate and overwhelm social duties and concerns. Too great a preoccupation with the "I" may cause a sense of isolation and loneliness; it can put too much pressure on the individual to determine what counts; it can cause a person to lose touch with his or her cultural roots and shared community values; it can lead to an insensitivity regarding the rights of others; it can promote a belief that life courses are based essentially on arbitrary personal decisions. Social theorists' perspectives on individualism are presented in the box below.

Individualism: Perspectives From Three Social Theorists

People are socialized, according to Bellah et al. (1985), to think of themselves as independent, as set on a course of life defined for and by themselves. They tend to ignore connections between themselves and their parents, culture, and traditions. They do not see themselves as part of a larger story, as contributing to some project that preceded and will probably postdate them. Their lives, in short, lack "coherence," "rich meaning," and generational, historical, and religious "context" (p. 82).

Local and idiosyncratic traditions and meanings—for example, folk stories and heroes that inspire people and give them strength—are too frequently changed and replaced by myths that are more in line with ruling class values and interests (Gruneau, 1983). Particularly where local traditions reduce interest in profitable consumption and fail to produce agreeable, productive workers, these special ways of looking at the world are both intentionally and unintentionally modified. Workers, in such a situation, lose a sense of solidarity with tradition and community and experience life as solitary laborers.

Lasch (1979) argues that Americans have lost their sense of history and any vision of a unique destiny or future based on it. They lack a commitment to firm, traditional values. For example, many individuals are unwilling to stand behind the ethics of love, faithfulness, and duty. Without this historical-social support, the focus of attention shifts to individuals and their present needs. Immediate personal gratification replaces deferred individual and community progress.

Runaway individualism may have some of the same causes as excessive survivalism. In a world where there is less cause for long-range optimism, people may become more preoccupied with the short term, with their own success here and now. In an environment where people have less confidence in the existence of objective right and wrong, they may be thrown back on themselves as the arbitrary source of all decisions. But regardless of the specific causes of increased individualism, if it has indeed taken hold as many social theorists think it has, we should be able to find symptoms of it in our profession.

Individualism in Physical Education

There are a number of ways in which excessive individualism might show up in contemporary physical education. I have listed only a few of them here.

Rise of Individual Sports

Individual sports have been on the rise for many years, and team sports have become less popular. Among the most crowded activity courses in colleges these days are golf, tennis, jogging, skiing, racquetball, and the like—all of them activities that a person can do alone or with a single opponent. The emphasis in many physical education programs has been to develop a personally active lifestyle. This is much easier to do, of course, if physical activity is dependent only on one or two people being available for a workout or game.

Similarly, in the area of exercise and fitness the focus has been upon individual health, not corporate or community well-being. The question in our culture is, How do I get fit? not, How do *we* get healthy? Most fitness activities are (or can be) done alone—jogging,

walking, weight lifting, cycling, hiking, and so on. Even group fitness classes, like aerobic dance, involve relatively little interaction and few, if any, shared goals. In many ways, they are simply individual exercises in a group setting.

Lack of Common Values and Direction

The field of physical education is not a model of disciplinary coherence. We often seem to be more a collection of individuals than a community with common values, interests, and goals. Within our university departments, for example, we have skill teachers and research professors, physiologists and historians, dancers and athletes, fitness people and sport people. These and other subgroups often have different agendas, and they even speak different languages.

Physical education, as of this date, is still not sure what its mission should be. The profession supports a bewilderingly broad array of goals and objectives. Physical education's purposes fall over much of the educational, recreational, health, and service landscape. The result is a lack of clear mission and purpose, as can be seen in the following (Kretchmar, 1988):

This past summer our national association supported "Senate Concurrent Resolution 145—Relating to Daily Physical Education Programs for All Children." This statement, written with what most of us would regard as a noble goal of encouraging legislators to support required physical education in our public schools, stakes out a claim for no fewer than eleven instructional purposes. Included are cardiovascular endurance, muscular strength, bone development, posture, diet and weight control, skillful movement, mental alertness, active lifestyle habits, leisuretime management, self-esteem and overall health and longevity education. From this laundry list

How can *I* get fit? How can *I* excel? Much of today's emphasis in athletics is on the individual.

of educational and quasi-educational functions we could argue alternately that we are primarily a school-related paramedical operation (helping children to avoid illness and physical injury and to recover more quickly from the same), a recreation education department (helping youngsters adjust to an adult world that includes large amounts of free time), a quasi-psychological organization (helping people to relax, like themselves, improve their abilities to concentrate), an adjunct health education unit (helping folks to achieve wellness through an active lifestyle), or a basic skills enterprise (helping students learn fundamental human skills).

While all these diverse areas are related, they entail nonetheless very different kinds of missions. What then are we (primarily) according to Resolution 145? Medical personnel? Recreationists? Movement psychologists? Health educators? Basic skills educators? All of the above? (p. 50)

Such an array of purposes and underlying values suggests that there is something here for everyone—take your pick! It does little to suggest that there are a few important values around which *we* gather, that hold *us* together as a unique community of movement-related professionals, that give *us* at least a partly common vision of the future.

Decline in Sport Ethics

Many sports have a long and honorable history that includes numerous stories of personal sacrifice, ethical heroism, duty, responsibility, rule following, and other proper behavior. That history, however, has relatively little affect on the attitudes and behaviors of many coaches and athletes today. Even if that history is known (and often it is not), it is regarded as irrelevant, quaint, and thus unrelated to sport as it is practiced today.

Rather than inheriting a tradition of clear rights and wrongs, coaches and athletes are

What price victory?

left very much to their own devices in deciding what should and should not be permitted. While there are still boundaries, they seem to have been arbitrarily established and thus more vulnerable to change. This places more pressure on the individual to choose for himself or herself what is right today, and then to check it all again tomorrow. Just how far should one go in the quest for victory? The answers today are shifting, uncertain, and to a great extent personally determined.

PHILOSOPHIC EXERCISE

By responding to the following questions, see if you can identify some ways in which physical education might combat excessive individualism.

1. Should individual sports be de-emphasized?

2. How might individual sports like hiking and cycling be given group, community, or team qualities? Can you come up with ideas related to how these activities could be structured? How they might be taught or presented?

3. How might individualized fitness be developed into community fitness? How could this be accomplished, for example, in a high school gym class? In an adult health-center aerobics class?

4. Are there traditions, values, and goals that could and should pull us together professionally? If so, what are they?

5. Do you follow the maxim, "You should do your own thing!"? Is this good or bad advice? How might it be both?

Oppressive Rationalism

Rationality, just like survivalism and individualism, is a positive value. We rely on reason, in its various forms, for much of human progress. However, reason is also capable of harming people and society, particularly when its limitations are not appreciated.

Rationalism, as I am picturing it here, takes at least two different forms. One is the product of scientific thinking, and its credo goes something like this: "I will do only what empirical science has shown to be correct, safe, or optimal. When I have decisions to make as a physical educator, I will look to the findings of science for my answers. When I need to get better performance from an athlete, I will look for the scientifically optimal way to produce it." The other form of rationalism comes from social reformers, who say, in effect, "Every activity, including play, must have a good purpose. If sport, games, and dance are not improving people in significant ways, these practices must be reformed and their services put to better use."

Excessive rationalism produces a number of potentially negative effects. People lose their ability to be spontaneous and just play. (They must always have good reasons for doing things.) Coaches treat their athletes more as machines than human beings. (There must be biologically optimal ways of manipulating diet, exercise, training, and so on.) Sport and play become useful rather than meaningful and fun. (People should not waste their time with mere play and games.) In short, excessive rationalism may promote a life that is too measured, dehumanized, and prudent. Perspectives on rationalism are presented in the box on p. 104.

Rationalism received a strong boost with the rise of science in the 19th and 20th centuries. Many people, in fact, looked to science as the prime source of solutions for all human problems, from disease to hunger, from anxiety to depression. Individuals began to assess problems primarily in terms of their scientifically measurable features. In other words, all problems became largely technical or scientific problems.

In today's sport we sometimes forget to let play be an end in itself.

In such a culture, ritual, folk stories, local values, and personal meaning do not fare very well. Because they are not as accessible to the tools of science (private thoughts have always been difficult to measure and manipulate), they tend to be ignored or dismissed as unimportant.

Rationalism also received a boost from any number of optimistic social-reform movements. Two examples that have affected our field are so-called muscular Christianity, an initiative designed to promote moral development through sport, and physical fitness for military preparedness, a movement generated by concerns for national defense during the cold war. These social programs were

Rationalism: Perspectives From Social Theorists

People in our world, says Lasch (1979), are losing their ability to play. This is making life dull and spiritless. Everything is becoming measured, calculated, planned. From the mystery, captivation, abandon, fascination, and refreshment of play, society is moving to the science, control, planned recovery, and "moral rightness" of rational behavior. A world that provided provocative, interesting, and meaningful invitations is now offering sensible opportunities. Lasch thinks that people are losing their ability to fall in love with their games. Individuals have been taught that they must seize sport and make it their servant, not meet sport and regard it as their prince or princess.

Technology, according to Gruneau (1983) and Sage (1990), is too frequently glorified; people and their interests are too often subordinated to "the machine." Today's high performance sports medicine is "aimed at nothing less than finding the physiological limits of the living organism" (Hoberman, 1992, p. 15).

Bellah et al. (1991) argue that educators are tempted to pursue what is scientifically right over what is culturally and historically meaningful, and that scientific education too often is divorced from moral education. The pursuit of athletic excellence has taken on the "quality of an obsession" and is "often corrupt." What science can imagine, it seems destined to do, or at least attempt. Thus, an important moral project in our contemporary world is to understand where "biological heroism ends and biological fraud begins" (Hoberman, 1992).

based on the notion that planning, organizing, and designing activities for positive change were good, perhaps even moral obligations. Thus, play was co-opted to serve good ends. Reason was employed to purge life of its excesses, frivolities, and useless practices. No time should be wasted; no trivial activity should be tolerated.

Rationalism in Physical Education

Rationalism, as you may already see, permeates our profession. In what follows I identify some of the ways in which it operates, and you may well be able to think of others.

Science Over Culture

Physical educators too often build programs around what is scientifically right and good and too infrequently around what makes

sense historically and culturally. Some activities, like softball for instance, receive generally poor marks in physical education because they do not make significant contributions to cardiorespiratory fitness, strength gains, flexibility objectives, or other good ends. Many physical education curricula, in fact, are devoid of such activities for very rational health, safety, or other educational reasons.

The result is often a set of experiences that is too culturally sterile, too disconnected from students' and clients' day-to-day lives. Such a curriculum does little to further peoples' understanding of where, historically speaking, they came from and where, philosophically speaking, they should be headed. This brand of physical education provides, in effect, scientifically sound but culturally barren education and service.

Similarly, physical education has been relatively unwilling to mold its curricula and programs to meet local cultural conditions.

Sport, dance, and recreational activity are diverse across America and across various subcultures that congregate in different regions, states, cities, or neighborhoods. These groups of people were raised on various traditions, rituals, and games that distinguish them from others. There are parts of the country, for example, where there is disproportionately high interest in and cultural attachment to activities like horseshoe pitching, horseback riding, quoits, kite flying, wilderness tracking, table tennis, camping, curling, ice hockey, lacrosse, mountain biking, trout fishing, beach volleyball, softball, rhythmic gymnastics, ethnic dance, hunting, archery, limbo dancing, ax throwing, square dancing, pole or tree climbing, and so on. Yet, they are not seized and embraced as rich and useful educational resources, but are often rejected on the basis of scientific understanding as outdated, quaint, useless, or dangerous. A national curriculum that represents the best in scientific understanding is considered preferable.

Absence of Play

Physical education is too often conducted by the clock, from a lesson plan loaded with good outcomes, by educators who are sober and serious. As prudent people, we do not want to waste time on mere play and games. So we put play to work for us. We make sure that it serves rationally defensible ends—like fitness, moral development, socialization, knowledge, health, and so on.

Many physical education teachers, by personality and operational style, have been far closer to drill instructors than playmakers. They line up students, shout out commands, threaten punishment if showers are not taken, and demand strict compliance with their orders. Physical education class becomes an experience in order, discipline,

Too much order and discipline can rob physical education of its meaning and value.

and decorum, not one of spontaneity, celebration, surprises, meaning, or much fun.

A Focus on Citius, Altius, Fortius

These three Latin words, meaning "faster, higher, stronger," depict the current rational/scientific fascination with what can be done. How fast can runners run? How high can people jump? How strong can athletes become? Performers are implicitly viewed as machines that can be molded, manipulated, and perfected through chemistry and physics—by means of pills, optimal training, and ideal mechanistic technique.

Logic is used like a sledgehammer. If a little bit of sport psychology, enriched diet, regimented training, or steroid usage provides some improvement, imagine what large doses of these interventions might produce! Never mind what negative side effects these excesses might have on the human being who is experiencing them. Never mind questions of right and wrong. Pursue *citius, altius, fortius* systematically, scientifically, single-mindedly.

An Interest in Records More Than in Heroes

We still have heroes. But there are fewer of them (see Crepeau, 1985), and fascination with star athletes has shifted from who they are to what they have done. Today we are more interested in the record than the person and the noble qualities that person symbolizes. We are able to dissociate the athletic feat from the whole person who produced it. This has evolved to the point where accomplishments are often revered even when they may have been gained illegally. This trend represents a rational, scientific focus on what is measurable and concrete. A person's reputation, values, motives, ethics, ideals, feelings, and personal observations are "squishy," and nonquantifiable. An athlete's record is solid and objective,

or so it is believed. Thus, today's heroes are often cut off at the knees. An aspect of their accomplishments, a segment of themselves, is put on a pedestal. But a large portion of who they are is kept out of play.

PHILOSOPHIC EXERCISE

Respond to the following questions related to combating excess rationalism:

1. How might science complement culture rather than threaten it? Take the example of softball: Are there ways to preserve the game and its significance while improving its safety, contribution to health, or relationship to some other educational goal?
2. Can physical education be spontaneous and playful and still accomplish other good ends? What ground rules would be needed to make sure that such activity does not become sober, regimented, and uninteresting?
3. What criteria might replace the quantitatively measured "higher, faster, stronger" as benchmarks of progress? If you think that *citius, altius, fortius* has at least some value as criteria for human achievement, how might it be amended and improved?
4. Are physical educators in a position to identify and promote heroes? How might they do this? How might they help their students or clients place less emphasis on the record and more on the whole person?

Review

There are at least three reasons for having taken this break in our philosophic journey to observe the actual condition of our society.

First, by acknowledging the power of both individuals and institutions, we think that our philosophy will be more realistic and potentially useful. Second, by examining our enculturation, we may be alerted to biases that we bring to philosophy. Finally, we should know what people need, not just in general, but also here and now. This will help our philosophy to be timely and thus more useful.

Three weaknesses of contemporary society are excess survivalism, runaway individualism, and oppressive rationalism. The footprints of each can be found in current physical education practices. Therefore, intentionally or unintentionally, the profession reinforces and perpetuates these problems. On the other hand, physical education has considerable potential for combating harmful forms of survivalism, individualism, and rationalism. Adjustments may need to be made in both mission and daily practice for this to come about.

Katie Freedman's situation (in the example at the beginning of the chapter) turns out to be a very interesting one. It shows some symptoms of the excesses and harms identified in this chapter—a very individual quest for excellence, too great an interest in winning and being the best, perhaps a willingness to trade elements of family and tradition for a life devoted to "higher, faster, stronger." The problem is that she wants to do it. She loves basketball. She is genuinely dedicated to excellence. Her family is willing to support her.

Has her life already been distorted by survivalism, individualism, and rationalism gone out of control? Or is she a balanced human being making a free choice to pursue a noble value like excellence? Perhaps we do not have the perspective necessary to see clearly which it is or if it is a little bit of both.

Looking Ahead

We will now return to our task of understanding philosophically how sport, dance,

exercise, games, and play can make people's lives better. The sociological, empirical side trip that you just completed has produced results that must be noted, cataloged, and saved for future use. But attention must be turned to understanding the intrinsic and extrinsic value of various goods that we produce. It is not enough, in other words, to observe cultural excesses, weaknesses, and needs. It is also necessary to ask more fundamentally (and philosophically), What do people in general need to make their lives go well? And how might the content of your field—sport, dance, exercise, games, and play—contribute to the achievement of the good life in general?

Checking Your Understanding

1. Why should philosophers, at least occasionally, look through the glasses of sociologists at the actual condition of their culture? What are the dangers of a philosophy that ignores the opportunities and constraints presented by individuals and institutions in society?
2. How can positive values like survival, individuality, and rationality become harmful? Can you find an example from your own experiences where each of these values has brought on problems or harm?
3. Has physical education actually contributed to the excesses of survivalism, individualism, and rationalism? If so, can you cite specific ways in which this has happened?
4. Does physical education have the capacity to combat these problems while still remaining faithful to its subject matter? Once again, can you cite specific ideas for bringing about these reforms?

Key Terms

Further Reading

For an overall analysis of society, see Bellah et al. (1985, 1991), Lasch (1979; 1984), Bloom (1987), and MacIntyre (1984). For discussions related specifically to sport, Hoberman (1992), Sage (1990), Gruneau (1983), and Coakley (1990) provide useful resources.

Chapter 5

Sport, Dance, and Exercise Values

At an interview for his first job, Sam was asked by his prospective employer just why he thought vigorous activity was so important for people. She asked Sam if he thought he could really make a difference for the individuals in their program and, if so, exactly what that difference would be. While Sam was thinking this over, the employer tried to help out by putting the question another way: "What do you stand for? What values does your profession promote, and which ones are the most important?"

Sam shifted uneasily in his seat. The professors he had in college spoke of many different values. He remembered that the physiologists and physical fitness instructors focused on stroke volumes, lean body mass, and health; his philosophy professor always talked about sportsmanship and character development; most coaches seemed to be dedicated to discipline and victories; several theory teachers emphasized research and knowledge.

Sam realized that he had never thought about which values were most important. Without a ready answer, he decided to say that he supported all these good things, and leave it at that. He cleared his throat. "I believe in the importance of physical fitness and health. In addition, I support motor skill development, winning, success, sportsmanship, self-development, knowledge about human movement, the building of character, and fun."

There. That ought to do it, Sam thought to himself. *I've included just about everything, and it sounded pretty impressive.*

Is it possible to distinguish the relative importance of values like health-related fitness, knowledge, motor skill, and fun on the basis of their importance in life? How would a person like Sam even begin to do this, and why should he have any confidence in the conclusions that he drew? Should people seeking jobs in the movement professions be able to say what counts most and give some reasons for their judgment?

You just completed a search for individual and institutional needs from a sociological perspective. You took this loop in the trail to make sure that your personal philosophy is realistic, timely, and thus useful. Your travels here will allow you to understand the dangers of promoting traditional values blindly and provide you with a technique for distinguishing their importance. This is your first step in gaining some philosophic distance from values that you may have taken for granted and rarely thought about.

IN THIS CHAPTER, YOU WILL

- **define what values are and see how they contribute to the good life,**
- **understand the dangers of promoting traditional values blindly,**
- **encounter four traditional values of physical education,**
- **learn why it is important to distinguish the significance of different values, and**
- **discover a technique for doing this.**

Philosophy should include attempts to identify what is good and say what should be. Without this effort to find out what counts in life, people become the passive victims of their circumstances. They usually do what everybody else does, whether this is good, bad, or in between. This is like the hypothetical land I described in the introduction, the place where everyone travels but no one knows where they are headed. Our work in this chapter will begin to answer questions that keep us from traveling without direction:

What values are most important in your life? Are many of them realized or experienced in movement activities?

Should a value like fitness, for example, be promoted over skill? Or should it be the other way around?

Have you ever tried to defend a certain lifestyle or value system to your parents or a friend? When you did so, were you using arguments or merely sharing an opinion?

Life's Important Values and Physical Education

In one way or another all teachers, coaches, health personnel, and businesspeople in the field of physical education have opportunities to improve people's lives. In fact, this can be considered a fundamental obligation of all professionals, whether they work in physical education or not. Hopefully, you selected this vocation not only to make a living but also to make a difference. You may even find that making a difference—improving people's lives in some way—is far more satisfying and rewarding than earning a wage or making a profit.

As a professional you must make judgments about the ways your different products and services can affect your students or clients for the better. You must attempt to understand which values in your arsenal are most powerful—which goods will help your athletes or customers achieve something called the good life.

The Good Life

The Good Life refers to an overall life condition and set of experiences that we regard as desirable. While most everybody aims at good living, there is considerable disagreement about what exactly it is. Some picture it in considerable detail. For them it includes things like owning a home in a nice neighborhood, having two cars, being happily married, raising two healthy and well-adjusted children, and enjoying a successful career. For others there are fewer criteria. For them the good life is being healthy and happy, or perhaps rich and famous. Some describe the good life in more philosophic terms. They might think that it includes loving one another, having faith in God, or dedicating oneself to the truth.

There are probably hundreds of ways to achieve something called the good life, and there are undoubtedly many patterns that are comparably good. One person might emphasize excellence, another truth, another friendship, another achievement, and all of these lives can reach high levels of goodness.

But what does all of this have to do with our professions—the ones related to sport, exercise science, and physical education?

Values and the Good Life

The good life is not produced by magic or any other particularly mysterious process. It is built value by value. In other words, the good life is a composite of many individual values that are woven into a person's life.

Values are goods; they are things that human beings find desirable. Two classes of values exist. Moral values are certain personality traits and human motives. They describe what we often call a morally good person. These are traits like honesty, conscientiousness, affection, prudence, industriousness,

For many, simple pleasures are part of living the good life.

and courage. **Nonmoral values** are things that we desire from life. Rather than describing a person or a person's motives, they identify items that people want—things like pleasure, knowledge, wealth, security, excellence, and friendship.

On most definitions of the good life, we can find a number of both kinds of value. For example, it might be difficult to live a good life without integrity and a good reputation, as well as security, friendship, and pleasure.

PHILOSOPHIC EXERCISE

How would you define the good life for yourself? Here is a list of values provided by Frankena (1973, pp. 87-88). First, try to reduce this long list to the five values that you believe are most central to the good life. Second, see if you can then rank those five choices from the most to the least important. Finally, take another look at the entire list of values and check those you believe can be directly and reliably promoted by the movement profession into which you are headed.

Life, consciousness, and activity

Health and strength

Pleasures and satisfaction of all or certain kinds

Happiness, contentment

Truth

Knowledge and true opinion of various kinds, understanding, wisdom

Beauty, harmony, proportion in objects contemplated

Virtues

Aesthetic experience

Mutual affection, love, friendship, cooperation

Just distribution of good and evil

Harmony and proportion in one's own life

Power and experiences of achievement

Self-expression

Freedom

Peace, security

Adventure and novelty

Good reputation, honor, esteem

It is not hard to find good values. If anything, it is probably difficult for you to reduce the previous list to five top choices. Nor should it be difficult to see that your anticipated vocation can foster any number of them—even all of them, at least to one degree or another.

But how did you defend your definition of the good life? We will look at one method for doing this later in the chapter. And what will you do with all of the values that can, at least to some extent, be promoted by the movement professions? Support them all as Sam did in our account at the beginning of this chapter? Or select some that should receive priority attention?

Physical Education's Contribution to the Good Life

Physical education has shown a great deal of consistency in describing its primary values. Below I have listed three formulations: one that was popular as long ago as the early 1900s, another that has been written to lead us into the 21st century, and a third one that identifies the root values in the other two formulations.

Formulation 1: The Four Prime Ends of Physical Education (Hetherington, 1910, pp. 350-357)

- **Organic ends** are biological objectives. *Examples*: fitness, health, longevity, life itself, strength, power, endurance, lack of pain or discomfort, and ease in moving or functioning.
- **Psychomotor ends** are skill objectives. *Examples*: skill, effective action, competence, freedom and expression (in and from the experience of skillful movement), participation or involvement (in cultural forms of sport and dance, for example), and creativity.

- **Affective ends** are attitudinal, experiential objectives. *Examples*: character development, appreciation, meaning, enjoyment, and fun.
- **Cognitive ends** are knowledge objectives. *Examples*: knowledge, facts, wisdom, freedom (in and from wisdom), insight, understanding, and truth.

Formulation 2: The Physically Educated Person (NASPE, 1992, p. 7)

Unranked and taken as a whole, a physically educated person

- *has* learned skills necessary to perform a variety of physical activities,
- *does* participate regularly in physical activity,
- *is* physically fit,
- *knows* the implications of and the benefits from involvement in physical activities, and
- *values* physical activity and its contributions to a healthful lifestyle.

Formulation 3: Four Prime Values

In many ways formulations 1 and 2 point in the same direction. The best terms I have found to capture these values are health- and activity-related *fitness, knowledge*, motor *skill*, and *pleasure*. In my judgment, these nonmoral goods have been and continue to be the four most significant values in our profession. Each needs some clarification so that you can see how they rest on very different parent values and how they make their appearance in sport, exercise science, and physical education.

- **Fitness** refers to biological values and corresponds to the organic ends of formulation 1. *Related values*: life itself, survival, perpetual youthfulness, and longevity.

In our profession the high value placed on fitness shows up in concern for such matters as organic well-being, aerobic and anaerobic fitness, strength, flexibility, weight reduction, youthful appearance, and lower blood pressure. This commitment to biological health and, more fundamentally to life itself, is promoted by the President's Council on Physical Fitness, AAHPERD's Physical Best, various physical fitness tests, exercise-and-diet programs, courses in aerobic dance and jogging, and a multitude of self-help books and other products related to diet, youthfulness, physical beauty, exercise, and health.

• **Knowledge** refers to informational values and corresponds to the cognitive ends of formulation 1. *Related values*: truth, scientific fact, understanding, enlightenment, wisdom, and the freedom that comes with illumination.

In our profession the high value placed on knowledge shows up in concerns for research, attaining academic respectability, eliminating the "dumb jock" stereotype, disseminating theory, and various types of learning about human movement. These values—and ultimately, a commitment to uncover the truth—are seen in the following: cognitive approaches to learning, the Basic Stuff curriculum, academic majors programs, the downplaying of athletics or an activity program, the use of games and play for experimental purposes rather than as ends in themselves, and efforts to make sure that students learn principles related to play and not just motor skills or habits.

• **Skill** refers to action or performance values and corresponds to the psychomotor ends of formulation 1. *Related values*: Practical wisdom, know-how, cleverness, doing and making, achievement, and the freedom that comes with creative capability.

In our profession the high value placed on skill shows up in concerns for motor skill development; the learning of sport, dance, exercise, play, and game skills; the acquisition of general movement and postural habits and skills; and the achievement of athletic excellence. This commitment to practical wisdom is reflected in curricula that are dominated by objectives related to skill development. It can also be seen in countless books, films, videotapes, and coaching tips devoted to improving exercise, play, dance, and sport skills.

Our profession has an obligation to generate and share knowledge.

• **Pleasure** refers to experiential values and corresponds to the affective ends of formulation 1. *Related values*: Satisfaction, fun, sensuous enjoyment, excitement, meaningfulness, relaxation, and playfulness.

In our profession the high value placed on pleasure shows up in concerns for fun, meaningful involvement, self-development, excitement, and aesthetic satisfaction of various sorts. These values, and more fundamentally a commitment to satisfaction, are reflected in programmatic emphases on play (particularly in contrast to threatening competition), self-improvement, and safe challenges. New Games programs, the casual approaches to grading physical education in schools and colleges, and low-key recreational and intramural opportunities also typically reflect concerns about the promotion of widespread enjoyment or pleasure.

PHILOSOPHIC EXERCISE

Try to identify some alternatives or additions to these four values and then look for ways in which these value commitments show up in our profession. For example, are excellence, winning, moral development, and artistic expression values that can be promoted by physical education? Can you find ways in which they are already being fostered?

After you have completed this exercise, take a look at Table 5.1. There I have listed a number of well-known authors and some of the principal values they have championed.

SUMMARY BREAK

Philosophers have an obligation to ask, What values are best? What values produce the

good life? Many moral and nonmoral values, in different combinations, can be selected to produce different styles of good living. Likewise, many different moral and nonmoral values are be promoted in relationship to your profession's content of sport, dance, exercise, games, and play. Three formulations of physical education's values showed that the values of fitness, knowledge, skill, and pleasure have been, and still are, claimed as prime goods by the profession.

Why Prioritize Values?

If the movement professions are comfortable with the four broad values just identified, why is it necessary to rank them? It would not be unreasonable to pursue goals in each of these four directions. In addition, most professions related to activity would seem capable of producing all four values to one degree or another. And finally, all four are probably important elements in the good life. Why can't we keep fitness, knowledge, skill, and pleasure—side-by-side—at the top of our list?

There are at least three reasons, discussed below, for prioritizing values: (1) different prioritizations make a difference, (2) prioritization is unavoidable in life, and (3) prioritization provides focus for professional and political purposes.

Value Choices Make a Difference

Value preferences are powerful things, and they are not to be underestimated, trifled with, or quickly dismissed as unimportant. What caused Martin Luther King to fight for racial equality? Was it something he ate for lunch, or a *principle* in which he believed? What is it that has caused repressed individuals

Table 5.1 Philosophers of Sport and Some of Their Prime Intrinsic Values

Philosophers	Intrinsic values
Arnold, P.	Knowledge, moral values, creativity, self-expression
Best, D.	Dance, artistic expression
Fraleigh, W.	Propositional knowledge; fairness, justice and other moral duties
Harper, W.	Individuality, self-development, play, wonder, reason
Hellison, D.	Individuality, self-expression, meaning
Herrigel, E.	Harmony, intuitive knowledge
Hyland, D.	Play, friendship, openness, fun, growth, fulfillment
Kleinman, S.	The body, artistic expression
Lenk, H.	Self-control, achievement, mythic meaning
McCloy, C.	Fitness, health, strength, skill, holistic education
Meier, K.	Freedom, play, challenge, reflection, love
Metheny, E.	Personal meaning, creativity, nonverbal knowledge
Morgan, W.	Play, freedom, individuality
Nash, J.	Education, democracy, play
Novak, M.	Spiritual strength, play, perseverance
Osterhoudt, R.	Philosophy, knowledge, ideas, excellence
Parry, J.	Education, knowledge, professional integrity
Simon, R.	Excellence, fairness, and other moral virtues
Slusher, H.	Freedom, responsibility, courage
Suits, B.	Challenge, uncertainty
Thomas, C.	Freedom, individuality
Weiss, P.	Excellence, contemplative knowledge, dedication
Wertz, S.	Expression, beauty, art
Williams, J.	Democracy, positive socialization, knowledge
Wood, T. & Cassidy, R.	Nature, curiosity, play, education
Zeigler, E.	Ethics, moderation, professionalism

around the world to risk their lives to fight for freedom? Was it a chemical in their heads, or a *vision* of what could be? What has caused some athletes and dancers to dedicate themselves to their craft well beyond any reasonable call of duty? Was it the physiological structure of their right knee, or a *dedication to excellence*?

If you fully comprehended the nondualistic material presented in chapters 2 and 3, your answer to all three questions will be "It was both." The inspiring thoughts people have are influenced by lunches, chemicals in brains, and the anatomy of knees. Likewise, their metabolism, chemicals, and anatomy are influenced by their ideas.

However that may be, the critical point here is that your drives and interests and commitments cannot be reduced simply to physical causes. Values cannot be dismissed because they are not physical things. Wrestling with "mere" ideas and making judgments on "mere" values have a tremendous effect on what you plan, where you go, and what you do. In short, value choices make a difference!

If you have any doubts about this, take another look at the four traditional values promoted by sport, exercise science, and physical education. See how dramatically different your professional focus would be if you were to give priority to only one and secondary attention to the other three. Let us look at each of the four possibilities.

A Fitness-Oriented Philosophy

This philosophy holds that the focus of physical education should be health-related fitness. What is more important than health and life itself? What more than overall health and good physical fitness, allows people to enjoy life?

A profession committed to physical fitness is on firm footing, for scientific evidence on the beneficial effects of exercise—from lower heart rates and blood pressure to increased muscular strength and flexibility—is mounting. In schools, on athletic teams, in corporate fitness programs, and service-oriented fitness businesses, teachers, coaches, and trainers can have a measurable, beneficial effect on people's fitness levels and their overall health. This thrust for the profession is timely because North America and much of the world needs preventive health-related practices now more than ever before. Current leading causes of death are related more to unhealthy behavior than to infectious disease. Large numbers of adults are known to lead sedentary lives. And high health care and insurance costs present a clear economic danger to the country. Some data show that exercise programs, particularly when combined with sound dietary practices, reduce the incidence and delay the onset of various chronic diseases. Also, some employee fitness programs have proven to be effective in raising productivity and reducing health care costs.

There has never been a time in history when people have been more concerned about their health and conscious of their appearance. The profession should take advantage of that fact and make sure that its members provide the expertise needed for the various growing demands for fitness education and of the fitness industry. Such responsibilities belong to this field, and this profession's reputation is damaged when untrained practitioners present themselves as fitness or exercise specialists.

An emphasis on fitness need not produce programs that are devoted exclusively to exercise. Many sport and dance activities, for example, have cardiovascular benefits. The goal in a fitness-oriented physical education profession is to promote a lifelong, active lifestyle so that a reasonable degree of physical fitness is continuously maintained.

Finally, there is no value in this field that can be sold as well as physical fitness. A good portion of the public is concerned about it; school boards will buy it; even Congress has supported it. Some people unfortunately associate physical education with fun and games and think of the contributions of this field as trivial. But there is nothing trivial about enhancing the health of a nation and helping to extend the lives of its citizens.

A Knowledge-Oriented Philosophy

This philosophy maintains that the focus of physical education should be the development and transmission of the body of knowledge about the human body, health practices, sport, dance, exercise, play, and games. Physical education has always been held back because it has refused to consider itself an academic field. The profession is top-heavy with practitioners who want to coach not think, teach not theorize, promote push-ups not science, produce athletic robots not intelligent players. There is nothing wrong with activity itself or with the professions of coaching and skill teaching, but an overly pervasive anti-intellectual tone in physical education has produced generations of gym teachers who are far more trained than educated and like to operate more on personal hunches and intuition than on solid information. Sport, exercise science, and physical education have an obligation to generate knowledge about human movement and to share it with others—even athletes, fitness clients, and the students in activity programs.

A profession dedicated to the development and transmission of knowledge is on firm footing because American society in general, and education specifically, recognizes the fact that science and technology hold many of the keys to the future. In today's world, elite athletes cannot afford to ignore the fruits of scholarship and research any more than can practitioners working on pollution, world hunger, or other complex issues. As physical education heads into the 21st century, the potential of this field to alleviate such problems as chronic disease, rising health care costs, and debilitation in an aging population must be more aggressively studied and researched, and the results must be more clearly communicated and put to use.

We need to reemphasize physical education and exercise science as an academic field of study now. First, there is a general mood in the country that supports a rededication to the basics, and the basics are generally understood to be academic skills and knowledge—not health and recreation. Second, if teaching, professional preparation, and research units in this nation's colleges and universities are to survive, they must present an increasingly solid academic image. During the present time of declining resources, almost every field of study is being placed under the closest scrutiny for scholarly potential and productivity, and some of our programs have been eliminated because they have come up short on this score.

A field that focuses on the generation and transmission of knowledge need not abandon the practices of sport, dance, and exercise. These are important, too, but they must not be allowed to dominate and define the field. Good practice follows from good science. Practice should not precede science or take its place.

Finally, there is no value in the profession that can be sold as well as knowledge. Today, society is spending millions of dollars on sports medicine, how-to books and tapes, health literature from topics like diet and exercise to safety while jogging, and volumes on aerobics, body engineering, stress reduction through exercise, and so on. People want to know how to live longer, how to stay young, how to win Olympic gold medals, how to dance and play better. Ours is the profession that can and should provide many of those answers.

A Skill-Oriented Philosophy

This philosophy holds that the focus of physical education should be skill development in such activities as sport, dance, exercise, games, and play. This is what the profession does best and is its unique contribution to society. Professionals must stop trying to be something they are not. They must stop jumping on the health and academic bandwagons just so they can say that they are important and respectable. They should stop trying to be like the others and start being themselves.

A profession devoted to the development of skills is on very solid ground, for skills are the foundation for so much else that people do and accomplish. Movement skills are basic skills every bit as much as reading, writing, and arithmetic. People who don't move well are afraid to play, and dance, and engage in sport. More than that, their very ability to explore the world and express themselves is

Movement skills are basic skills every bit as much as reading and writing.

limited. When asked to picnic, vacation, re-lax, vacation, re-lax, exercise, learn, or recreate in physical ways, they typically participate reluctantly and uneasily or simply decline the invitation. They lack the basic skills needed to engage in very fundamental human activities. Literally and figuratively, they remain undereducated and on the sidelines.

There has hardly been a time in history when the teaching of skills has been more important. This society is "movement crazy." While large numbers of people participate in vigorous activities on a regular basis, there is even a larger number who might like to do so—except for the lack of physical skills and perhaps some motivation. Little wonder that in a physically oriented culture like this one, there is so much obesity and so many who do not participate. Without basic movement skills, physical activities just aren't much fun. Thus, the clientele are there, and so is the need. The only question is whether or not this profession will answer the call.

A focus on skills is crucial for yet another reason. When instructors teach dances and

games, they teach culture. They prepare citizens to enter this society, complete with its values, stories, and myths. It has been said that if one wants to understand a people, one should study them at play. Thus, it can also be said that if one wants to educate people to participate successfully in their culture, one should educate them to perform the movements, play the games, and dance the dances of their society.

An emphasis on skill development will not produce programs that exclude such goals as physical fitness, knowledge, and pleasure. These values are by-products of skillful behavior, and to some extent the acquisition of skill depends on health, knowledge, and pleasure. But this must not be allowed to derail this profession from its unique function and service in American society—instruction in basic movement skills with an emphasis on those of sport, dance, exercise, games, and play.

Skill development can be successfully promoted for society, in front of school boards, and in corporations. However, the profession will have to show that it can make a difference. Physical educators can no longer roll out the ball and expect skill to appear magically. They can no longer tolerate gym classes that are more recreation than education. They can no longer spend excessive time on theory and repetitive physical fitness exercises. In short, physical educators do not need to be like the other guys, for teaching liberating movement skills and preparing students to take part in their culture need no further justification.

A Pleasure-Oriented Philosophy

This emphasis suggests that the focus of physical education should be pleasure or, more simply, fun. When people say that this field is the toy department of service, business, and education, professionals should accept that as a compliment, not turn away in embarrassment. People have always wanted, as much as possible, to lead pleasurable, fun-filled lives. Members of this profession should be delighted that they have been identified as major contributors to that end.

A profession committed to fun and the playful activity that spawns it is on solid footing, for much scientific evidence now points to the fact that people are suffering from many work- and stress-induced diseases. Play, it has been discovered, may not only be a good value to have in one's life but also a necessary one. People are finding out, sometimes too late, that much that is valuable in life is not related to fame, fortune, and extra hours on the job but rather to the ability to relax, experience freedom, and enjoy themselves.

In a workaholic culture, people need help in slowing down their frenzied lives and recapturing the ability to play fully and completely. Professionals should take advantage of this fact and present their games and activities as valuable in their own right—not as a

Play may be not only valuable but *necessary*.

means to a longer life or a laboratory for theory. Whenever sport, dance, and games are made to work for other values, instructors risk deflating them, removing a degree of their charm, making them less enjoyable. By presenting them as important and useful, professionals suggest to their children, athletes, and clients that participation in activity is rational, prudent, even obligatory. They snuff out freedom, exploration, play, and much of the meaning and fun that can be found there.

People who have fun when they move in dance, games, and play will, of course, return to the profession's fields, gymnasiums, and playgrounds. And because they are there and actively involved, they will gain fitness, develop their skills, and probably pick up some knowledge. Thus, a program that is oriented toward fun does not stand in opposition to these other values. It may even be good from time to time to promote directly the values of fitness, skill, and knowledge in order to make future participation in an activity even more fun than it has been with lower levels of these values. Problems emerge, however, if these and other serious values are introduced as the real goals and purposes of activity. For when this happens, physical education and recreation become just more work—a time and place to do important things—not an interlude in which to smell the daisies.

Why is it that so many school-age children report unsatisfactory experiences in their physical education programs? Perhaps it is due in part to the fact that this profession has been too structured, too drill oriented, too concerned about making its gymnasiums and fields into laboratories for the improvement of people and society. At the same time, professionals may have been too little concerned with making their teaching and service environments what these, on their own, tend to be in the first place—playgrounds!

There may be no value that sells as well as pleasure or fun, for it is a key element in almost everyone's definition of the good life. In a culture that is fascinated with productivity and achievement, it is particularly useful. In a culture that is also fascinated with enjoyment and pleasure, it is attractive. Thus, the best thing teachers can do with and for their subject matter is to let it be, for sport, exercise science, and physical education is and ought to be the home of fun and games.

SUMMARY BREAK

Value prioritization results in real-world differences that are significant, not trivial or inconsequential. A profession that chooses as its prime value one from among the four presented here (fitness, knowledge, skill, pleasure) will be noticeably distinct from a profession that chooses one of the others. Depending on which value is judged as primary, the professions related to sport, exercise science, and physical education will make very different contributions to what we have been calling the good life.

PHILOSOPHIC EXERCISE

Review the four priority choices and rank them from your most to your least favorite. What does this say about your value system? What does it say about the way you view life?

Now attempt another important step. Rather than simply identifying and describing your value choices, can you also defend them? Try to give at least one justification for your choices. See if your friends or classmates have similar rankings and provide the same reasons for their choices.

Value Choices Are Unavoidable

You may have realized from the preceeding exercise that you have already made some value commitments, whether you ever set out to do so or not. Perhaps one or more of the four philosophies you just reviewed hit home and got your blood moving. It had you saying to yourself, "Yes, yes! That's it!" Others may have been attractive in varying degrees, and one or more of these statements may have even left you wondering why anyone would want to aim their professional activities in that direction.

If this was the case, then you are not a novice at committing yourself to some values over others. Even if you had no particular reaction to any of these statements, you undoubtedly have made thousands of value decisions in your life. Because all humans are valuing beings and quite naturally prefer home runs to strikeouts, a graceful and expressive plié to an awkward and mechanical dance movement, and good physical fitness to poor health, it is quite impossible to be conscious and honestly claim that you do not make value judgments.

The only question then is whether or not you have given, and continue to give, careful and thoughtful attention to these commitments. For example, have you forfeited your right to make further choices by choosing to follow the crowd? Are your decisions automatic, emotional, and based only on what feels right at the moment? Or are your decisions more deliberate, thoughtful, and based on reason?

Value Choices Provide a Focus

Even though you have already made value decisions and probably favor one or more of our four values over others, it is likely that you found all four values to be good things in themselves and worthy of at least some support. Who of us wants to speak out against fitness and long life, knowledge and truth, artistic skill, or pleasure, fun, and play?

But you are still not forced to say that they should all be promoted equally. You can say that, while all of these values deserve attention and support in your profession, one or more of them should be emphasized over the others. The problem is that many of your predecessors have been reluctant to make these tough decisions. Many adopted Sam's approach (at the beginning of the chapter) and tried to be all things to all people. This prevented them from having a clear professional focus, and this can have serious consequences. Some of these consequences, described below, affect daily professional activities. Others have broader political implications.

Professional Problems

Time with students, heart patients, YMCA clients, athletes—whomever it is you are serving in your professional role—is limited. Classes are large; equipment and other resources are frequently in short supply; the attention span and motivation of students and clients are finite. Even if you want to do everything for them, you cannot. Given these limitations, you must plan your interventions carefully.

Sport, exercise science, and physical education are not unique in this regard. All teachers, managers, medical personnel, and leaders face limitations. All of them have to target their energies and prioritize their values and related objectives to make sure that what is most important gets done and gets done well.

We have a pressing need in our profession to convince others that we can accomplish what we promise to do and to carefully document our successes. Too often we have been satisfied with getting people moving and trusting that this alone will produce positive results. But in avoiding a prioritization of values, we have not been careful in deciding *how* people should be moving. Our unwillingness to focus our energies has, in short, contributed to our lack of accountability.

One of the goals of the National Association of Sport and Physical Education (NASPE) Justification Project a few years ago (Seefeldt, 1986) was to gather scientific evidence that would suggest that we can and do actually achieve various outcomes. Vogel (1986) identified 23 areas in which current research indicates that physical education makes concrete contributions to human development and healthful living. These areas run the gamut from aerobic fitness, strength, agility, and maturation to social gains, perceptual motor development, attitudes, and knowledge. The problem, of course, is that a pursuit of all 23 objectives without any prioritization may guarantee that none of them is accomplished well. Accountability and credibility again suffer.

Political Problems

Politically, in a world where we need to court and enjoy the support of taxpayers, boards of education, investors, businesspeople, students, and clients, it is strategically foolish to swim aimlessly in a sea of competing values. From the perspective of these much-needed supporters, it could appear as if we do not really know what we are doing. Before these people invest in us, most will want to be assured that we have direction and that clear values provide compass points for moving one way and not another. They are interested in knowing whether we embrace fitness over skill instruction, enjoyment and recreation over knowledge, victory over excellence, good character over strong bodies—and why.

The answer, of course, will depend partly on the specific activity-related profession toward which you are headed. Many physical educators support all four values, but this does not absolve them from the responsibility of showing clients and supporters what their primary functions are, what their most significant missions are. Anything less can send mixed messages and confuse those whose support we need.

It has been said that those who value everything in fact value nothing. While this would appear to be a contradiction in a strict logical sense, it contains an important truth. Professionals who fail to prioritize their values, who talk and behave as if they value anything and everything, are often seen as lacking insight (they do not know what they stand for), energy (they are too lazy to come to grips with their commitments), interest (they may be in sport, exercise science, and physical education simply to make a living), direction (they flip-flop unpredictably), courage (they may have secret commitments but lack the fortitude to stand behind them), or any combination of the above. Such perceptions, whether accurate or not, obviously can have devastating effects on a profession and on individual careers.

SUMMARY BREAK

In one way or another—whether thoughtfully and carefully or mindlessly and automatically—you have already prioritized the values of your profession. In other words, to prioritize or not to prioritize values is not truly a human choice. The relevant question is whether you will do it well or poorly.

Focusing on some values and outcomes in contrast to others is a practical necessity. Because professionals should be held accountable, they must aim at a limited number of objectives and do them well. It is also politically unwise to suggest to those outside the profession that we are not sure what our specific mission is.

Making Value Choices

We need a method that will produce persuasive reasons for our value choices. Such a procedure should not allow us to impose local or personal values and parade them as if they are, or should be, everyone's values. But it must be sufficiently discriminating to keep us from concluding that people can value anything they choose to value. This method must negotiate a balance between needs for prescriptions about what is good for everyone and tolerance for different individual choices, tastes, and preferences. (Prescriptions will come later, from our work in chapters 6 and 7. There we will attempt to determine which of our contributions are the best ones.)

The issue of tolerance deserves our special attention because prioritizing physical education values objectively results in prescribing what is best for others as well as ourselves. We will be claiming, in effect, that we have some ideas that apply to all human beings about how movement activity should lead to better lives.

Reasons for Tolerance and Caution

There are at least three reasons for being very cautious in making judgments about values in different lifestyles and national traditions:

1. *Sound values show up in many different ways.* The same values wear many different costumes around the world. Yet, because these costumes are strange to our eyes, we may not recognize the old, familiar values that lie beneath them. Many people, for example, do not appreciate the slow British game of cricket, or they think that the practices of Zen archery are strange, or they see traditional African tribal dances as too emotional and somehow inferior. But could familiar and objectively sound values (values like patience, excellence, meaning, and tradition) be lurking there? Could some of them (like peace and tranquillity) be the same values

A method is needed to negotiate a balance between overprescription and blind tolerance.

that we honor, but in different clothing? And might they even be supporting some important values that we have missed or underemphasized (such as honoring wisdom and the aged)? If so, we must look for the best values but realize that they will not always look as we expect them to look. And we must hold open the likelihood that other cultures emphasize good values that would extend, provide alternatives to, or complement our own traditions.

2. *Sound values can be emphasized to different degrees.* Different life circumstances warrant emphases on different values and different life patterns. In some cultures and for some individuals, health concerns should take priority. For instance, in some third world countries basic health and nutrition ought to be highest order concerns. In other cultures or for some other individuals, health concerns probably should be kept more in the background. However, because we may have difficulty taking others' perspectives, there is always that danger that we will be insensitive to the goodness in different value patterns. We thus must look for the best values but acknowledge that our prescriptions must allow for considerable variation.

3. *Sound values are difficult to prioritize.* We may well make some mistakes in carrying out our analysis. We can be wrong about the objective significance of given values. And we can be wrong about which values should receive specific attention in a particular culture. For instance, if we end up ranking pleasure over fitness, will we be sure that this judgment is correct? Will our arguments be so strong that we can confidently claim, for all time, that we are right? And will we be able to tell what needs people in society really have? What if society has partly programmed people to think and say that they have needs that, for their own well-being, should not be fed or supported?

In any case, there is more than ample cause for caution here. As we try to negotiate this tricky thinking, we have many good reasons for being cautious in prescribing our conclusions for others.

Reasons for Intolerance and Boldness

Even though tolerance and caution are needed, we should not be intimidated into a blind affirmation that anything goes. Traditions, per se, do not merit tolerance, affirmation, or even basic respect. Only good traditions and decisions do.

It is possible to see variation in contemporary American culture between the good, the bad, and the uncertain. Sport can foster such values as friendship, freedom, and personal expression. This is undoubtedly good, and these practices deserve our support. But sport has also reinforced traditions of racism by expecting whites to play quarterback in football, for example. Sexist practices, such as the suggestion that women not participate in certain rugged sports, have been upheld. This is undoubtedly unfortunate, and such traditions and practices do not merit our support.

The third category of traditions and practices is probably the largest one. It includes activities that may be both good and bad, such as the emphasis on winning in sport, having children specialize early in a single sport for the sake of excellence, and the health and safety risks that Olympians take for the sake of high-level participation. Are these the practices of a healthy society that values individual excellence and achievement? Or are they practices of a society gone astray with imbalances and excesses? We may not be sure if such traditions merit much tolerance and support.

It is easier to be bold in supporting traditions that are clearly sound and to condemn practices that are clearly misdirected. It is harder to be bold in making the more difficult decisions on ambiguous cases. Nevertheless, our emphasis on tolerance does not relieve us of this responsibility to think boldly about what is right and wrong or better and worse, to report our conclusions, and to incorporate them into our actions.

A Procedure for Ranking Values

Baier (1958) suggests that at least two steps must be taken in order to rank values effectively. The first requires that we survey the facts, the second, that we weigh the reasons. Each needs some explanation.

Surveying the Facts

Surveying the facts involves describing and cataloging the characteristics and known benefits of each value. This will include (1) short- and long-term benefits, (2) benefits for ourselves and others, and (3) benefits as ends in themselves and as means to other ends.

This process is currently threatened by the state of research on the benefits of sport, dance, exercise, games, and play. Some, and perhaps many, of the good outcomes of the profession's activities and understandings are not yet known. Consequently, it is necessary to proceed on the basis of partial information and currently known benefits.

Fortunately, our four values of fitness, knowledge, skill, and pleasure are so broad and fundamental, so commonly experienced, and so well researched that we believe we can produce them to one degree or another. To be sure, we do not understand all there is to know about how to produce them or to what degree we bring them into being. And it might be good to get into the scientific

details on these issues (for further information, see Seefeldt, 1986). However, ours is a philosophic journey. Here we must be content with the realization that fitness, knowledge, skill, and pleasure are realistic values for us to prioritize. We can proceed with confidence that we are spending our time wisely by reviewing values that we can produce.

In chapters 6 and 7 we will survey the facts by reminding ourselves of the good things that are associated with each of our four values. For example, we will remind ourselves of what people who are more fit can do, of how people who have knowledge about activity can avoid common errors, and so on.

Weighing the Reasons

In the second step, weighing the reasons, I will propose three criteria for determining what Baier (1958) calls the *rules of superiority*. These criteria will allow us to evaluate the evidence gathered from surveying the facts. For example, suppose we now have a list of all the known benefits of skill and knowledge in front of us. The problem is that both lists appear impressive. Under *skill* we see "freedom to move," "ability to express oneself creatively," and many other important benefits. Under *knowledge* we notice "capacity to understand and play by game rules," "ability to avoid mistakes in dieting and exercising," and other good things.

Our tendency here may be to fall back on our hunches, personal biases, tastes, and whims. And it is conceivable, especially if we have fine tastes, that they would serve us well. But because we are doing philosophy, we need to look for a set of defensible rules for determining which of these good things should count more. In other words, we have to be able to give objective reasons for our choices. This is a critical and difficult step to take. When these rules are applied to the factual evidence, they will largely commit us to certain conclusions. If we do not like the conclusions, in other words, our primary recourse may be to dispute the original rules of superiority. However, if you want to change the rules, you must have good reasons for doing so.

The following principles will serve as our rules of superiority:

Rule 1 (Criterion of Intrinsic Value). *Values that are good in themselves are superior to values that lead to good things* (Frankena, 1973).   The traditional way of saying this is that intrinsic values are superior to extrinsic values. **Intrinsic values**, or **end values**, are regarded as good in themselves. Excellence, happiness, and knowledge, for example, are commonly thought to be strong end values. Thus, if we were asked the question, What is the realization of excellence, happiness, or knowledge in dance good for? we could respond, "Each one is good in itself. Dancing out, experiencing, or living such things as excellence, happiness, or knowledge needs no further justification. Such encounters themselves are the things at which we aim. We are satisfied when they fill our days, even if they do not lead to anything else."

Extrinsic values, or **means values**, are regarded as good because they lead to or somehow contribute to values that are good in themselves. Sport practice sessions, for example, are often thought to have primarily means value. Thus, if we were asked the question, What is routine drill, sacrifice, and painful fitness activity good for? we could respond, "They are not much good in themselves, but we think they are still valuable because they lead to things that we really want, things like the experiences of improvement and excellent play."

All experiences of life can be regarded as having both intrinsic and extrinsic value, or at least possibilities for such values. Experiences of fitness training and even drill can, upon occasion, be encountered as enjoyable in their own right, even though they also lead

Practice sessions primarily have extrinsic or means value—they lead to good things.

to further intrinsically valuable activities or experiences. On the other hand, the pleasure of playing or dancing well, while having strong intrinsic value, also has components of extrinsic merit; for example, pleasure can serve as motivation for further practice or the acceptance of additional challenges. Thus, while values may have greater or lesser components of intrinsic and extrinsic goodness to them, it is possible to think of virtually any experience or activity in both intrinsic and extrinsic terms.

It is unlikely, therefore, that any values can be cataloged simply as wholly intrinsic or wholly extrinsic. The four values emphasized in this chapter—fitness, knowledge, skill, and pleasure—have both intrinsic and extrinsic merit to them. But they may not have equal amounts of each kind of value. This first rule of superiority, therefore, will allow us to examine these values on their relative strength as intrinsic and extrinsic values. We will judge those that have greater intrinsic strength, all else being equal, as superior.

What permits us to establish this rule? Are there any good reasons for preferring end values to means values?

Rationale. End values have what may be called independent worth. They carry their cash value, as it were, on their own persons. They lack nothing; they wait for nothing. Their merits are self-contained. Means values have what may be called dependent worth. Their value is derived from the end values to which they lead. Their glory is not self-contained. They need end values for their own potential worth to show itself.

This one-way relationships of dependency presents end values as superior to means values. It acknowledges that we want to experience the good life, not just spend our energy getting there. It also acknowledges that, from time to time, we are willing to endure experiences that are not part of the good life, so long as they eventually lead us to this destination. It does not, however, depict extrinsic values as necessarily unimportant or insignificant. Experiences, exercises, or various disciplines that lead to intrinsically satisfying states of affairs may be tremendously valuable—but again, valuable primarily as means to those more important things that we experience as valuable in themselves.

In chapter 6, when we review the extrinsic power of each of our four values, we will discriminate between greater and lesser extrinsic value on the basis of its utility. That is, how useful are fitness, knowledge, skill, and pleasure as a *means* to something else, as a *tool* for producing other good experiences? Four criteria will be employed to answer this question:

1. Whether the means is necessary or optional
2. Whether the means is narrowly or broadly useful
3. Whether the means leads to important intrinsic values or trivial ones
4. Whether the means are pure (without significant cost) and durable (likely to be of continuing value)

Rule 2 (Criterion of Satisfaction). Experiences that include satisfaction (all else being equal) carry more intrinsic power than those that do not. Happiness, or what Frankena (1973, p. 89) calls "satisfactoriness," is a broader concept than pleasure. It is not limited to highly excited emotional states, nor is it limited to the so-called lower or animal pleasures. It can even include experiences that have a measure of discomfort to them (long distance races, long hours of productive work) but that are lived with an overall feeling of contentment. Satisfaction, in many cases, comes from doing what we want to do, even if such projects introduce difficulties or hard work.

Two corollaries accompany this rule:

1. Corollary of Purity. Satisfaction that brings little or no harm into the world is to be preferred to satisfaction that is accompanied by greater amounts of harm. We may experience some satisfaction, for example, while soundly defeating a weak opponent. The experiences of succeeding dramatically, scoring effortlessly, and winning convincingly may be pleasurable and intrinsically valuable for that reason. Yet the behavior itself may still not be defensible because it is done at the cost of another person's pain and, possibly also, harm to one's own integrity. This sort of behavior is less valuable than one that would include the same experiences of succeeding, scoring, and winning but without hurting the opponent—for instance, in a close, well-played game against a worthy competitor.

2. Corollary of Durability. Satisfaction that is durable or dependably recurring is preferred to satisfaction that is temporary or erratic (Fraleigh, 1989; Parker, 1957). When we experience success by winning the big game, for example, the satisfaction turns out to be very temporary. To, be sure, the good feeling lasts a while and sometimes can even be dredged up again years later through recollection. But there is another game to be played; there is another challenge to be met. Fans' memories are short, and today's heroes are often forgotten tomorrow. This experience of success is less valuable than one that lasts or is recurring. The more steady and repetitive satisfactions that come with good skills and a good reputation, for instance, would be preferred over pleasures that come with the relatively short-lived flush of victory.

Are there good reasons for adopting this second rule of superiority and its two corollaries? Will this criterion help us objectively to discriminate values that more directly produce the good life from those that are less effective in this regard?

Rationale. Rule 2 places a fair amount of importance on what some have called the pleasure principle. It is based on a recognition that experiences that are satisfactory, pleasant, enjoyable, agreeable—call it what you may—are intrinsically good. This is so because experiences that are pleasurable would seem to need no further justification. We seek pleasure because we want to experience it, not because we want it to lead to something else.

However, I have tempered this pleasure principle in two ways. First, the notion of pleasure has been broadened from narrow,

Pleasure is its own reward.

short-term, or sensually oriented experiences to broader, more durable, sensuous and non-sensuous satisfaction. Satisfaction encompasses more of life than pleasures do and seems to get closer to the heart of what it means for an experience to be good for its own sake. We would not normally want to claim, for example, that the experience of playing baseball is enjoyable only when we are having some particularly fine sensuous experience, like hitting a fastball on the meat of the bat. Baseball can also be enjoyable when we conjure up some strategy, wonder how an opposing pitcher will throw to us, review game statistics, or watch a pitcher from the on-deck circle—that is, when little or nothing sensual or aesthetically important is going on in our immediate experience.

Second, I am not claiming that satisfaction is the only thing that makes an experience worth having. That is why I had to include the phrase *all else being equal* in rule 2. This is important because it keeps us from having to judge experiences simply on the amount of pleasure that they contain or the balance of pleasure over pain that they produce (Frankena, 1973). It seems reasonable to claim that experiences, for example, that include enjoyment *and* excellence (e.g., using fine technique in hitting a golf ball out of the deep rough onto a distant green) are superior to those that are only enjoyable (e.g., feeling a delightfully warm breeze blow through your hair as you prepare to hit a shot from the rough). Similarly, experiences that are characterized by satisfactoriness *and* creativity (e.g., doing a compulsory dive well and with unusual style or personal flair) are superior to those characterized simply by satisfactoriness (e.g., doing the dive extremely well but unimaginatively).

The two corollaries also require justification. The first is based on the recognition that pleasure or satisfactoriness is not absolutely good. That is, satisfactory experiences are not self-justifying to the extent that any manner

of producing pleasure or enjoyment is acceptable. An extreme example will make this point clear. There is a baseball pitcher who, as strange as it sounds, derives a great deal of pleasure from hitting opposing batters with 90-mile-an-hour fastballs. Whenever his team gets a comfortable lead, he can be counted on to seek pleasure in this unconventional way. However, everyone knows that this behavior is entirely unethical. No matter how pure the enjoyment is, and thus, no matter how intrinsically valuable the experience of hitting opposing batters is for the pleasure it creates, this behavior is unsupportable. It makes sense then to allow for factors like harming another human being to detract from the overall strength of satisfying experiences.

The second corollary also seems to be sensible. Given our limited time, energy, and ability to find and experience satisfaction, we want to invest our resources wisely. We do not want to waste our talents chasing something that gives a very temporary high but then leaves us chronically empty, bored, or tired.

Rule 3   Criterion of Coherence. *Satisfactory experiences that build a coherent and meaningful life take precedence over those that are isolated moments of pleasure.*   What qualities or types of experiences tend to produce durable satisfaction that is not harmful to others? The answer proposed here is that the experience of a coherent, meaningful life—one that is headed somewhere—brings with it these durable satisfactions. This criterion is about making sense of our lives, of seeing and living a pattern in daily activities that is interesting and worthy of development. When we say that life has **meaning**, we are indicating that it coheres, is reasonably consistent, has poignancy, is moving somewhere, has a goal, and is recognizably ours.

Perhaps the most fundamental and customary experience of a coherent life comes with developing and living a story. A story has a beginning, a middle, and an end, and all three are related to one another. A story leads someplace. Its characters have roles to fulfill, work to do, celebrations to hold, and love to experience. In short, its characters belong; they have a place in the world. A story line does not develop on its own. History and culture are two prime sources of plots, goals, and aspirations that can add drama to life. Consequently, rule 3 implies that cultural traditions (particularly good ones) will take precedence over cold mathematical solutions, antiseptically correct scientific recommendations, or impersonally pure philosophic ideals.

Early chapters in life stories are often written on playgrounds.

To be sure, there are countless numbers of different stories, and we are not entirely free to choose the ongoing account or plot that we wish to take up or join. Parents, ancestors, upbringing, talents, and genes have much to say about which stories will suit us. As we mature, move through school, prepare for our life's work and play, make commitments to mates or choose to remain single, and start families and careers, we continue to define our stories and achieve, hopefully, increasing degrees of meaning, satisfaction, and at-homeness with our choices. We refine our goals and gain a good sense of what fits and what does not.

On the other hand, if we have no narrative operating in our own lives, if our activities are experienced as somewhat arbitrary and disconnected, it is more likely that we will see the world as confusing and at least somewhat meaningless. Our day-to-day actions would occur more by happenstance than on purpose, or they would be controlled by appetites and other forces that operate largely apart from rooted meaning. In short, our lives would lack direction. As disconnected from our past, meandering through our present, and uncertain about any future directions that would be uniquely right for us, we would experience ourselves as living in a strange land. The incapacity to deal with the world would give our lives few if any attractive possibilities.

Rationale. We need rule 3 for breaking ties because rule 2 presents us with several problems (Frankena, 1973, pp. 90-91). Different kinds of satisfaction are difficult, if not impossible, to compare with one another. How, for example, would we evaluate the pleasure gained in watching a ballet in contrast to the satisfaction achieved in understanding, for the first time, how the Krebs cycle works and why people feel pain in conditions of oxygen debt? It is possible that they are incomparable and thus simply may have to be appreciated for what they are. We need a way to choose between incomparable satisfactions. Rule 3 helps us do this.

Some pleasures, however, are similar and comparisons would seem to be possible. But here a second problem shows up. It is very difficult to measure the amount of pleasure or joy that accompanies an event. How would we ever determine the exact quantity of pleasure that is present in a given experience or, worse yet, is likely to be present in some future event? For instance, how could we ever be certain that we had effectively measured the amount of pleasure in each of 10 lacrosse goals we had scored during the season or be certain that a goal in the play-offs would offer more enjoyment than all of these goals combined? It is therefore highly impractical to discriminate greater from lesser intrinsic values on the basis of quantity of pleasure (or balance of pleasure over pain) provided. Once again, rule 3 acts as a tiebreaker.

But why should this standard be coherence and meaningfulness? Why not exellence, for example? This is not an easy call, but several reasons can be given. First, meaning seems to be a doorway through which virtually all human behavior must pass. If I score a winning goal and thereby achieve a bit of excellence, its value (at least for my life) seems to be uncertain until I know that this is important to me, that it means something. If I gain some excellence as a part of a lifelong, passionate journey—that is one thing. But if I gain it as a result of pushy parents or a selfish, demanding coach, if it is an angry or reluctant reaction to a negative set of circumstances—that is quite another. In short, excellence on its own may be cold, even if it is impressive. However, when it is woven into a story, its powerful intrinsic values can strike home.

Second, a coherent, meaningful life typically includes and fosters excellence. That is because people care about those things that are meaningful and important. And they are

likely to get good at whatever those things are. If parenthood is deeply meaningful, parents will likely spend the time and energy necessary to achieve a degree of excellence in that role. If kicking soccer goals is meaningful, players will likely practice until they get it right.

On the other hand, there are many forces that would promote excellence: economic necessity, guilt, fear, a blind sense of duty, to name only four. While it is true that some people will eventually develop a love for the activity they do so well (even though it was forced upon them), many will not. They will continue to produce excellently even though it means little to do so. Or they may eventually rebel, change jobs, or drop out. In sum, meaning seems more often to bring along excellence than vice versa. Consequently, if forced to choose what value I would want to start with, I would pick a coherent, meaningful life.

Finally, meaning is a very democratic value in contrast to excellence; excellence has an elitist ring to it. Not all of us can achieve much that is truly excellent. Most of us cannot even approach the achievements of the best athletes, the best actors, the best writers, the best of anything. If we attempted to reach the highest levels of participation in the name of excellence, we might have to neglect much else that can embellish life—things like friendships, family, an appreciation for the arts, even an ability to relax. But as regular humans, we can fight for and find meaning, struggle to have passion about something, and mold an interesting narrative out of our lives. We do not have to be abnormally gifted or put our lives out of balance to experience meaning. But we do have to be true to ourselves, attentive to those invitations that are right for us, dedicated, interested, given to those things that make up our narrative.

While these sorts of arguments may be persuasive, I must admit that they are not conclusive. Coherence, meaningfulness, a sense of place and direction, lived connections with culture and history—as a complex standard or criterion for intrinsic value—these cannot be proven to offer the most powerful measure for intrinsic value. Nevertheless, they provide a useful measuring stick. As you will see, this criterion will have some very important effects on how we prioritize fitness, knowledge, skill, and pleasure. It also carries some exciting implications for the practice of sport, exercise science, and physical education.

PHILOSOPHIC EXERCISE

The identification of Rule 3 may have the most important and far-reaching consequences of any judgment made to this point in your journey. The fact that it may be a controversial judgment makes it all the more important that you hesitate at this junction in your philosophic travels.

On your own or with the help of your instructor, you may want to do some experimental hiking down another path by substituting another criterion for my third rule of superiority or by adding one or two more rules to the list. Two criteria for the good life that have received perhaps the most attention in our literature are (1) experiences of *freedom*, authenticity, choice, and responsibility (Meier, 1988; Slusher, 1967) and (2) experiences of *excellence* (Novak, 1976; Simon, 1985, 1992; Weiss, 1969). As we attempt to prioritize fitness, knowledge, skill, and pleasure in the next two chapters, you may want to apply these different or additional criteria for purposes of determining the objective strength of these four values.

Review

Your work in this profession should be aimed at making some contribution to the good life.

Four traditional values of sport, exercise science, and physical education—health- and activity-related fitness, knowledge, motor skill, and pleasure—are prime candidates for such contributions.

At least three reasons can be given for prioritizing these values:

1. Making one value primary to the other three can make a tremendous difference in the scope and nature of your work.

2. You have already made value judgments on these and many other matters of worth. Because valuing is unavoidable, it might as well be done on the basis of reason and reflection in contrast to blind tradition or unexamined feeling.

3. A profession that has not committed itself to a direction by prioritizing values may accomplish much—but none of it very well. It may also appear to lack a focus, and this can place it in jeopardy in educational and other settings.

The process of ranking values can be accomplished in two steps: surveying the facts and weighing the reasons. Surveying the facts involves a description and cataloging of the good things that come with or are produced by fitness, knowledge, skill, and pleasure. Weighing the reasons requires an identification of criteria for good living. Three such criteria can be used: (1) intrinsic values should count more than extrinsic ones; (2) intrinsically valuable experiences that include pure and durable satisfaction should count more than those that lack it; and (3) intrinsically valuable experiences that promote and are part of a coherent, meaningful existence should count more than those that are pleasurable but less well connected with a person's life.

From this discussion of values and priorities, it becomes clear that the question Sam's potential employer asked (in the example at the beginning of the chapter) was a shrewd one. She wanted to know if Sam had any passion for his career, if he knew what he really wanted to do for people through his profession, and if he could give any reasons for his choices. His response that everything counts equally and that he had no reasons for placing any of these values above others probably told her a great deal, no doubt to Sam's detriment.

Looking Ahead

In the next two chapters, you will use the method you picked up here to evaluate the worth of fitness, knowledge, motor skill, and pleasure. Your goal is to produce a reasoned judgment about which of these good things should count most in your professional life. The purpose is to provide you with a philosophic road map for your daily actions and overall professional priorities.

Checking Your Understanding

1. What is the difference between moral and nonmoral values? Give some examples of each. Which moral and nonmoral values are most important to you? That is, how would you define the good life for yourself?
2. What are four of the most prominent traditional values of physical education? Describe examples of their presence in the profession today. Which of the four philosophies do you find most attractive and why?
3. Why is it important to prioritize values? Give at least three reasons for taking this responsibility seriously.
4. How can values be prioritized? What does it mean to survey the facts and weigh the reasons? Identify three criteria that can be used to weigh the reasons.

Key Terms

The good life, p. 111

Moral values, p. 111

Nonmoral values, p. 112

Fitness, p. 113

Knowledge, p. 114

Skill, p. 114

Pleasure, p. 115

Surveying the facts, p. 126

Weighing the reasons, p. 126

Intrinsic, end values, p. 127

Extrinsic, means values, p. 127

Meaning, p. 130

Further Reading

For further information on values and the good life in general, see Frankena (1973), Parker (1957), MacIntyre (1984), and Bellah et al. (1991). For examples of contributions to the good life from exercise, sport, and physical education see Fraleigh (1989), Arnold (1988, 1991), Simon (1985, 1992), and Williams (1964). For more detail on the importance of prioritizing values in our profession, see Kretchmar (1988, 1990c).

Chapter 6

The Extrinsic Value of Fitness, Knowledge, Skill, and Pleasure

Susan James is the head of a physical education department at a large high school in the Midwest. She is responsible for all physical education classes and after-school intramurals. She has five full-time faculty in her unit, four of them head coaches. Susan must work closely with the athletic director as well as the head of the Health Education Department in order to carry out her duties.

As department head for six years, Susan has developed a successful program oriented around two primary purposes—the promotion of health through physical fitness and the development of an active lifestyle through an emphasis on lifetime sports. The health/fitness purpose has been advanced by the addition of a required aerobic fitness class; jogging, cycling, and hiking electives; and the initiation of a new theory course that focuses on the general physiology of fitness and on personal fitness assessment and prescription. The active-lifestyle goal has been advanced by giving intramural sports a high profile in the school and by purging the curriculum of activities that are not lifetime sports. Susan has reason to be proud of the changes she has made.

These successes have not gone unnoticed by her principal, Dr. Shea. With the district facing budget cuts and the need to find ways to effect savings, Dr. Shea has asked Susan confidentially to consider serving as head of a new and larger unit—one that would include her own department and some combination of the departments of Health Education (an academic service department), Interscholastic Athletics, Driver Education, Intramurals, and School Clubs (nonacademic/extracurricular departments).

Susan is flattered by Dr. Shea's confidence in her abilities, but she is bothered by the options facing her. Health education, while an academic department, provides a service that leads to better health. The content of health education is not usually regarded as valuable in its own right, at least not like information in literature, history, or the arts. Susan is worried about aligning physical education with a department that is grounded in extrinsic value alone.

On the other hand, athletics, driver education, intramurals, and school clubs are not even regarded as academic or central to the educational mission of her school. She does not want physical education to be associated with departments that are considered auxiliaries to education.

What should Susan do? Should she suggest that the new unit include all of the departments named by her principal? Or should she look for an alternative? If physical education were seen both as academic and the source of intrinsic values that are part and parcel of the good life, would other alignments for her department make more sense?

In the last chapter you met the four traditional values of fitness, knowledge, skill, and pleasure. Each of these can be considered as valuable in its own right (intrinsically good) or valuable as means to other ends (extrinsically good), that is, as tools. In this chapter the focus will be on fitness, knowledge, skill, and pleasure as tools. Using the rules of superiority delineated in the previous chapter, the question will be, Which of these four values best *leads* to a life that is experienced as satisfactory and coherently meaningful? Which educational acquisition—becoming fit, knowledgeable, and skillful, or experiencing pleasure—is best able to transport us to activities and experiences that we enjoy for their own sake?

IN THIS CHAPTER YOU WILL

- examine the extrinsic value of fitness, knowledge, skill, and pleasure;

- speculate on their relative power to produce important ends; and

- develop a ranking of fitness, knowledge, skill, and pleasure based on their extrinsic values and, on this basis, establish a tentative road map for your own future.

The primary goal in this part of your journey in philosophy is to see the fundamental values of sport, exercise science, and physical education as tools. When considered as tools, they are good because they lead to good things, not because they are good in themselves. And like most tools, they are not all created equal. Some tools simply have the capacity to do more than others. If you and I were building a house and were forced to choose between a radial arm saw and a pair of pliers, we would probably select the saw.

As a young professional in exercise science, you will be helping others build a good life. Thus, you need to consider the merits of health- and activity-related fitness, knowledge, motor skill, and pleasure as four important power tools for your professional tool box. Which of these tools do you expect to be using most? Which tools do you want most to protect, highlight, and enhance?

What are the ways in which fitness, knowledge, skill, and pleasure can promote other good things in your life?

If you could keep only one of them as a pathway to the good life, which would you retain?

Aren't fitness and good health the basic foundation on which all else in your life rests?

How would your life develop if pleasure were not present? What would this do to your chances for achieving a satisfactory and meaningful life?

Examining Extrinsic Values

Before we can make judgments about the relative importance of our four values, we must see each one clearly. In other words, we need to examine fitness, knowledge, skill, and pleasure as tools and look at what they can and cannot do. This step was referred to in chapter 5 as surveying the facts.

The Extrinsic Value of Health- and Activity-Related Fitness

Health- and activity-related fitness is a condition of biological well-being that permits normal, physically active functioning, enhances chances for a long life, and improves one's appearance. Accordingly, physical fitness would seem to have outstanding credentials as an extrinsic value. In fact, to the extent that physical fitness is related to the continuation of biological existence itself, it is a tool that is probably without a serious rival. Without our health, as we say, we have nothing. Without our lives, all projects and stories, all hopes, all satisfactions, and all experiences of meaning come to an end.

Even if fitness is taken less dramatically to signal only the presence of moderate degrees of energy and endurance, it still shows itself as a very powerful and virtually necessary means to good living. Even individuals who have chosen relatively sedentary lifestyles must have threshold levels of energy and endurance because their writing, painting, reading, reflecting, desk work, walking, sitting, and concentrating all take degrees of energy and endurance even if they do not require high cardiovascular efficiency. People who tire quickly, who become uncomfortable after sitting for only short periods of time, who cannot concentrate for long, or who are generally lethargic or sleepy cannot even lead satisfactory quiet lives.

Fitness is also related to our physical appearance and our self-concept. The more fit we are, the better we look and the better we feel about ourselves. Because fitness can affect self-confidence, it can also influence our success at work and our social lives. Particularly in a culture that praises youthfulness, thin bodies, tight skin, and vitality, physical fitness can play a major role in shaping a positive self-identity.

Along with the strengths of physical fitness as a means value, a few weaknesses also exist. Fitness is a very temporary possession if it is not tended to. Unlike well-learned motor skills that can remain a part of oneself for a lifetime, high fitness levels may be lost in a matter of weeks, if not days. In addition, fitness (at least for some) is difficult to maintain. Because it must be worked on regularly, and because a degree of stress on one's biological systems is needed to maintain or improve fitness, the cost of this value may be high. When fitness activities are experienced as boring, distasteful, or painful, the costs can be very high.

A brief review of physiological-anatomical factors (Vogel, 1986) fostered by physical education programs will help to clarify the nature of physical fitness. I have added examples of activities made possible by the acquisition of each factor so that it is possible to appreciate fully their appearance in daily life.

These examples of activity, it must be noted, have both intrinsic and extrinsic value. Some fit individuals, for example, may enjoy working in their yards for its own sake. The experience of working-as-a-fit-person is its own reward. Others do not much like the experience itself and use their fitness to get their mowing and weeding over with as quickly as possible. Fitness has extrinsic value in this latter case.

However, because we are looking at our four values as means to other ends in this chapter, I conclude each description with a sample of the factor's extrinsic power.

You are encouraged to add examples of activities from your own life that are made possible by physical fitness. You may also find samples of fitness's extrinsic power that are more in line with your own goals.

- **Aerobic fitness** refers to the ability to move with moderate to low intensity, where energy is produced with oxygen. *Examples resulting from good aerobic fitness*: working on a physically demanding yard project that will consume the better part of the afternoon, taking a 2-hour bike ride; walking three miles to get gas for a stalled car; playing 30 minutes of basketball with one's child on a driveway court. *Samples of extrinsic power*: can promote high levels of productivity at work, longer periods of fun while at play, even a longer life.

- **Anaerobic fitness** refers to the ability to move with high intensity, where energy is produced without oxygen. *Examples resulting from good anaerobic fitness*: meeting the demands of an emergency situation by running for help; moving a piano; sprinting for the winning score in touch football. *Sample of extrinsic power*: can allow one to save a life in a physically taxing, emergency situation.

- **Agility** refers to the ability to move one's whole body quickly and gracefully. *Examples resulting from good agility*: taking part effectively in virtually any sport or game; working in many outdoor and physically oriented vocations; reacting to an immediate danger, like jumping out of the way of an oncoming cyclist. *Sample of extrinsic power*: can lead to competitive success and fame in basketball.

• **Body composition** refers to the combination of elements that constitute one's body—particularly the mixture of fat, bone, and muscle. *Examples resulting from good body composition*: being able to move quickly and gracefully because of a lean, fit body; playing a demanding game such as basketball, one in which excess amounts of fat or insufficient musculature is disadvantageous; enhancing chances for a long life by maintaining an optimal weight. *Samples of extrinsic power*: can promote vitality for all of life's activities; can affect appearance.

• **Body size** and **shape** refer to one's weight, height, body composition, and body design. *Examples resulting from good body size and shape*: having a good self-image or a sense of confidence; fitting into narrow places; wearing attractive clothes; relieving or avoiding back pain. *Sample of extrinsic power*: can lead to or promote self-acceptance and good social relationships.

• **Flexibility** refers to the capacity to move one's appendages through their full range of motion. *Examples resulting from good flexibility*: doing simple household chores that involve bending, reaching, and stooping; taking off tight boots; stretching for a wide throw at first base in a picnic softball game; getting into and around the crawlspace in one's basement. *Samples of extrinsic power*: can lead to greater productivity; can promote self-reliance and independence among the elderly.

There are many other parameters of physical fitness that could have been included in this list (Vogel, 1986). Nevertheless, this description of embodied vigor and healthful appearance shows that the extrinsic values of fitness are ubiquitous and significant, even for those who do not regard themselves as physically active people.

SUMMARY BREAK

There are at least three very compelling reasons for giving health-related fitness a high score on extrinsic value.

1. In that fitness preserves life itself and promotes longevity, it is *the* tool required for any of life's projects and experiences.

2. In that fitness provides threshold levels of energy and endurance, it is important for virtually all people in a wide range of occupations with many different lifestyles, even those who lead a more sedentary existence.

3. In that fitness affects appearance, it plays a role in shaping a positive self-image and influences how we feel about ourselves.

Weaknesses of fitness as a means value include its temporary nature and the discomforts and other costs of maintaining good levels of fitness.

The Extrinsic Value of Health- and Activity-Related Knowledge

Knowledge takes the form of theories, propositions, and statements. Knowledge is something that can be called to mind, mulled over, symbolized in words, stated, and restated. It is abstract in the sense that it has a life or existence apart from the particular situations or circumstances that it describes or explains. If we have knowledge about how to swing a baseball bat correctly, for example, we can talk about it away from ballfields and without actually moving a bat.

It is not easy to gain a clear view on the extrinsic merits of health- and activity-related knowledge in general or in the profession specifically. On the one hand, it is known that knowledge has tremendous utility value for much that we do. It helps us avoid repeating the errors of our predecessors. It provides us with principles that can be applied to an infinite variety of new situations. It relieves us of much time-consuming and potentially harmful trial-and-error activities. It liberates us from inferior practices that produce inferior results. It gives us access to things without requiring us to see them with our own eyes.

On the other hand, it is also known that the acquisition of knowledge does not always result in improved practice. This is particularly important in health-related fields. For example, knowing that smoking causes cancer does not always result in a decision to stop smoking; knowing that seat belts reduce traffic deaths does not always result in habits to use them; understanding that high-fat diets are generally unhealthy is not the same thing as having low-fat eating patterns.

The extrinsic value of knowledge may be cast into doubt even further when it is noticed that positive behaviors and fine skills are not dependent on prior knowledge. We can develop smokeless lifestyles whether or not we understand the chemistry of cancer or know statistics on smoking and lung disease. We can develop habits of using seat belts whether or not we know about traffic fatalities. In sport, a baseball batter can develop a major league stroke under the guidance of a coach even if he does not understand the principles of physics that underlie his swing. This, of course, is not to say that knowledge never leads to more efficient practice, practical inventions, or strong motivations for behavior change. But knowledge as such is often not needed for these.

An additional limitation must be noted. It has to do with the significance of knowledge related specifically to our profession. Although health- and safety-related facts might be given high utility ratings, information about sport, dance, games, exercise, and play

Right practice does not automatically follow knowledge.

would probably receive a lower score. Learning the rules of different games, the cultural traditions of various folk dances, the etiquette of golf, the advantages and disadvantages of various types of weight-training protocols, the history and heroes of different sports—this kind of information, while still having some utility for the ability to function successfully in society, does not seem to be as crucial as health and safety knowledge.

Some might even argue that, relative to information in other subjects, sport, dance, game, and play knowledge is relatively trivial. For example, if we were high school curriculum coordinators and were forced to choose between the following types of theory, which would we select? Principles of democracy or the origins of baseball? Life and times of Shakespeare or strategies for breaking a full-court press? Workings of a free-market economy or mechanics of a golf swing? As much as we movement people might enjoy the latter, it would be difficult to defend the second choices in each pair—particularly if it meant that our students would know nothing of the first ones. If a major goal of education is to prepare students to function effectively as citizens in society, it might be difficult to convince a school board, for instance, that background information on baseball is as important as an understanding of the principles of democracy. Health knowledge, particularly about life-threatening practices or illnesses, would fare better. But even then, many educators would argue that this should not replace basic academic subject matter.

With these limitations in mind, let us look at some areas of knowledge and add personal examples of extrinsic uses for each.

• **Health knowledge** refers to the comprehension of psychobiological factors that influence human vitality and longevity. *Examples of good health knowledge*: understanding AIDS, pregnancy prevention (from knowledge of birth control), illness (from knowledge of drug abuse and sound dietary practices). *Sample of extrinsic power*: can lead to a longer life.

• **Safety knowledge** refers to the comprehension of specific behaviors that influence physical well-being and longevity. *Examples of good safety knowledge*: understanding procedures that maximize well-being in automobiles, at work, at home, and in sport. *Sample of extrinsic power*: can prevent unnecessary pain and suffering.

• **General performance knowledge** refers to the comprehension of factors that promote efficient and effective movement. *Examples of good general performance knowledge*: learning principles of practice technique, concentration strategy, the effective distribution of practice sessions, and the proper sequencing of learning tasks; having information that will allow people to learn games and dance techniques more quickly and efficiently. *Sample of extrinsic power*: can lead to more efficient movements, less wasted energy.

• **Specific performance knowledge** refers to the comprehension of factors that promote efficient and effective participation in particular dance, sport, game, play, or work activities. *Examples of good specific performance knowledge*: learning principles of a specific activity; getting tips on how to improve a swing, stance, reaction, movement, or flow in a given dance or game. *Sample of extrinsic power*: can lead to more victories in competition, more satisfaction in play.

• **Competitive performance knowledge** refers to the comprehension of one's competence relative to others. *Example of good competitive performance knowledge*: learning, by means of a sport contest, who is the better player or team on a given day. *Samples of extrinsic power*: can lead to more accurate assessment of one's progress, one's status, the effects of a certain practice strategy.

• **Rules knowledge** refers to comprehension of the prescriptions and proscriptions that define a game. *Examples of good rules knowledge*: understanding the do's and don'ts of softball, golf, tennis, and other games. *Sample of extrinsic power*: can allow individuals to join friends and play culturally popular games.

• **Game spectator knowledge** refers to comprehension of the factors that permit the intelligent observation of performances by others. *Example of good game spectator knowledge*: understanding how to watch a game on television or in parks and stadiums. *Sample of extrinsic power*: can permit individuals to enjoy the company of other fans and join in their discussions, analyses, and fun.

• **Sport history knowledge** refers to the comprehension of previous events, forces, and individuals who influenced the domain of human activity, particularly sports and games. *Examples of good sport history knowledge*: understanding the lore and traditions of a culture's sports, games, and dances; knowing who the sport heroes are and being familiar with their exploits. *Samples of extrinsic power*: can help persons analyze factors that led to a current sport problem; may point to solutions or at least the avoidance of past mistakes.

• **Sport strategy knowledge** refers to the comprehension of techniques that can produce superior performance results. *Examples of good sport strategy knowledge*: understanding the principles of playing a game successfully and unsuccessfully; having information on how to counter different techniques used by an opponent. *Samples of extrinsic power*: can lead to additional victories, success, fame.

SUMMARY BREAK

Knowledge has clear and important utility value in directing practice, avoiding dangerous or wasteful hit-and-miss strategies, and promoting inventions of new and better practices. Health and safety knowledge probably has the clearest and most forceful means value among the various kinds of information for which we are responsible in our field.

However, the overall utility of health- and activity-related knowledge is only moderate. At least three reasons can be given for this conclusion:

1. Good theory does not necessarily lead to good practice.
2. Good practice is not dependent on a prior understanding of good theory.
3. Sport, exercise science, physical education, and even health knowledge may, in certain cases, deserve a lower priority ranking in our schools than other sorts of knowledge.

The Extrinsic Value of Motor Skill

Motor skill is a form of knowledge, often referred to as procedural, practical, or how-to knowledge. It brings with it the capacity to negotiate complex or problematic procedures, but it does not necessarily include the ability to theorize or talk about them. In this sense, skill is context-dependent, not abstract. It is useful only at the scene, in the face of the problem. Motor skill allows people to solve concrete problems in the movement world of time, space, and force.

The extrinsic merit of motor skill is considerable, for much that we do in life depends on movement skills of some sort. Even people who do not choose sporting, dancing, or exercising lifestyles need motor skills for activities like grooming themselves, working around the home, typing, driving a car, walking, gesturing, making love, cooking, and so on.

However, several mitigating factors must be kept in mind here. These limitations parallel those that were uncovered in the earlier

Motor skill allows you to solve problems in the movement world of space, time, and force.

discussion of activity-related knowledge. First, our profession, at least in much of the world, has been focused largely on one subset of activity—that associated with sport, dance, exercise, games, and play. Movement per se, as a conceptual framework for the profession, has not caught on. Our profession does not for the most part promote the teaching of general movement skills.

A second limitation on the rating of extrinsic value of motor skill comes with the realization that many day-to-day movement activities are learned fairly well apart from formal educational intervention. Walking, for example, is "taught" to us by our parents, and most of us develop sufficient skill in walking without further education. Likewise, penmanship and basic drawing skills are largely self-developed, and the acquisition of a wide range of skills and styles of moving normally causes no problems. Around-the-home climbing, reaching, pushing, pulling, lifting, and dragging skills are also generally acquired without specific training, and, again, we do these things well enough that our lives are not much the worse for the lack of formal training and the absence of serious and dedicated practice.

A third limitation has to do with the relative independence of exercise activities and health-related fitness benefits from motor skills. That is, people do not need finely honed movement skills or long periods of training to lift weights, walk, jog, hike, swim laps, or engage in other health-promoting exercise activities. So, it cannot be claimed that extensive motor skills are a prerequisite, and least of all a necessary means, for the achievement of health benefits or the so-called active lifestyle.

Finally, it must be noted that the value of motor skill as a tool depends to a great extent on the significance of sport, dance, games, and play in culture. In other words, because the profession emphasizes skills for these activities, it stands to reason that skills' utility value would increase or decrease in the degree to which people are thought to live well or poorly given their having or not having skills in sport, dance, games, and play.

The significance of such skills is difficult to assess. Some believe that good sport skills, for example, are helpful in the development of a healthy self-concept and good social skills (Sage, 1986; Vogel, 1986; Weiss & Bredemeier, 1986). Also, given the centrality of sport and recreational activity in society, there is certainly an enhanced level of acceptance that comes with skills in playing with others in school, in the neighborhood, or at work. This used to be particularly true for young boys, but it has become increasingly important for youngsters regardless of gender.

The overall utility score for motor skill should probably be fairly high given the difficulty in contemporary society of being insulated from skillful (motor-oriented) games, play, and recreation. But it should not be as high as the utility rating of body weight, shape, and appearance—factors related to physical fitness—for everyone is affected (and usually significantly) by how they look and feel.

Positive self-concept and good feeling are probably not tied as tightly to the capacity to play a game well. It is entirely conceivable that people could lead very successful, enjoyable, and productive lives without having much in the way of sport, dance, game, and play skills. They may even have motor skills in other areas—like playing a musical instrument, doing calligraphy, sculpting, and so on. Success in the workplace (planning, typing, discussing, convincing), satisfaction at home (preparing and consuming good meals, cleaning, washing the car), and enjoyment in recreational pursuits (reading books, gardening, listening to music) are entirely possible in the absence of the particular activity skills with which professionals in physical education typically must concern themselves.

A review of a list of different types of activity skills should help to clarify the scope and significance of movement skills. You should attempt to provide additional examples for each category from your own experiences.

• **Sport skill** refers to the procedural knowledge that allows successful participation in physically active, competitive games. *Examples of good sport skill*: playing softball, baseball, golf, tennis, or any number of other popular sporting activities with some success and satisfaction; being able to join sport leagues or clubs with friends, co-workers, or neighbors. *Samples of extrinsic power*: can be a means to fame, financial success, and self-confidence.

• **Dance skill** refers to the procedural knowledge that allows successful participation in a variety of modern and traditional dance forms. *Examples of good dance skill*: participating with some success and personal satisfaction in social dance opportunities throughout a lifetime; becoming involved in specialized dance organizations, such as modern dance companies, square dance clubs, ethnic dance societies. *Sample of extrinsic power*: can lead to experiences of oneself as free and expressive.

• **Exercise skill** refers to the procedural knowledge that allows successful participation in activities designed to have beneficial physical and psychological effects. *Examples of good exercise skill*: having the ability to swim, jog, bike, play sports, and generally move in ways that allow for the taxing of cardiovascular, muscular, and other physiological and anatomical systems. *Samples of extrinsic power*: can lead to health and good levels of physical fitness; can be a means for self-improvement.

• **Recreational skill** refers to the procedural knowledge that allows successful participation in informal games and other leisure activities (e.g., horseshoes, picnic volleyball, fishing, hunting, hiking, skiing, and the like). *Examples of good recreational skill*: having the ability to participate in informal play and outdoor activities; being able to refresh oneself through such activity. *Sample of extrinsic power*: can allow a person to avoid burnout and return to work with greater productivity.

• **Health- and safety-related skill** refers to the procedural knowledge that allows successful participation in potentially dangerous activities or situations. *Examples of good health- and safety-related skill*: being able to work and play (e.g., balancing, climbing, lifting) to promote health and avoid injury; having the ability to assume healthy postures when sitting and standing. *Sample of extrinsic power*: can lead to a longer life with fewer injuries.

• **Expression skill** refers to the procedural knowledge that fosters successful communication. *Examples of good expression skill*: being able to use gestures, stance, and posture effectively to supplement or enhance verbal communication; having the capacity to express meanings nonverbally through dance, sport, or some other form of movement; feeling at ease and moving without embarrassment as others watch these skillful expressions. *Sample of extrinsic power*: allows person to say things that words alone cannot communicate.

• **Exploration skill** refers to the procedural knowledge that fosters successful discoveries. *Examples of good exploration skill*: being able to explore the physical, sense perceptual world effectively; being able to discriminate subtle physical distinctions in shape, color, texture; being able to climb, hike, bicycle, or otherwise locomote to new and interesting places. *Samples of extrinsic power*: can lead to new inventions, better methods for doing things, the development of a personal style.

SUMMARY BREAK

Three concerns are raised about the utility value of the activity skills taught and promoted by our field:

1. Our profession in much of the world has largely limited itself to a subset of movement skills, namely, those associated with sport, dance, and exercise. In many cases, there is little carryover to the movement requirements of life in general.

2. Many day-to-day movement skills (like walking, riding a bike, and reaching) are learned by people on their own.

3. Fitness objectives can be achieved without the possession of high-level movement skills.

Nevertheless, sport, dance, exercise, game, and play skills are culturally important—especially for the growth and development of children, but also for adults in an activity- and sports-oriented society. While the achievement of the good life at home, at work, and at leisure is possible in the absence of some repertoire of motor skills in sport, dance, games, exercise, and play, it may not be as likely.

The Extrinsic Value of Health- and Activity-Related Pleasure

I have defined pleasure in broad terms to include any kind of general satisfaction. It includes not only fun and what might be called positive emotional experiences, but also meaningfulness, and thus a group of experiences that may be deeply satisfying without being much fun. Certain efforts to help others, for example, might not be much fun but are still experienced as satisfying. I count these as pleasurable.

Pleasure has a considerable degree of utility value in most educational and service professions. The field of sport, exercise science, and physical education is no exception. The value of pleasure as a tool stems primarily from its role in promoting repeated or continued behavior. We tend to continue with or return to what we like or enjoy. In physical education, if we want our students and clients to become healthy or fit, if we want them to learn lifetime sports, if we want them to develop active lifestyles, if we want them to learn and remember important knowledge—we must promote repetitions. One of the best ways to do this is to make the activity fun.

When it is said, for example, that it is important to make learning enjoyable, we are paying tribute to the utility value of pleasure. When it is said that successful physical education often occurs in an atmosphere of play, we are probably paying tribute to the utility value of pleasure. When it is said that competition may spice up a physical education class or exercise protocol, we are undoubtedly paying tribute to the utility value of pleasure. When managers spend considerable amounts of time and money to make sure that their fitness clubs are aesthetically pleasing and that the exercise itself is personally satisfying and socially enjoyable, they too are undoubtedly paying tribute to the utility value of pleasure.

Pleasure is also the value that fosters cultural literacy. It gets people back to the games and dances of their country, region, or town. This pleasure-motivated repetition leads to socialization in the values, goals, and meanings of a people. A way of life becomes something of a habit through these repeated encounters.

Concerns about pleasure as an extrinsic value are related to its transitory or temporary nature. Pleasure is influenced, for example, by familiarity. Activities that were once a great deal of fun sometimes grow stale. People have mood swings that influence the degree of enjoyment that is experienced. External factors, like the attitudes of other participants in a group activity, can dramatically affect the level of enjoyment. There are also possibilities for physical problems of pain or discomfort that can interfere with many sensuous pleasures in sport and dance.

Thus, if continued participation or repeated involvement were to be based only on pleasure, it might be on very unsure footing. Cardiac rehabilitation trainers would certainly not want heart patients to stop their potentially life-saving walking routine simply because it was becoming a little tiresome.

We saw earlier that this concern can be countered to a degree by broadening the idea of pleasure to one of satisfaction. This would allow the expansion of the relatively narrow and fluctuating utility of pleasure to the relatively broad and stable utility of generally positive or satisfactory experience. This would also support the claim that people will repeat

Pleasure fosters socialization into the games and activities of your region.

activities they find satisfactory, whether or not each repetition is entirely pleasurable. Heart patients might then persevere with their walking routines because they find such self-control and self-improvement satisfactory, even though, on given days, they may not receive a great deal of pleasure from the walking per se.

There are many kinds of satisfaction that inhabit our various movement domains and have the capacity to serve as means for continued participation or other ends. A listing of some of these should give us a more complete picture of the potential of pleasure as an extrinsic value. Once again, see if you can add examples from your own experiences to each category.

- **Testing pleasure** refers to the satisfaction related to the uncertainty and challenge of solving problems. *Examples of testing pleasure*: playing a game like golf—one that is challenging, not too easy yet not impossible; making progress in finding new answers or techniques that work; anticipating whether or not a good score can be achieved or at least a better score than was earned last time. *Sample of extrinsic power*: can provoke long periods of arduous practice.

- **Contesting pleasure** refers to the satisfaction related to the uncertainty and challenge of trying to perform better than someone else. *Examples of contesting pleasure*: enjoying the closeness of a hard-fought game; appreciating victories; finding some satisfaction in the achievements and future challenges that go with defeats. *Sample of extrinsic power*: can lead one to improved performance, success, fame.

- **Sensuous pleasure (sedate)** refers to the satisfaction related to comfortable body states or experiences. *Examples of sedate sensuous pleasure*: enjoying the feeling of the body after a long run; experiencing the sensation of hitting a golf ball on the "sweet spot," of catching a baseball or softball squarely in the pocket, of a long shower after a strenuous workout. *Samples of extrinsic power*: can bring one back to these settings again and again; can promote cultural literacy.

- **Sensuous pleasure (dramatic)** refers to the satisfaction related to ecstatic body states or experiences. *Examples of dramatic sensuous pleasure*: feeling the thrill of careening down a ski slope, of free-falling from an airplane, of rappelling down a 200-foot cliff, of driving a shoulder full force into an oncoming football running back. *Samples of extrinsic power*: can lead to remarkable levels of devotion and commitment; can refresh and inspire; can make the rest of life seem more worthwhile.

- **Aesthetic pleasure** refers to the satisfaction related to experiences of beauty. *Examples of aesthetic pleasure*: sensing in dance, sport, or exercise such factors as harmony, grace, balance, right expression, evenness, flow, proper force, accurate direction, tension, and closure. *Samples of extrinsic power*: can lead to experiences of peace, a sense of well-being.

- **Ascetic pleasure** refers to the satisfaction related to experiences of deprivation and sacrifice. *Examples of ascetic pleasure*: enjoying confrontations against impossible odds; reaping the benefits of self-denial, strict training regimens, successful dieting, and physically and psychically painful attempts to reach goals or win a contest. *Samples of extrinsic power*: can promote feelings of self-worth, self-control, power.

- **Ludic pleasure** refers to the satisfaction related to experiences that are appreciated for their own sake. *Examples of ludic pleasure*: enjoying activities in which there are no serious or long-lasting consequences of playing, winning, or losing; appreciating doing something because it is freely chosen, rather than because it must be done; relishing the absence of work pressures or real-world consequences. *Samples of extrinsic power*: can lead to repeated activity and thus to the development of traditions, culture, rituals, customs; promotes a culturally embedded and meaningful life.

SUMMARY BREAK

Pleasure is a useful pedagogical tool because it promotes the repetitions that foster learning. Whether the educational goal is truth, knowledge, excellence, or something else, pleasure may be needed to sustain the practice and attention required to reach those ends. For similar reasons, pleasure is a powerful socializing agent. Value-laden and culturally affected games, play, and dance may be repeated to the point where individuals embody a cultural perspective and find its way of life meaningful. On the other hand, the delicate and temporary nature of pleasure may reduce its utility value.

Ludic pleasure is the appreciation of experience for its own sake.

Prioritizing the Four Extrinsic Values

You have had an opportunity to examine four values, or tools, that can be used to help your students, athletes, or clients build a good or better life. While these tools are all useful, they are not equal. As noted in chapter 5, they undoubtedly have different capacities as tools to build conditions for satisfactory, coherent, meaningful lives. Having surveyed the facts, you now have a perspective that will allow you to make judgments as to their relative utility.

PHILOSOPHIC EXERCISE

Attempt to prioritize health- and activity-related fitness, knowledge, motor skill, and pleasure. Your only concern here is the extent to which each of these values has the ability to make other good things happen. That is, you are to judge the importance of each as a means to what we called the good life, or at least a better one. Remember the four criteria presented in chapter 5:

1. Are the means necessary or optional?
2. Are the means narrow or broadly useful?
3. Do the means lead to important intrinsic values or trivial ones?
4. Are the means pure (without significant cost) and durable (likely to be of continuing value)?

After you have completed your ranking, try to show where there are larger and smaller gaps between the values. For example, are your top two finishers close to one another, or is your top pick an easy winner? Then attempt to give at least one reason for your ranking of each value.

One Possible Ranking

My own ranking, from greatest to least extrinsic value, looks like this:

1. Fitness
2. Pleasure
3. Skill
4. Knowledge

When I take the second step, and attempt to indicate their relative importance, my ranking changes to this:

1. Fitness ³
2. Pleasure ₁
3. Skill ⁴
4. Knowledge ₂

In other words, fitness is something of a runaway winner in the first position. Pleasure and skill are tightly grouped, indicating

that I found little to choose between them. Yet I think I have a reason for giving the edge to pleasure. Finally, knowledge resides as far away from skill on the low side of the ranking as fitness does from pleasure on the high end. As a tool or means to other ends, knowledge does not have much clout.

Fitness: Our Most Important Extrinsic Value

There are two arguments that, in my estimation, show fitness to be the top means value in the field of sport, exercise science, and physical education. First, fitness appears to be broader in scope than the other values. Second, it appears to be more nearly a necessary means to other end values than pleasure, skill, or knowledge.

Fitness is more broadly useful than any of the other three values. Threshold levels of energy and endurance are prerequisites for

Fitness is a necessary means to virtually all end values.

all tasks—thought-tending and motor-intensive, sedentary and nonsedentary, sport and nonsport. Likewise physical appearance and attractiveness are important factors in developing a sound self-concept for virtually all people. Physical fitness, in these ways, affects all of us, athlete and nonathlete alike, by modifying what we can do, how long we can do it, how we feel, and how well we regard ourselves.

Fitness is also the closest thing we have to a necessary means value. In that fitness promotes continued life itself, it is absolutely necessary to all end values. Without life, we can no longer experience excellence, wisdom, truth, respect, security, or anything else. As much as we may value these or other goods, we risk becoming foolishly imprudent if we ignore the critical means for having them at all—namely, life itself.

The costs of health-related fitness are considerable in terms of time spent and, sometimes, discomfort experienced. Additionally, fitness is a fragile and temporary acquisition. However, these two negative factors can be mitigated by developing an active lifestyle, one in which exercise, dance, and sport are built into one's weekly schedule and are experienced as fun—not as a painful duty.

Fitness Versus Pleasure

In some ways the pleasure that results from play and games is comparable to fitness. Nearly everyone has been socialized, to a degree, by physically active play and games—if not as adults, at least as children. And this socialization, to the extent that it embeds people in a culture and provides a foundation for a meaningful life, may be close to a necessary means for experiencing the good life. It has been said that people cannot survive without myths, meaning, or direction (Rue, 1989).

However, the argument that everyone is or has been affected significantly by pleasure-motivated, physically active games and play

is not as convincing as the parallel argument about physical fitness, because some people are enculturated in very sedentary ways. Likewise, the claim that human survival is at stake where pleasure-motivated play has not generated myth and meaning is weaker than the similar claim about the absence of biological health. Consequently, as important as pleasure is as a pedagogical and socializing tool, it is not as broadly useful and powerful as physical fitness.

Pleasure Versus Skill

Motor skill, of course, is pervasive as a means value as well. It is difficult to imagine the achievement of excellence, fame, knowledge, wisdom, freedom, or other end values in the absence of motor skills. Walking, speaking, typing, writing, sculpting, and even reading involve motor skills. We cannot live or do much of anything without a good number of well-developed motor skills.

However, it is not too difficult to picture the achievement of satisfaction, a meaningful life, excellence, and other end values in the absence of the sport, dance, exercise, game, and play skills that physical educators typically teach. There are a multitude of alternative routes to good end states of affairs. Physical education provides an important one, particularly for those who are blessed with a strong body and good motor genes, but it is nevertheless only one avenue. It would seem that motor skill is a more optional means to good ends than is motor-related pleasure.

Because pleasure that stimulates repeated encounters with physically active games and play affects nearly everyone, and because the socialization into cultural meaning that comes with such repeated encounters may well influence the overall direction and meaning of a person's life, activity-related pleasure is a more powerful tool than motor skill. This judgment is reinforced by noticing that pleasure is more a necessary means for the development of motor skill (people who do not like an activity will generally not repeat it) and vice versa (people do not have to have high levels of motor skill to get pleasure from an activity).

Knowledge: The Weakest Extrinsic Value

Knowledge is ranked last, and I assigned it a place at some distance from pleasure and skill. Knowledge, as we noted earlier, has an uncertain relationship to behavioral change. Thus, even health-related knowledge does not guarantee healthy behavior in day-to-day life. Habits and attitudes may be pointed in the right direction by knowledge; their formation may also be given a motivational boost by some frightening or hopeful knowledge, but their presence is not coextensive simply with knowing the facts. Consequently, knowledge, even for important health ends, is useful, but it has only limited power as a means.

In addition, people can have proper skills, right habits, and good attitudes before becoming aware of the theory that supports or explains them. Some fine performers and some individuals who have marvelously healthy lifestyles may never come in contact with the knowledge that would explain their status. Some researchers now openly admit that they have more to learn from elite-level performers than such athletes or dancers have to learn from them.

Also, knowledge seems to have the most narrow utility value of our four values. Knowledge of sport rules, game strategies, and dance origins pales in significance relative to other kinds of knowledge—for instance, knowledge about how government works, about differences between one culture and another, about economic laws, about religion and family. This may be one reason for the apathy and resistance that has accompanied some efforts to infuse physical education with more sport-,

dance-, and exercise-related knowledge. This theory, this knowledge, these scientific facts, while important, are not as important as other facts and propositions.

PHILOSOPHIC EXERCISE

If your ranking is different from mine (even if you have the values in the same order but see larger or smaller gaps between them), now is the time to decide if you want to stand behind your conclusions. Identify arguments that support your alternative. You may want to check some of these arguments with your instructor or classmates to see how much persuasive power they have.

My ranking, for example, could be seen as unfairly skeptical of the powers of science, because knowledge is ranked so low. Perhaps, then, knowledge should be placed higher. Others might claim that I have not given enough credit to the power of play, that I have not taken seriously enough the claim that culture develops through play (Huizinga, 1950).

Review

Health- and activity-related fitness, knowledge, skill, and pleasure have extrinsic value; they are useful tools for achieving the good life or, at least, significantly better living. There are reasons, therefore, for retaining all of these objectives in our programs and services. Nevertheless, some of these values have more means or utility power than others. Because of limited resources, the importance of having a clear professional direction, and the need for passion and commitment in our work, we need to pay attention to these differences.

One possible ranking shows fitness with the greatest extrinsic power, followed at some distance by pleasure and skill, and then by knowledge. If this prioritization is sound, we should commit more of our energies, for example, to physical fitness than knowledge. We should show far more excitement about physical vitality and good appearance as pathways to good living than about knowledge of sports, dance, exercise, health, and games. This prioritization, however, does not take into account the intrinsic value of physical fitness, knowledge, or other activity- and movement-related values.

This analysis would give Susan James (in the example at the beginning of the chapter) some of the answers she needed in determining the best alignment for her department. Given the power of health-related achievements as prerequisites to the good life, she might choose to head a new unit that included health education and, perhaps, driver training. However, this decision might be premature given a lack of information about the intrinsic values of physical education. Would such an analysis still support a realignment with health education?

Looking Ahead

In chapter 7 you will again visit the values of fitness, knowledge, skill, and pleasure in an attempt to rank or prioritize them. This time, however, it will be on the basis of their power as ends—that is, on their intrinsic value. Near the end of this chapter you will attempt to pull together information on extrinsic and intrinsic value. This should allow you to make comprehensive philosophic judgments on a priority ranking for these values and the direction you think your field should be taking.

Checking Your Understanding

1. What is the difference between intrinsic and extrinsic value?
2. Describe at least two ways in which health- and activity-related fitness, knowledge, skill, and pleasure can be regarded as tools for achieving other good things.
3. Which of these four values has the broadest value as a tool for good living? Which is most nearly a necessary means to other good things in life? Which has the greatest purity? Which has the greatest durability?
4. Among these four values, which are the most important as extrinsic values? Give at least one argument for your judgment.
5. Can you generate any passion or excitement for your profession were it to emphasize the extrinsic value of physical fitness? Why or why not?

Key Terms

Extrinsic value, p. 137

Health- and activity-related fitness (extrinsic value), p. 137

Health- and activity-related knowledge (extrinsic value), p. 139

Motor skill (extrinsic value), p. 142

Health- and activity-related pleasure (extrinsic value), p. 145

Further Reading

For a general survey of the values of the physically active lifestyle see Seefeldt (1986) and NASPE (1992). For more philosophic treatments of the relative importance of different values and their effect on professional concerns, good sources include Fraleigh (1990) and Arnold (1988).

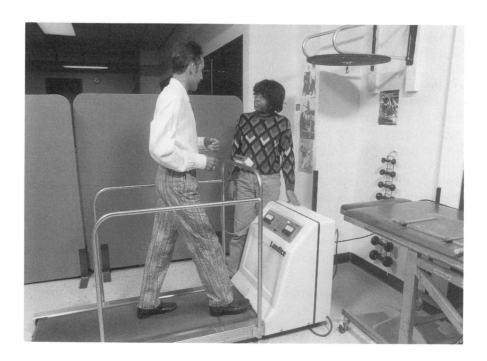

Chapter 7

The Intrinsic Value of Fitness, Knowledge, Skill, and Pleasure

Kim Stanton has been a cardiac rehabilitation specialist in a hospital in a large metropolitan area on the West Coast for 11 years. She works closely with cardiologists, internists, and general practitioners. It is her responsibility to do cardiac testing on their patients and then prescribe lifestyle interventions, often having to do with a combination of relaxation, exercise, and diet. Kim is thoroughly versed in modern sport and exercise therapies, and she usually gives them a central place in the prescriptions for her clients. Kim has a reputation throughout the city for being one of the best at her profession, particularly for being able to match the cardiovascular condition of patients with the right level of physical activity.

Kim herself, however, is not entirely satisfied with her practice. She has noticed over the years that many of her clients would exercise for a period of time and then eventually return to their old ways. She never ceases to be surprised by this, for she stresses to her patients the life-and-death consequences of their sedentary lifestyles. She emphasizes the important effects that exercise can have in arresting and even reversing circulatory diseases. She explains to her cardiac patients the logic of prescribing certain levels of exercise and not others. In short, she gives them every reason she can think of for continuing their exercise programs. Yet, many of her patients regress, and some of them have additional circulatory crises not long afterwards.

Kim reminds herself that she should not feel guilty over a client's decision not to follow her advice. After all, patients are free people, and she can hardly force them to exercise if they lack the discipline needed to do so. Still, she feels uneasy. Has she been doing all that she can to promote behavior changes? Is she a good motivator? Is she presenting exercise, sport, and dance in the right way to her clients? Should she know as much about human rehabilitation as she does about cardiac repair?

Is it possible that she is on the wrong track altogether? Is her strategy to present sport, dance, and exercise as means to better health sufficient? If she wanted to promote fitness as an end rather than a means, how would she accomplish that? Would Kim's cardiac rehabilitation efforts actually improve if she stopped emphasizing the rational importance and seriousness of moving and focused instead on the many joys and poignant moments of active living?

Your reflections in chapter 6 on extrinsic values put you in a position to make preliminary judgments about the mission of your field. In this chapter you will see the ways in which your field contributes *directly* to the good life. These deliberations about the relative importance of experiencing health- and activity-related physical fitness, knowledge, motor skill, and pleasure should have a tremendous effect on the shape and direction of your profession and its practices. Combined with your reflections in chapter 6 on extrinsic values, it will put you in a position to make final judgments about what ends are most important, what should produce a sense of professional mission, and which goals in your field should receive priority attention.

IN THIS CHAPTER, YOU WILL

- **examine health- and activity-related fitness, knowledge, skill, and pleasure as intrinsically satisfying experiences;**
- **evaluate the strengths and weaknesses of these values;**

- rank the four values on the basis of their intrinsic power; and
- rank the four values on the basis of their combined intrinsic and extrinsic power.

Many of us in sport, exercise science, and physical education have been trained to think of our field primarily as a service profession. We set the stage, clear the path, build a foundation, provide an avenue—use whatever metaphor you wish—for what people really want out of life. We saw in the last chapter how easy it is to picture ways in which our fitness activities, knowledge about movement, skill development, and play lead to other good things.

But why don't we focus more on how the goods that we produce in our gymnasiums, fitness centers, ball fields, and dance studios are good things in themselves?

Why is it more difficult for us to say (and to argue clearly) that when we are dancing, sporting, and exercising in certain ways that we *are* living the good life?

Have you ever wondered why you rarely hear the following boast about experiences of excellence in sport or dance artistry: "Life does not get any better than this"?

Have you ever wondered why people engaged in meaningful play do not often say, "This is what it's all about!"?

Examining Intrinsic Values

We will once again be reflecting on the traditional physical education values related to organic objectives (fitness), cognitive objectives (knowledge), psychomotor objectives (skill), and affective objectives (pleasure). However, this time we take a different perspective. Instead of asking how these services lead to good ends, we now ask how these values are important in their own right. How, in other words, are these values good in themselves and, on this basis, which ones are more important than the others?

Once again, we will be using the rules of superiority and corollaries presented in chapter 5 (see pp. 127-133; note that rule 1 is not being used yet). *Rule 2* states that experiences that include satisfaction carry more intrinsic power (all else being equal) than those that do not. Its first corollary is that satisfaction that brings little or no harm is to be preferred to satisfaction that is accompanied by greater amounts of harm. Its second corollary is that satisfaction that is durable or dependably recurring is to be preferred to satisfaction that is temporary or erratic in nature. *Rule 3* states that experiences that fit into and promote the development of a coherent life course (of ongoing stories or narratives) take precedence over those that are freestanding, directionless, or otherwise disconnected from one's history. Such experiences of a coherent life course are often described as meaningful.

Once again we need to survey the facts. In the following section, I provide types of experiences that are associated with the acquisition of each of our four values. The examples that follow can be taken intrinsically *and* extrinsically. However, because we are focusing on the intrinsic power of each value in this chapter, I then offer a statement about each experience as an end in itself.

The Intrinsic Value of Health- and Activity-Related Fitness

First, we must gain a clear picture of what health- and activity-related fitness, as an intrinsic value, would be. Remember that intrinsic values are experiences that are lived as enjoyable or, more broadly, satisfactory or worthwhile in themselves. If they also include the related experiences of coherence, important life goals, or meaningfulness, they are to be regarded even more highly. A number of experiences of life and health, of being fit, and of having threshold levels of energy and endurance can at least minimally satisfy these criteria.

• **The experience of simply being alive**. *Examples*: We enjoy being alive, being on this earth, existing, awakening each morning, experiencing the new day. *Intrinsic strength*: The continued experiences of consciousness, human opportunity, thought, and action are good in themselves.

• **The experience of embodied power, energy, and endurance**. *Examples*: As our fitness levels improve, we embody more power and energy. We can move things we could not move before (such as opposing football players), make things that previously were too difficult to make (such as an illusion in dance based on a physically demanding series of moves), and experience higher levels of control and staying power both at work and play. *Intrinsic strength*: Experiencing increased power and energy can be very satisfying and even exhilarating.

• **The experience of lightness**. *Examples*: When we are physically fit, we are free of our body. We objectify it less regularly and need to attend to it less often. It automatically supports what we want to do, but it remains in the background, out of consciousness. *Intrinsic strength*: We feel an embodied freedom and lightness, and that experience is wonderful.

• **The experience of living with an absence of pain**. *Examples*: When fit, we are usually able to face life without being sidetracked or impeded by aches and pains. When we sit for long periods of time, our back does not hurt. When we run, our lungs do not burn. *Intrinsic strength*: We appreciate life more when it does not include experiences of pain or discomfort.

Based on these characterizations, it is clear that fitness qualifies as an intrinsic value, one that all people embrace to one degree or another. The experience of merely existing in a well state can be appreciated for what it is. Experiences of aliveness, power, lightness, and pain-free living can also be relished for their own sakes. These must be counted as important strengths of fitness as an intrinsic value.

Critical Analysis of Fitness

Most human beings are not satisfied with merely existing or surviving, even if such day-to-day living is free of pain. This may be due to a recognition that mere existence says little about human potential, about what people can be or become. Thus, the satisfactions of fit living seem to have a minimalistic quality to them. We all know that it can be intrinsically satisfying to be alive and fit, but this may seem more like a starting point in living the good life than a final goal.

Fitness does not measure up well on the criteria of meaningfulness and coherence in life. By itself the experience of living has nothing to do with a sense of place, things to do, roles to play, or goals to achieve. The experience of life—even a healthy and fit one—is hardly tolerable if we are bored, confused, alienated from friends and other loved ones, or lost in some psychological or spiritual sense. If we have nothing to do, no function to serve in improving matters in the world, no context or home in which to celebrate and kick up our heels, no playgrounds that invite us to while away some time, no way to revitalize the world and meet it as interesting and intriguing day after day—if we have none of these, experiences of embodied lightness, power, or vitality may hardly be noticed through the haze of boredom, disenchantment, or even anger.

We saw in the last chapter that fitness is a far stronger value when considered as a means to a full, vibrant, and meaningful life. Base levels of energy and endurance open up many possibilities for active living that are closed to those who have lower levels of health and who are less well able to move. But as an end value, fitness does not seem to carry human beings very far. People want more out of life than experiences of mere survival, physical power, or even good health.

PHILOSOPHIC EXERCISE

You can check on the validity of the judgments that I made above by using the forced-choice inventory that follows. For each of these pairs, select the experience that is more important to you. Even in cases where both options are good and the choice is difficult to make, choose one.

When you select one member of each pair you guarantee that value for your life. The other option is left uncertain. For instance, if you were to choose "living 90 years" in the first pair below, you would be guaranteed a life of at least 90 years. The other experience (that of being an excellent and respected coach, teacher, or other movement professional) may or may not come your way. You simply do not know, nor can you influence it.

Furthermore, in making these selections, you are ignorant of your other life circumstances. For example, you do not know if you are brilliant or slow, rich or poor, male or female, American or Russian, and so on. You could not say, I would choose 90 years of life over a good reputation if I knew I were rich and of sound mind. You do not know that. You could be poor and insane. This ignorance forces you to focus on the intrinsic power of the experience in question.

You can proceed by completing the following sentence: "Not knowing anything of the other characteristics of my life, and forced to choose between items that I can secure for myself, I would prefer to guarantee experiences of . . ."

Pair 1

a. living 90 years
b. being an excellent and respected coach, teacher, or other movement professional

Pair 2

a. living with a normal blood pressure and a general absence of pain
b. being accepted and loved by family

Pair 3

a. having important goals for life
b. having physical and financial security

Pair 4

a. an enjoyable life
b. a fit life

My own choices (1-b, 2-b, 3-a, and 4-a) show that I strongly favor an array of values over mere existence. Check my reasoning to see if it corresponds with your own.

Pair 1.   The prospect of a 90-year life is both exciting and frightening. The excitement comes from both intrinsic and extrinsic values of healthful living. Because life per se is good, the more of it the better. And because life has such great utility value, the more of it I have, the more things I can experience, do, and achieve. But the fear comes from not knowing any of the qualitative aspects of that long life. If it is a lonely or anguished life, the prospect of living 90 years is not an entirely good one. If my life has little or no excellence in it, if I enjoy no respect from my colleagues, or if I am actually disliked for some reason, the guarantee of a long life is a mixed blessing at best.

On the other hand, excellence is something that is known to be good or valuable. If I am an excellent coach, teacher, trainer, or other professional, I stand apart from the crowd; I am respected or even admired. I might do something special, approximate an ideal that relatively few people achieve. If I have to choose, I will lock in a life that includes day-to-day experiences of professional excellence and self-respect—and take my chances with existence.

Pair 2.   A life that proceeds under the handicaps of chronic high blood pressure and physical pain or discomfort is much the less for it. I would never freely wish such a condition on myself or others. However, the prospect of facing life without family (even extended family) love, support, ties, and roots is a more bothersome one. When I go even further by picturing not just an absence of love, but family hatred, alienation, or abuse, the second choice becomes all the more preferable.

Love from family has been a powerful force that allows and even inspires individuals to endure high blood pressure, physical discomfort, or worse. If I have love, strong family ties, a constant support system, I can survive many a setback, get through many a difficulty, and probably even celebrate in the process. On the other hand, if I have normal blood pressure and an absence of physical discomfort or pain, this would have little power to sustain me were I alone, disliked, unclaimed, unrelated, free-floating, part of no ongoing history, lost, or isolated.

Certainly, I would like to experience both family love and an existence with normal blood pressure and an absence of pain. But if I can guarantee only one for my life, I will take love.

Pair 3.   This comparison pits a goal-oriented, meaningful, and interesting life against one that guaranteed safety or security. Security, to be sure, is a powerful end value, particularly in light of contemporary socialization, which places a considerable emphasis on it. Many people go to college to get good jobs—that is, ones that pay well and provide security. They eat health foods and exercise to secure continued health. They spend thousands of dollars on insurance to buy peace of mind. They hire therapists and seek out many forms of immediate gratification to help them survive psychologically. They like the warmth and equilibrium and the predictability of security. Life feels good when it is solid and secure.

Nevertheless, a life oriented around security could still be a deadly boring one—one that is headed nowhere, has no purpose, is frightfully drab and tedious. Waking up in the morning would be no fun if I were secure but utterly disinterested in everything. What would I do? Why would I even get out of bed?

The alternative sounds more attractive. I want to start each day with fascinating projects at hand, with a sense that there may not be enough hours in the day to accommodate all my interests, with the notion that what I will do that day matters. If I must worry about various things—my health, guarantees about keeping my job, whatever—that is unfortunate, but at least I am vital. I find the world and my life full of meaning. Thus, I will take my chances with security.

Pair 4. The comparison of fitness and enjoyableness, perhaps more than any of the other value contrasts, allows me to see the relative weakness of health-related fitness as an intrinsic value. The image of an enjoyable life seems to leave far fewer questions about its goodness than the picture of a life lived with an ample amount of physical fitness.

It is true that an enjoyable life may not be one that is entirely satisfactory. It is possible to picture a shallow, selfish, sexually preoccupied, or food-oriented life as being somewhat enjoyable—at least insofar as it contains repeated pleasures. But even with these insufficiencies of enjoyment as an end value, it would seem that a life that only guarantees experiences of fitness leaves many more questions unanswered. The first might be simply, Is it also an enjoyable life? If the answer to this is yes, many qualms about the goodness of that existence might be put to rest. It would seem to be more important for me to know that my guaranteed fit life is also enjoyable than to know that a guaranteed enjoyable life is also a fit one.

Again, the vote here would have to go to the intrinsic value of enjoyableness. Fitness can add to and be a part of enjoyable living and I would undoubtedly like to have both, but if I can be sure of only one, I would select repeated experiences of enjoyable living.

In addition to its inability to make more than minimal contributions to the good life, fitness scores poorly on the two corollaries of the second rule. The satisfactions it provides are temporary, and they are won at the cost of some discomfort (if not pain) and, for many, no small degree of inconvenience.

Energy and endurance potentials decline quickly and dramatically if we do not actively maintain them. To regain the satisfactions of health-related fitness, we must tend to our body, take time out of our day to exercise, prepare meals properly, and so on. We may wish to do something interesting or important, but we are hungry and must eat; we

are tired and must sleep; we are unfit and must exercise. In a sense our biological functions control us. If nothing else, they use up precious hours in our days that could be devoted to more interesting or important matters.

Moreover, some exercise is distasteful. "No pain, no gain," we remind ourselves. "No overload, no improvement," the fitness books tell us. Our joints ache; our muscles are sore; we are tired. But if we are not to lose our current level of aerobic fitness and muscular endurance, we must once again lift, run, bicycle, or swim.

To this criticism a supporter of fitness could reply, as we saw in chapter 6, that fitness activities can be enjoyable, and significant pain or discomfort is not required for many health gains. Hiking in local hills or mountains, for example, effects at least some fitness gains, and such activity is not usually painful. However, it could still be argued that it is not the gain of fitness in hiking that is enjoyable, but rather experiences of the hiking and exploring and observing of nature itself. We hike not to experience fitness, but rather to experience the mountains and nature.

Experiences of motor skill, activity-related knowledge, and pleasure are not as temporary or fragile in nature as fitness. Motor skills, while they do take some time to develop, are relatively durable. Once we learn how to ride a bicycle, we will always be able to return to bicycle riding experiences. Once we learn some information that is interesting or of critical importance, we are likely to retain it. At worst, we may need to be refreshed from time to time, but usually we do not have to work at understanding a concept all over again. Activity-related pleasures, because they are often grounded in skills, are also reasonably durable. For example, we know that we can return to tennis tomorrow, next week, or next year and that it is likely to be fun once again.

SUMMARY BREAK

Health-related fitness has some intrinsic power but more as a base-level or minimal value than a maximal one. The good life should be a healthy one, but it must be far more than that. Forced comparisons show fitness to be a weaker value than several others on criteria of satisfactoriness and life coherence. Fitness per se has only a limited effect on life satisfactions. And by itself, it has very little to do with lifetime coherence. Fitness also fares poorly on the corollaries of satisfaction—those having to do with durability and cost.

The Intrinsic Value of Health- and Activity-Related Knowledge

Knowing can be considered as a satisfying experience of insight. When we are uncertain, ignorant, in the dark, intellectually lost, wandering about, living by trial and error, or confused, we are fundamentally "off center." We live with the uneasiness of knowing there is unfinished business ahead. When will we find out? When will we really know? What is the truth? How can we get this right? While there may be some validity to the notion that ignorance is bliss, living in the dark of misconceptions and unexamined prejudices is not usually a satisfying experience. If we were ignorant and had absolutely no idea that we were blind, that would be one thing. But when we are ignorant about something in this life, we typically receive clues to that effect. We know that we do not know, and that is frustrating!

In contrast, when we learn, when we find something out, a light shines on a given matter; we move "on center." We know, see, have direction; we are in balance. For any issue fully understood, there is no unfinished

business left. We experience the closure of insight, and the experience is a good one.

Imagine the satisfying insights that can be, and often are, reached in sport, exercise science, and physical education:

- **Insight in matters of health, safety, and understanding the workings of our bodies.** *Examples*: We may learn how our body works, how we can live longer, what are the safest ways to exercise. We might better understand our genetic endowment and whether it is an asset or liability regarding our future health, our desires to be a professional athlete, or our hopes to become a dancer. *Intrinsic strength*: Our curiosity is satisfied, and that experience is good.

- **Insight in matters of skill and learning.** *Examples*: We might come to know what the best practice strategies and techniques are and how much progress we can make in our sport through mental practice. We might find out if there is such a thing as performance burnout and, if so, what its causes and characteristics are. *Intrinsic strength*: Uncertainty about these things is removed, which is comforting.

- **Insight from testing ourselves and by entering contests with others.** *Examples*: We can find out if we are improving and, if so, by how much. We may learn how good we can get and if we are better than our competitors. We can understand how well we can play under different weather conditions, under different training regimens, or under guidance from a new coach. *Intrinsic strength*: We are enlightened about these things, and the experience is good.

- **Insight as spectators.** *Examples*: We may learn whose team is best, whether or not our team will improve this year, if our sport hero can still perform well now that she is 35 years old, whether our team will finish higher this year than our hated rivals. *Intrinsic strength*: We are free from ignorance regarding these matters, which is satisfying.

In sport participation we gain information about ourselves.

The process of enlightenment is among the most satisfying experiences human beings encounter. We often say to ourselves, sometimes in eager anticipation, sometimes in exasperation, "We just want to know!" Anything would be better, we believe, than continued doubt or uncertainty. We are curious, trapped by ignorance, and uneasy until we get answers. When we find something out, we almost sigh audibly with relief. We are pleased, comfortable, free to act with understanding, delighted to be in the company of some bit of truth or information. We like it so much that we often go out looking for more. Both our appetites for curiosity and our hunger for the enjoyment and freedom that comes with insight would seem to be insatiable.

Fraleigh (1984, 1986) argues that knowledge is the prime value of sport in that it is the only value that is guaranteed in the sport setting. He depicts people in sport as questing to get information about themselves—in particular, the status of their own game and the level of their own skill in relation to the skill of others. Consequently, ties in games (the frustration of not coming to closure and thus delaying knowledge of who is best) are experienced as unsatisfactory. Contestants must play again just so they will finally know.

There is also a considerable degree of interest in transmitting preexisting knowledge to students as an end in itself. Through the Basic Stuff curriculum (Dodds, 1987) and a variety of other resources, teachers at all levels—grade school through college—are encouraged to share facts about sport, dance, physiology, psychology, human movement, and other topics. Consequently, some of what is called "the body of knowledge" in sport, exercise science, and physical education is now finding its way to practical activity settings and to students and clients.

In addition, there are some instructors who teach games in part by emphasizing concepts and a variety of theoretical approaches (Kirk, 1983). This produces performers who are free to perform intelligently, who can apply principles to their play, who understand a game and know its context. Again, understanding can be viewed as good in itself, whether or not it leads to better play, world championships, and personal fame. It is simply good to understand a game.

Critical Analysis of Knowledge

As satisfying as knowledge is, and as much as people study, compete, dance, exercise, and play to learn more and to satisfy their curiosity, this value has its limitations as an intrinsic one. On both criteria for intrinsic value—satisfaction and meaningfulness—knowledge shows only moderate strength. Knowledge, to produce a satisfying life, must be lived, not just contemplated. Furthermore, knowledge produces only partial satisfaction and meaning for many in sport.

Most of us are not particularly attracted to contemplating the truth. We would rather live it. For example, rather than know the factors that lead to good performance in sport, most of us would rather embody them—that is, have the sense-perceptual abilities, motor skill, and tutored muscular strength needed to play well. We learned in chapter 2 that holistic human liberation and full satisfaction are not gained by "minds" that meditate on the truth or through reflective-sedentary skills, but rather by persons who embody and live what is right and good.

Is Sport Knowledge Alone Satisfying? Are we attracted to competition, as Fraleigh contended, primarily because it allows us to know what we can do? Perhaps there is satisfaction in sport that complements or even eclipses the experience of knowing how good we are or who is best. We could argue, for example, that sport is captivating largely because it places human beings in a realm of controlled or safe uncertainty, possibility, and risk. We search out games in general and often sport specifically when our world

becomes too predictable, too well understood, too much under our control, too boring. We intentionally put ourselves at risk by trying to solve a puzzle (even though we don't have to), by trying to climb a mountain (even though our job does not require that we do so), by trying to take fewer strokes on a golf course than a friend (even though nothing really depends on our succeeding in this venture). We intentionally take on unnecessarily difficult problems. In this culture we have done so regularly, as have previous cultures (Huizinga, 1950; Suits, 1978).

Do we behave this way simply to secure relatively trivial knowledge about ourselves and our opponents? Possibly, in part. But this

When life becomes routine, we seek challenges.

cannot be the entire, or even the best, answer. Why? Because we do not like it when our games come to an end or when uncertainty is lost because one side has gotten too far ahead. We do not search out uneven or lopsided contests. We handicap, reconstitute, and in many other ways embellish and reestablish uncertainty of outcome in our games. In point of fact, we spend most of our time in games experiencing a delicious uncertainty as we try mightily to solve difficult problems or strive courageously to outdo a worthy opponent.

If I were forced to choose between a game in which I learned early and absolutely that I was the better tennis player and one in which knowledge of superiority was not gained even after two hours of keen and even play, I would select the latter. The experience of uncertainty at the hands of a skilled opponent would be far more satisfying than knowing that I am better (or worse) in a game that lacks any component of doubt and tension. Of course, such poor contests also limit my knowledge because I do not learn much about my skill. Nevertheless, games without uncertainty are simply not much fun.

This is an argument in favor of pleasure, fun, and play over knowledge. Human beings are so taken or carried away by experiences of challenge and uncertainty that they even delay some closures (who will win?) and some understandings (on the whole, who played better today?). The tension and uncertainty of play may be more important than the tranquillity and security of knowledge.

How Meaningful Is Sport Knowledge?   Knowledge does not receive particularly high marks on the matter of coherence, or meaningfulness. This is so for at least two reasons. First, and by far most importantly, we do not encounter our place in life or experience meaning for living primarily in the form of facts, information, logical alternatives, or knowledge. Rather, we sense it, feel it, intuit

it, and live it in purposeful day-to-day activity. It is often after the fact that we reflect on our lives and abstract certain statements about why life has been or is so meaningful. The experience of coherence, therefore, is at least partly independent of the acquisition of formal knowledge.

We grow into coherence as children by listening to stories and slowly, intuitively picking up different values and trying them out. We subjectively experience our parents and their choices rather than analytically examine their lives and reduce them objectively to lists of *do*'s and *don't*'s. We become steeped in the values of our culture; we pick out heroes and try to emulate them; we hear the myths that are transmitted through society's rituals. Gradually, for most of us, life begins to hang together. We realize that there are important and interesting things to do, places to explore, traditions to cultivate and preserve during our lifetime. Certainly, the coherent, meaningful life may include a good amount of contemplation, knowledge about traditions, information about family trees, or facts about our history. The acquisition of such understandings might even serve as a means for promoting life coherence. But the truth is that connectedness or meaningfulness is not assured simply by encountering such information. There are students of culture, for example, who themselves are not effectively in a culture. There are students of meaning and history who have not incorporated these good things into their own lives.

The second problem in meeting the criterion of life coherence relates to the fact that the knowledge propounded by the activity sciences is often not personal in nature. It has to do with rules, strategies, anatomy, health concepts, biomechanics, levers, and general learning patterns. Much scientific knowledge in this field applies equally to everybody— the anonymous dancer or any athlete. Much sport strategy is thought to be effective or not so effective in principle, abstractly. Facts about skeletal structures or exercise and cholesterol levels, for example, may or may not contribute much to our particular goals, our unique dreams.

SUMMARY BREAK

Knowledge is an important end value for sport, exercise science, and physical education because it is easily understood as an intrinsic value (the experience of knowing needs no further justification), it is capable of providing satisfaction (the equilibrium and freedom of knowing is comforting), and it is able to provide some experiences of life coherence, particularly where such knowledge is personal in nature. Nevertheless, it also shows serious limitations. In general, we gain more satisfaction from living the truth than contemplating it; fascination with sport contests has more to do with relishing experiences of uncertainty than knowledge; much sport, exercise science, and physical education knowledge is impersonal; and propositions or facts found in a book or elsewhere may or may not lead to experiences of actual, lived, internalized coherence and meaningfulness.

The Intrinsic Value of Motor Skill

As noted in the previous chapter, skill is a form of knowing—it is practical knowledge. Because skill has something to do with discovery, accuracy, rightness, or roughly what might be called the truth, it shares many of the intrinsically satisfying qualities as the propositional, theoretical, factual, laboratory, and book knowledge discussed above. Below I have listed some examples of intrinsic satisfactions related to motor skill.

• **The experience of ease and simplicity.** *Examples*: We do not have to think or worry

The experience of ease and simplicity: effortlessness during great effort.

while playing basketball; everything falls into place; we sense openings and opportunities with great precision. *Intrinsic strength*: We experience a paradoxical effortlessness even when our activity requires a great deal of effort, and this experience is exhilarating.

• **The experience of creative power.** *Examples*: We move so well on the golf course that we accomplish new feats. We hit our drives farther; we draw a shot around a tree; we feather a soft pitch shot to within three feet of the pin. We experience a transition from working at making the right shot to creatively letting the shot make itself. *Intrinsic strength*: We experience hitting a golf ball with personal style, grace, and flair, and this feeling is wonderful.

• **The experience of harmony and tranquillity.** *Examples*: We swing the tennis racket so well that it seems to be a part of ourselves—a virtual extension of our arm complete with its own nerves and sensations.

Intrinsic strength: We are no longer trying to manipulate the racket, and this experience of coordination and integration is good.

• **The experience of rightness and truth.** *Examples*: We are able to sense subtleties in distances, wind direction, and effects of the grain of the grass on golfing greens. Mostly intuitively, we react correctly to these variations, and our subsequent shots are true. *Intrinsic strength*: Our "statements" in golf are on the mark, and this experience of being right or truthful is extremely satisfying.

When we get a skill right in sport and can repeat it largely at will, there is a sense of closure, a feeling of equilibrium, of comfort. When faced with a game problem or a difficult skill in creating a movement illusion in dance, there is a sense of confidence. Without perhaps knowing exactly what we will do beforehand, we trust from past experience that the right things will occur to us at the right times. We know that we can do it, and this gives us confident feelings of authorship and control both before and during the contest, exercise routine, or dance.

There is also a newly won sense of freedom. We can go where we could not go before, do what we could not do, see what we could not see. We become inventive and creative. We break the chains of mere reflex and habit. We spread our wings and fly. We move to the right side of the behavior scale in Figure 3.2 (p. 78); we experience ourselves as smooth, coordinated, and unpredictable because our behavior is so intuitively insightful. [Skill provides a kind of analog to the peace, tranquillity, and freedom experienced when reflecting on book knowledge, facts, or propositional truths.] We noted that when we are enlightened by information, when we are no longer confused, frustrated, and ignorant about something, we typically feel some relief. When we develop a movement skill to a high level, a paradoxically similar experience

may be had. It is paradoxically similar because we are anything but tranquil in terms of our activity. We may literally be sweating, straining, and expending large numbers of calories. Nevertheless, because we are sensitively skillful, we experience an ease, a kind of tranquillity in action. Our relished truths are met moment by moment in the process of moving artfully. These truths are encountered rather than reflected upon; they are highly visible at the performance moment but then fade away and may be difficult to recall after the activity is over. Yet this experience of in-process knowing is peaceful (Herrigel, 1971).

This quality of experience is highlighted in what some have called peak experiences (Maslow, 1962), deep-flow encounters (Csikszentmihalyi, 1975), or, more recently, experiences of living in the so-called zone. Many of us have had occasions during which our movements are effortless, right, spontaneous, and perhaps even experienced in altered states of consciousness such as slow-motion action or images that are larger than life. Such encounters with the movement domain are rare, unforgettable, and difficult to recreate. However, those who have been fortunate enough to have had one or more of these extraordinary sport, dance, or exercise experiences understand how intrinsically satisfying they are and, more broadly, how rewarding the tacit form of knowledge is. It would be wonderful to live more of life in this kind of enlightened, graceful euphoria. (Indeed, many individuals following Eastern traditions, such as Zen Buddhism, systematically try to do so.)

Motor skill consequently would seem to deserve high marks for its capacity to serve as an intrinsic value, marks that are comparable to those given to propositional knowledge. It would also seem to deserve high marks for the satisfactions that it produces. This enjoyment is highlighted in peak experiences and often at the upper ends of skillful practice, but it can be experienced across the spectrum from beginner to advanced performer.

Critical Analysis of Motor Skill

In the previous section I argued that the good life needs to be filled with experiences of skillful competence, that is, with living the truth, not just contemplating it. This, of course, gives an advantage in our rankings to motor skill over knowledge about health and physical activity.

However, this still does not guarantee a high place in the good life for the kinds of skill we teach. How would we ever argue that the satisfactions that come from hitting a baseball well are inherently superior to the pleasures that can be gained by solving an algebraic equation quickly, or reading a good book insightfully, or playing Mozart at the piano expressively? Satisfactions from different experiences are, as Frankena (1973) argued, incommensurable. They are simply different and good. Perhaps then, the good life should include a variety of skillful activities that produce satisfactions, but there is no reason to say that they must be sport skills rather than other varieties of procedural knowledge. Given different talents, tastes, and interests among people, it makes all the more sense to remain cautious about the place of satisfactions from motor skills in the good life.

A further limitation on skills related to sport, games, and vigorous play comes from individuals who think that these activities lack cultural significance, are more suited for children than adults, or both. While it might be good to fill one's days with experiences of skillful motor performances, it would be better to do so, some would argue, in the arts than in sport. This criticism is a serious one, and responses to it will have to be analyzed in the next section and in chapter 8.

If it is not clear that experiences of motor skills or sport skills are needed for the good life, it still seems relatively safe to argue that skills of some variety are important. The competent life that is characterized by artistry in some realm is to be preferred to the existence that contemplates wisdom but cannot act on it. For most, the actively insightful life will be filled with more satisfactions.

Skill Is More Durable.   Skill also has an advantage over knowledge on one of the corollary principles—the principle of durability. Retention of isolated facts or information that people come upon in lectures, by reading, through experimentation, or other means is often poor. Skills, by way of contrast, are relatively durable. Certain skills, like swimming and catching a ball, are virtually inextinguishable even though they may have gone unattended and unpracticed for many years.

This is one of the very exciting things about teaching motor skills. The changes that instructors stimulate and the skills that they help to develop will remain with their students, in many cases, throughout their lifetime. In retirement, these one-time students might be pleasurably rehearsing the same movements that were taught them on a junior high school tennis court, in a YMCA swimming pool, or on a college jogging trail. On the other hand, most facts or propositions that were taught in civics, or history, or English literature, or health and physical education will have been long forgotten.

Skill Is More Meaningful.   On the third rule of superiority—promoting experiences of coherence, meaning, direction for life, the experience of being part of a story—skill should once again be given a slightly higher score than knowledge. There is no question that information and facts can and often do help to give lives direction and meaning. They help give us a sense of place, personal identity, and worth. Information and facts help to free us from biases and other sorts of narrow thinking. But it is an exaggeration to suggest that ideas, propositions, or tips about a meaningful and coherent life are sufficient to produce one. Just as there are students of sport who can talk a good game but not play one, there are scholars of human existence who can talk a good life but not live one. The task in dealing with truths about life is always one of translating or converting a cold idea into a personal perception, belief, or habit.

Propositions about significant living are not difficult to locate. The Bible, the Koran, the Bhagavadgītā, Zen scriptures, hundreds of sages and wise people, and thousands of pop psychology and philosophy books can supply them. We can even purchase videotapes now that purport to tell us the true meaning of life. Or we can watch cable television all night to get tips on achieving wealth and total happiness. While the content of some of what passes today as wisdom is undoubtedly suspect, there is plenty of good information available. And it is far easier for individuals today in their media-rich culture to come into contact with these ideas than it was for many of our ancestors, who had to count on the memory of the elderly, on word of mouth, or, later, on the few books or manuscripts that were available.

If developing a meaningful and coherent life that is headed somewhere were simply a matter of getting in touch with the right ideas, there would not be so many people today wandering about looking for fulfillment. People would not experience as many moments of discontent, misdirection, and anxiety as they indeed experience.

The fact is that we grow into stories and meaning more than we encounter them as foreign propositions or theories. Cultural traditions, hobbies, dances, games, habits, crafts, and other activities point us in some directions and away from others. The skills we learn tell us implicitly that it is important to do this and not that. Moreover, these activities come loaded with values—with etiquette, with ways of behaving, with right attitudes, and so on. By learning play and game skills, we grow into rights and wrongs, values and disvalues, things that are important and other things that are not valuable. By learning play and game skills, we get important cultural bearings. Games and play resonate with the dominant messages of our time and place, and this builds a compass into our being that tells us the directions in which we should develop our personal stories.

The skills that professionals teach and the way that they teach them in sport, exercise science, and physical education speak volumes about what counts in life. Do coaches honor a lifecourse that coheres around the notion of power over finesse? Around winning or being number one over success? Around achievement over play and celebration? Around opportunity and advancement over certain moral values? Around perseverance over immediate gratification? Around the individual over the community?

Who are today's cultural heroes? What values do teachers highlight in their games and play? What models for living do they put up on the cultural marquees of professional sport and the Olympic games?

In developing sport, dance, and exercise skills, we spend a great deal of time with them. We live in the subcultures of tennis, swimming, soccer, baseball, folk dance, or other activity areas. We rub shoulders with the people who are the teachers, the masters, the coaches of those activities—the people who hold many of the keys to those particular kingdoms. We hear the stories of success and failure. We learn of the heroes and antiheroes. We begin to fit into the subculture and vibrate positively with its history and values. As athletes, dancers, and exercisers we become part of a family—if only distantly.

As we improve our skills, we experience a lived freedom to search, explore, express, invent, and create. This freedom is exhilarating, just as the freedom is that is experienced when a proposition or fact erases ignorance. We like ourselves as free, competent, perhaps even powerful. We want to return to the court, or pool, or dance floor, or exercise hall—wherever it is that we experience ourselves like this.

This skill-based and apprentice-guided freedom grounds performers more forcefully than the freedom of knowledge. We win this skill-based freedom over time, at a certain place, with specific people, in the context of our sport, dance, or exercise history. Our freedom grows up, as it were, locally. We experience freedom at a place, in a family, in the face of a specific opponent, doing the same sorts of things that many of our predecessors tried to do.

There is a good chance here to develop threads that tie various life acts and life periods together. There is a good chance here to develop threads that tie sporting, dancing, or exercising lives to the culture at large. There is a good chance here to advance and strengthen personal stories, even if tennis, modern dance, or jogging are not featured in these accounts.

SUMMARY BREAK

Even if competence is a critical element in good living, it is not clear that motor skills are needed by everyone. On the criterion of satisfaction, pleasures from different skills are incommensurable, and individual taste and interest need to be respected. In addition, some regard experiences of competence in sport, games, and play as trivial when compared to skill in the arts or various intellectual professions.

While both of the forms of gaining knowledge—propositional and procedural, theoretical and practical—are central components in the good life, and while both provide important degrees of freedom and peace (though in different ways), the edge must be given to skill because it shows itself as a superior source of satisfaction, as more durable, and as a stimulus for value, custom, tradition, and meaning. People who grow into skill concurrently grow into meaningful experiences, particularly when they return to that skill again and again. On the other hand, individuals who are presented with facts, theories, ideas, and books on meaning and value, may or may not incorporate them into their own lives. They may know about meaning, and they may be able to recite some facts or theories about a well-directed life, but they may or may not experience increased meaning and direction because of it. Thus, motor skill scores better on the criterion of lifespan coherence or meaningfulness.

The Intrinsic Value of Health- and Activity-Related Pleasure

In chapter 5, I defined pleasure in broad terms. I indicated that it is more than the mere absence of pain or even the presence of an experience that might be called satisfactory or agreeable. Pleasure is often associated with play—that is, with an experience that is intriguing, gripping, fascinating, captivating, one that is enjoyed for its own sake.

Pleasure often occurs in environments where something of a spell has been cast over its participants. They are given to the experience—so given, in fact, that they often forget what time it is. They are also taken by the experience—so taken, in fact, that they are not sure why they spent so much time there. When asked after the fact why they gave so much energy to dancing, playing field hockey, or riding a bicycle, for instance, these players will often say simply that they experienced a great deal of pleasure. Or more likely, they will just say that it was fun.

The terms pleasure and fun can be used synonymously, but here I take fun to refer to those experiences that have high degrees of emotional or sensuous content. Going down a roller coaster, breaking a tackle, winning a championship, getting a skill right—all these are fun. Pleasure, on the other hand, is used for the remainder of highly positive experiences—those that do not have high degrees of emotional or sensuous content. A good workout, the learning of a new play in basketball, a productive practice session in dance, a full season of play in retrospect, can be regarded as pleasurable. Pleasure or fun can be seen in the following kinds of experiences:

• **The experience of sensuous joy.** *Examples*: We may hit a golf ball on the "sweet spot"; smack solidly into an opposing lineman; feel a delicious exhaustion after a long run. *Intrinsic strength*: We delight in what literally feels good, in what pleases the senses.

• **The experience of satisfaction over an accomplishment.** *Examples*: We may reach a new personal goal in a distance run; play tennis well for three consecutive games; get a hit off a certain pitcher for the first time. *Intrinsic strength*: We enjoy experiences of control or mastery, particularly when it was difficult to achieve it.

• **The experience of satisfaction because of good play.** *Examples*: We can play with efficiency and effectiveness, experience victory, participate with poise and confidence. *Intrinsic strength*: Experiences of excellence and freedom are usually encountered as pleasurable or fun.

• **The experience of meaning.** *Examples*: We may play in a way that is personally satisfying; interpret a sport or dance event in a way that fits into our life story; play a traditional game; play with a long-time friend and

Play often casts a spell over its participants.

competitor; play a game on which we have been raised. *Intrinsic strength*: When we encounter meaning, we are pleasantly carried away by it.

Critical Analysis of Pleasure

In terms of the criterion of satisfaction (rule of superiority number 2), there is little to choose between pleasure and skill. Experiences that are fun or experiences that are grounded in the freedom of skill are both satisfactory. It would be difficult, if not impossible, to determine which was more satisfactory. Again, as with the comparison between skill and knowledge, perhaps this matter is best left to personal taste or preference.

Likewise, with the two corollaries of satisfaction—its purity (lack of harmful or immoral costs) and durability (how long it lasts or how often it recurs)—there seems to be little to choose between skill and pleasure. Play habits are very durable, just as skills are. And the costs that go into producing such habits do not seem to be different, in principle or fact, from those that are needed for developing skill. Additionally, satisfaction that comes from experiences of skill or play can be impure (they can be had at another's expense, for example), but neither one need be so.

It is on the criterion of coherence or meaningfulness (rule of superiority number 3) that pleasure and fun may be seen to have a slight advantage over skill, particularly if these goods are associated with the phenomenon of play. Experiences of life coherence or narrative meaning, as I am thinking of them here, have a great deal to do with play. I agree with Huizinga (1950) that culture develops in and through play. A sense of history, of place, of people's roles in life, of the values that will guide their activities—all are enhanced, enriched, and otherwise furthered in environments of play. The more we play, the greater the opportunities we have to experience coherence rather than random sensations, stories in progress rather than

Skills learned well
remain a lifetime.

disconnected events, values that are part and parcel of ourselves rather than mere sensuous thrills.

There is a connection between play and experiences of coherence because the wellsprings of play are based in particular cultures and histories. We do not play because it is rational, or smart, or logical to be so engaged. We play because we are invited to play by the world around us. We play because we cannot help ourselves—we are intrigued, interested, fascinated, challenged, mesmerized by something or other. And that something or other has to be consistent with our humanity (with what it is to attract the interest of a human being) and with our history or culture (with what it is to get the interest of that human being in this time and place). Competitive and achievement-oriented play, for example, works in a competitive and achievement-oriented culture. Aggressive games that focus on the individual will not work in a passive society that is structured around community action.

Of course, sport, exercise science, and physical education do not own or dominate play. But movement domains are particularly ripe with intrigue, pleasure, and fun; thus, they are good for play.

The upshot of this is that skill is more dependent on pleasure than pleasure is dependent on skill. Imagine the teaching of skill in a barren, culturally impoverished environment where, for example, people are driven to win or to be excellent without knowing why, without owning this drive as part of their stories, even without having these ends as particularly meaningful. Skill and excellence apart from a rich cultural context do not appear to be very appealing. Wonderful, excellent performances produced by programmed robots do not constitute much of a good life. Skill (and the excellence and freedom that accompany it) needs context, culture, and meaning. Skill, in short, would

appear to be highly dependent on the meanings and pleasures of play if it is to have its full intrinsic value.

Pleasure, on the other hand, seems more self-sufficient. Particularly in the environment of play, pleasure and fun have a relative independence from skill. It may be true that those with the greater skill levels have more frequent or deeper experiences of play, but skill is not needed for play to take over people's lives. Children, with skant knowledge and very few skills (motor or otherwise), have rich and memorable play experiences. Many of us can still recall the special individuals with whom we played as preschoolers, the magical places in which some of this play occurred, and the themes or stories that kept us wonderfully preoccupied.

Culture develops in and through both skill and play, but the edge in this regard should be given to play. If forced to choose between a life with richer play experiences or experiences of higher levels of skill, I would choose the former. In play, in pleasure and fun, we are more likely to stumble across a whole host of values, purposes, and roles that we will slowly piece together into what we call our life. We are more likely to experience coherence.

Prioritizing the Four Intrinsic Values

You have now had an opportunity to examine the ways in which fitness, knowledge, skill, and pleasure contribute directly to the good life. As was the case with extrinsic values, in chapter 6, these values are not equal in strength. In light of the descriptions and analyses in the previous sections, let us attempt to rank fitness, knowledge, skill, and pleasure as to their intrinsic value.

In the environment of play, pleasure and fun are relatively independent of skill.

PHILOSOPHIC EXERCISE

Attempt to prioritize health- and activity-related fitness, knowledge, motor skill, and pleasure on their intrinsic strengths. Your

basic criterion here is the extent to which experiences of each of these things is satisfactory in itself. To help in discriminating between four things that are all good, you can also analyze the durability of such experiences, the degree to which each experience is costly or inexpensive, and the extent to which such experiences promote a meaningful, coherent life—one that operates like a narrative or story.

After you have finished with your rankings, try to show where there are larger and smaller gaps between the values and attempt to give at least one reason for your ranking of each value.

One Possible Ranking

My own ranking, based on the previous analysis, would look like this:

1. Pleasure
2. Skill
3. Knowledge
4. Fitness

When I try to show the relative distance between these values as ends in themselves, my ranking appears as follows:

1. Pleasure
2. Skill

3. Knowledge

4. Fitness

SUMMARY BREAK

Early in this chapter we made forced-choice comparisons between fitness and other values. If our thinking was accurate, we saw that fitness was given a ranking lower than a number of other values. Although fitness was stronger as a means value (chapter 6), it deserves the lowest ranking when we consider what we want to have as ends in our lives. We want more than health and long life. We are far from satisfied with experiences of life, survival, or health alone. By itself, fitness does very little to assure the good life.

We also noted a number of weaknesses of knowledge, particularly in its ability to assure meaning and coherence for our lives. We argued that sound propositions are not in short supply, yet many people do not experience a meaningful existence. We claimed that, while propositions may be able to describe coherence and meaningfulness and give any number of tips regarding the secrets of life, they do not necessarily change lives and make them coherent. In short, it is one thing to know about meaning and coherence and quite another to embody, have, or live it. Thus, knowledge is ranked well below skill.

Yet the experience of knowing facts, theories, and ideas; the satisfactions of finding something out through laboratory examination; the delight in reading and learning about sport—all these have important intrinsic value, and all can comprise a large portion of the good life. The experience of enlightenment does far more to assure good living than the mere experience of life itself. Thus, health- and activity-related knowledge is ranked well above fitness.

We gave the top position to pleasure because it seemed more sufficient for guaranteeing good living than skill. The experience of superb baseball skills, for example, in the absence of meaning, story, play, and their attendant satisfactions, appeared to be more lacking than a baseball-focused existence with experiences of coherence, a mission in life, and important roles to play in the game, even with a lifetime .250 average. Excellence at shortstop would grow tiresome without the magic of play.

PHILOSOPHIC EXERCISE

You are now faced with perhaps the most speculative and difficult task in this journey.

You must attempt to synthesize your evaluations of fitness, knowledge, skill, and pleasure as means or tools for various good ends with your judgments about them as good experiences in their own right, as ends in themselves. Remember that we gave reasons for counting intrinsic power as far more significant than extrinsic strength (Rule of Superiority Number 1). Thus, your final prioritization should resemble your ranking in this chapter more than your ranking in chapter 6.

Attempt to place gaps betwen your values and argue for their relative position. Share these with your classmates to see how your rankings and arguments compare with theirs.

An Overall Ranking of Extrinsic and Intrinsic Values

My final prioritization has produced two clusters of values, which are presented in Table 7.1. Pleasure and motor skill have risen to the top of the list in a virtual tie. Pleasure finished ahead of motor skill on both my extrinsic and intrinsic rankings, but skill was close behind in each case. It remains there in this final ranking. Health-related fitness and knowledge occupy a position of second rank and lower priority, again in a virtual tie with one another. Fitness pulled ahead of knowledge on the basis of its extremely powerful extrinsic value. (Remember, life- and energy-preserving health is *the* tool for everything else that you and I desire and enjoy.) But knowledge's superior intrinsic ranking kept it close to fitness in the final ranking.

Review

If we cannot be all things to all people, if we are to find direction for our professional

Table 7.1 An Overall Ranking of Intrinsic and Extrinsic Values

Value	Intrinsic	Extrinsic
1. Pleasure	Experiences of play, intrigue, delight, and cultural meaning in sport, exercise, dance, and games	Pleasure as a powerful means to better skill, health, learning, etc.
2. Motor skill	Experiences of confidence, peace, authorship, excellence, and power in sport, exercise, dance, and games	Skill as a means to more satisfactory play, health, and other good ends
3. Fitness	Experiences of bodily lightness, endurance, and strength	Fitness as a means to virtually all of life's achievements and pleasures
4. Knowledge	Experiences of enlightenment in knowing about sport, games, play, and healthy living	Knowledge as a means for promoting enlightened practice, improved sport skills, and better health

energies, and if we are to develop some passion over values and contributions that centrally and significantly change lives for the better, we may be ready to claim the following:

WE ARE DEVOTED TO PLAY!

We promote activities that are done for their own sake—that matter to individuals, to neighborhoods, to towns, to ethnic cultures, to traditions. We promote love affairs with games, dances, exercise, sports. We want these activities to enhance life stories by allowing individuals to rehearse and highlight the values that produce meaningful and interesting lives. We favor life-long companionship with these movement forms so that people and these crafts grow and change together. Moreover, we make no apologies for the fact that such involvement provides pure, unadulterated satisfaction and fun.

WE ARE DEVOTED TO SKILL!

We promote the impressive employment of intelligence in ways that emphasize human embodiment. We honor how-to knowledge—the shrewd pitch in baseball, the clever pass in field hockey, the insightful cut in football, the creative and fluid gesture in dance. Without a word spoken, without a single fact delivered, without one proposition on the table—we value truth in moving. In addition, we offer no apologies for the fact that such how-to knowledge has not been (and never will be) fully transmitted to books or that some performers are not also advanced theoreticians of movement.

In order to advance such a mission, we must be able to

✓ articulate clearly the errors of dualism and convince society that entirely whole, thinking persons are involved in movement activity;
✓ articulate clearly the fact that skill is a form of knowing and that this knowing can satisfy standards for higher forms of intelligence;
✓ articulate clearly the fact that this form of knowing is central to the development of human potential—for example,

that movement skills are no less significant than the more reflective-sedentary sorts of human skills that promote exploration, expression, inventiveness, and creativity;

✓ articulate clearly the fact that skill (even at the level of excellence) has human worth and significance primarily when it is meaningful, attractive, and fun; and

✓ articulate clearly the value of play as an essential wellspring of movement significance and importance.

By taking this stand, the profession will tilt toward human growth and education, not toward medical maintenance, recreational battery recharging, work-dominated productivity, and base-level biological survival. In short, the objectives of the profession will focus around persons, not bodies, and around intrinsic values, not utility services.

These conclusions might seem to put Kim Stanton, the cardiac rehabilitation specialist you met at the beginning of the chapter, in a bind. She has been hired to promote health and fitness with recovering and at-risk cardiac patients. But while her prescriptions might have been scientifically sound, they seemed to Kim to be humanly lacking. Many of her patients, for example, failed to continue with the exercise programs she had recommended. Perhaps Kim was trying to sell health and fitness as an end value, but her patients intuitively knew that other things were more important to them. Possibly, Kim could revise her prescriptions to better reflect the power of skillful activity and the strength of meaningful play. Paradoxically, such a strategy might lead to even better health than the program that was aimed more directly at producing it.

Looking Ahead

You are now ready to start on the third segment of your journey. Armed with an understanding of the holistic nature of human beings, the needs of contemporary society, and the extrinsic and intrinsic power of four traditional values, you should be ready to draw some conclusions about how sport, exercise science, and physical education practitioners can most effectively change their students and clients for the better.

Checking Your Understanding

1. Describe at least two personal experiences of health- and activity-related fitness, knowledge, skill, and pleasure that were intrinsically valuable.
2. Which of these four values is least able, on its own, to provide the good life? Give at least one reason for your judgment.
3. Which of these four values is most able, on its own, to provide the good life? Give at least one reason for your judgment.
4. Rank the four values on their combined extrinsic and intrinsic strengths. Are you willing to allow the intrinsic strength of these values to carry more weight? Can you defend this decision to support intrinsic over extrinsic strength?
5. Are you comfortable with a profession that would champion motor skill and play? Try to defend your answer.
6. Are we the only academic field that leans heavily on the intrinsic value of skill (all varieties) and play (in all environments)? If not, can you name any of these other fields and describe how and why they too rely on these values?

Key Terms

Intrinsic value, p. 155

Health- and activity-related fitness (intrinsic value), p. 156

Health- and activity-related knowledge (intrinsic value), p. 160

Motor skill (intrinsic value), p. 164

Health- and activity-related pleasure (intrinsic value), p. 168

(1950), Harper (1973-1976), Pieper (1952), and MacIntyre (1984). For analyses that are supportive of the intrinsic value of motor activity and excellence, see Weiss (1969), Novak (1976), and Simon (1992).

Further Reading

For discussions on the intrinsic value of meaning, pleasure, and play see Huizinga

Part III

Improving Life Through Our Profession: Applications of Philosophic Thinking

Philosophy is sometimes criticized for being too abstract and only minimally useful in the so-called real world. I mentioned in the Introduction that, as much as I like to muse, idealize, and imagine utopian solutions when doing philosophy, I am not willing to leave it at that. I want good thinking to change my life and the lives of others for the better—and to do so in very real, measurable ways.

Consequently, in the next three chapters, we will turn our philosophic thinking in more practical directions. You will use information gained from your travels in previous parts of this book, uncover some additional ideas, and try to apply both to the problems that professionals face in sport, exercise science, and physical education.

Chapter 8

Making Changes That Matter

Sally McIntyre was a new instructor at a junior high school. Like many new teachers, she was full of ideas, energy, and optimism. She wanted to have an educational influence on her students, one that might be as important as any other teacher in the school. In other words, she wanted to change their lives in significant ways. She believed that physical education is central to the growth, development, and overall education of each of her students. And she approached each class with the kind of purpose and determination that teachers have when they believe such things.

During one lunch period Sally was sitting with several veteran teachers—one who taught math, two who were in social studies, one English instructor, and the school's art teacher. As was frequently the case, the conversation had turned to frustrations with teaching. The math teacher grumbled, "What it comes down to is this. The kids just don't care. They are 10 times more interested in one another than they are in numbers and calculations."

The math teacher paused and noticed all the heads but Sally's nodding in sympathetic agreement. "Sometimes I wish that math were as much fun as the play and games that Sally teaches," he continued. "On the other hand, sport, dance, and play don't have much to do with real education, do they?"

Sally wondered how she should respond. Play and games did sound a little trivial next to such weighty subjects as math, social studies, English, and even art. Perhaps she should agree with her colleague and emphasize the importance of fitness and health rather than sport and motor skill. But everyone in the room knew that her physical education curriculum was designed to do much more than promote physical fitness and that sport, dance, games, and play were central elements in her program. Indeed, Sally was dedicated to these loftier educational goals herself. She felt trapped.

Why do Sally's colleagues not take her work seriously? If Sally wanted to argue that the educational changes she makes are important, how would she go about it? If she wanted to claim that "fun and games" are not trivial, would she find enough evidence to make a convincing case?

Earlier in this book you learned about the negative effects of mind-body dualism in your field, the needs of society that can be addressed by physical education, the importance of prioritizing professional objectives, and the strength of four traditional objectives. On the basis of the analysis in the last two chapters, I suggested that a profession dedicated to sport, dance, exercise, and game skill instruction in the context of meaningful play held the most promise for promoting good living. Here you will attempt to better understand why physical education is, in spite of its potential, often regarded as a fringe element in education and health services. This will include an examination of bases on which this unfavorable judgment can be reversed.

IN THIS CHAPTER, YOU WILL

- examine four claims that physical education is relatively unimportant;
- review responses to three of these claims;
- understand the seriousness of the fourth claim;
- identify two interpretations of liberal (mainstream) education; and
- determine ways in which changes promoted by physical education might qualify under both interpretations.

Our philosophic journey has allowed us to see different ways in which our profession can help people. This help, whether it occurs in education, business, recreation, or the health-related professions, is designed to change and improve lives. We have drawn some conclusions about which changes matter more than others. We have some reasons to believe that people who frequently experience play and who possess sport, dance, and exercise skills have very important resources for living the good life.

This optimism is not always shared by others. It is not that these individuals doubt our ability to be effective agents of change—to teach sport skills, to produce successful teams, or develop a familiarity with recreational activities, for example. Rather they doubt that these changes are truly significant. Apart from the improvement of health, our changes, some think, are relatively trivial ones. Physical education frequently labors under a number of unfavorable stereotypes.

Why is physical education often perceived to occupy one of the lower rungs of the education ladder?

Why do athletes, who often exhibit many of the skills of artists and who are often paid large sums of money, receive very little of the educational and cultural respect given to pianists, painters, and sculptors, for instance?

Should our profession de-emphasize games and play in favor of content that might be viewed as more educationally salable—content like movement, the theory of exercise, character development, or health-promoting exercise itself?

Do you ever think you will be able to speak of games and play to educators in other fields without a bit of anxiety and defensiveness?

Trivial Physical Education: Four Charges

For purposes here, we will define **change agents** as professionals who, through sharing information and providing services, intend to modify a person's status and behavior. While much discussion that follows concerning change and change agents will be about education, neither change agents nor their services are limited to schools. Physical therapists, cardiac rehabilitation specialists, and athletic trainers need to educate their clients as much as physical education teachers work to change their students.

While all of you are aware that physical education has a precarious status in many school systems and other institutions devoted to educational change, you may not realize that this lack of status has several distinct sources. As previously noted, one of them is not our ability to effect change in our students, athletes, physical therapy patients, or other clients. In fact, we are frequently honored for that. Negative biases are related more to the *kind* of learning and change we facilitate. These criticisms will sound familiar because we addressed several of them previously. But here the focus is on change, and critics say that many of the changes we produce do not much matter. Here are three such statements, to be followed shortly by a fourth one.

The Criticism From Dualistic Idealism

Dualistic idealism, you may recall from chapter 2, is a viewpoint that sees persons as composed of mind and body (a form of dualism) where the mind enjoys some independence from, and a superiority over, the body (a form of idealism). A critique from a dualistic idealist might sound like this:

> All of you are *physical* educators, or in service professions related to *physical* needs, or in business related to *physical* activity. While it may be impossible to completely separate minds from bodies, your profession focuses on the physical. You have very little to do with ideas, knowledge, or understanding. Mainstream education must be intellectual education, and you obviously cannot make any serious claims that you satisfy this criterion.

A Response.   You should be well-armed to react to this old dualistic claim. In chapters 2 and 3 you learned that it is not correct to describe human beings as body-plus-mind or to radically separate physical from mental education. You also saw that there are important and valid ways in which to describe good levels of muscle- and motor-oriented skill itself as intellectually impressive. In fact, through the horizontal image of persons and their behavior in chapter 3, you encountered a radical redefinition of what it is to be intellectual and how people might show their intelligence.

Thus, even if we were to agree with this critic that mainstream education is intellectual education, we are not forced to concede anything. We could even turn the last sentence of the criticism around like this: Mainstream education must be intellectual education, and we have every reason to think that we can satisfy that criterion.

The Criticism From Liberal Education

Advocates of liberal education may see our field of study as vocational, technical, and, as a result, unfortunately narrow. Physical skills are often viewed as work-related or useful for the daily, mundane necessities of life. People need to move skillfully, it is sometimes believed, primarily for responsibilities on the job or chores around the house and yard. Physical education, from this perspective, has the relatively low status of the manual arts. A critique from the perspective of the liberal arts might sound like this:

> Your field is useful but narrow. Learning how to dance, play games, and stay healthy is like learning how to cook, sew, clean, build things from wood, and repair automobiles. These skills may be handy, but they are hardly liberating. They are useful, but we would not want to call them ends in themselves. They may help one to hold a job or take care of necessities, but they do not enlighten, free, and eliminate narrow thinking, superstition, and bigotry. Mainstream education must be a broad and liberating education, and you obviously cannot make any serious claims that you satisfy that criterion.

A Response.   Sport, dance, and exercise education need not be vocational or otherwise narrow. Of course, a skilled athlete could be just a baseball player and not employ his movement capabilities to enrich the rest of his life. But a skilled writer could also be only a journalist and not employ his writing capabilities effectively in a variety of life circumstances.

However, neither writing nor moving well needs to be vocationally narrow in these ways. Writing and moving skillfully can liberate people to discover, explore, express, invent, and create in many aspects of daily life. The good writer may be better able to appreciate good literature, gain special enjoyment from reading the newspaper, carry on an enjoyable correspondence with friends, write poetry, play word games, and craft particularly humorous or clever sentences in

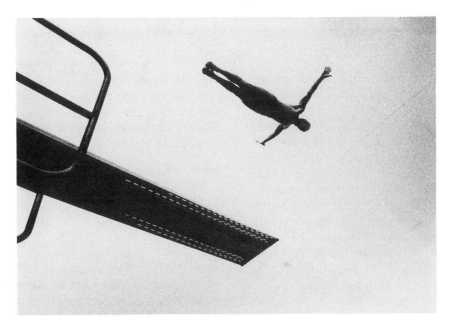

Sport skills enable one to reach places others cannot find.

conversation. Similarly, a person skilled in sport and exercise might be able to appreciate the countryside on a hike, reach places that others cannot find, play a variety of his culture's games with grace and creativity, and express himself through posture and gesture.

Thus, even if we were to agree with this critic that mainstream education must be broad and liberating, we would not be obligated to concede anything. We could even turn the statement around as follows: Mainstream education must be broad and liberating, and we have every reason to think that we can satisfy that criterion.

The Criticism From Humanism

Humanism places emphasis on the uniquely human elements of life in contrast to godlike, or divine, realities, on the one hand, and subhuman, animalistic, or mechanistic realities, on the other. Thus, the critique from humanism might sound like this:

Movement skill, as a form of knowledge, is a dependent and otherwise inherently inferior kind of understanding. You people in physical education tend to promote the development of habits rather than insight. Thus, your students and clients are predictable and in many cases act like robots. They may be able to perform specific motor tasks very well, but they are slaves to those few skill environments. They do not understand the principles or abstractions that allow them to generalize, to override habits, to manage new and different environments effectively. In an important sense, your students are not free. You people in physical education, apart from some modern dancers, have little ability to teach or promote human freedoms found in creativity, expression, exploration, and other higher-order behaviors, all of which are grounded in the capacity to deal with abstract principles.

A Response.   You have already learned that there are at least two planes on which human freedom is developed. One is more sedentary and tends toward reflection. It produces propositions and other abstractions that are typically communicated through verbal and mathematical symbol systems. A second plane of liberation is more muscle- and motor-oriented. It produces right movements and other abstractions that are typically communicated through sport, dance, exercise, and gestural symbol systems. If our thinking was sound in chapter 3, we have every reason to believe that skillful behavior transcends rote and habitual actions even though we do not achieve this primarily by teaching principles or theories about movement. The improvisations of athletes, no less than the improvisations of jazz pianists, can hardly be accounted for in terms of reflexes, habits, and mechanical principles alone. In short, we have every reason to believe that performance itself can reach levels of impressive creativity, uncanny truth, and exhilarating freedom.

Thus, even if we were to agree with the humanists that mainstream education should not be blind, thoughtlessly repetitive, and limited by habit, we would not be obligated to concede anything. We could turn their claim around and say: Mainstream education gives individuals knowledge that frees them in unique and ever-changing settings, and we have every reason to believe that we meet that criterion.

SUMMARY BREAK

Skepticism about the importance of the changes promoted by activity-oriented education comes from at least three distinct sources. Dualistic idealists are unable to see improvements in motor- and muscle-oriented skill as a form of intellectual development. Liberal educators are unable to

disengage motor behavior from narrow, job-oriented manual arts. And humanists mistakenly view activity skills as limited habitual activity and not flexible and insightful improvisation.

A successful response to the first criticism can provoke the second charge, and so on. The sequence of charges and defenses is summarized in Figure 8.1.

The Criticism From High Culture and the Arts

A fourth criticism remains, one that strikes closer to home than the other three. It is a more enlightened criticism because it does not rely on the worn-out biases of mind-body dualism, the mistaken belief that skills must be narrow and vocational, or the misconception that physical skills are nothing more than locked-in habits and reflexes. In fact, critics from this camp actually accept motor- and muscle-oriented skills as important avenues for human change, growth, and liberation. However, the activities they support and celebrate do not include sport, games, and play. The critique from the arts might go something like this:

> Your skill-based liberation is trivial. While motor skills may be a particularly powerful and liberating form of knowing, sport, exercise, game, and play skills are relatively unimportant activities. Granted, it is better to be a creative, expressive basketball player than a predictable, mechanical one. But it is better yet to be a good pianist, sculptor, artist, or actor. The fine arts are closely associated to some of the higher parts of culture. Sport, games, and play are not.

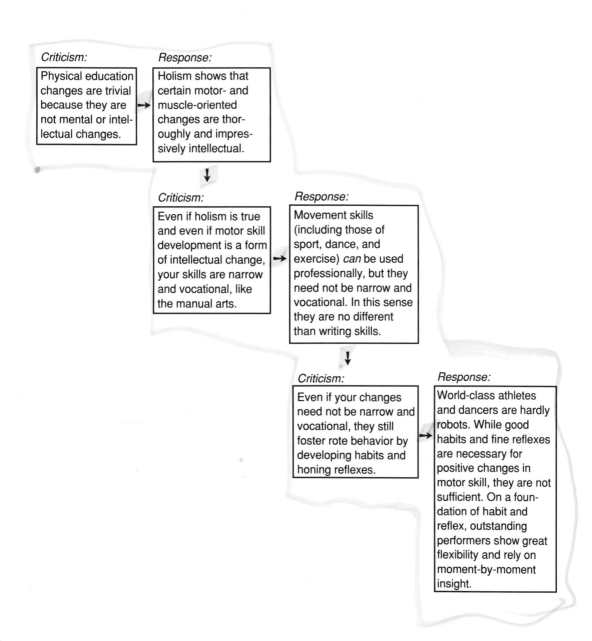

Criticism:

Physical education changes are trivial because they are not mental or intellectual changes.

Response:

Holism shows that certain motor- and muscle-oriented changes are thoroughly and impressively intellectual.

Criticism:

Even if holism is true and even if motor skill development is a form of intellectual change, your skills are narrow and vocational, like the manual arts.

Response:

Movement skills (including those of sport, dance, and exercise) *can* be used professionally, but they need not be narrow and vocational. In this sense they are no different than writing skills.

Criticism:

Even if your changes need not be narrow and vocational, they still foster rote behavior by developing habits and honing reflexes.

Response:

World-class athletes and dancers are hardly robots. While good habits and fine reflexes are necessary for positive changes in motor skill, they are not sufficient. On a foundation of habit and reflex, outstanding performers show great flexibility and rely on moment-by-moment insight.

Figure 8.1. Flowchart of charges against and defenses of PE.

PHILOSOPHIC EXERCISE

You face a number of options in light of this final criticism. You could

1. reject the criticism by showing that sport, games, and play are or can be aspects of high culture, that they can be art or like art;

2. accept the criticism by substituting movement for sports, games, and play;

3. accept the criticism by retaining a commitment to exercise and physical fitness but downplaying the importance of sport, games, and play; or

4. accept the criticism by downplaying the commitment to physical activity altogether and by emphasizing, for example, the research and theory of your field of study, or the lessons in morality that can be learned through participation.

Which option do you like best? When speaking with others about your profession, are you inclined to talk about human movement rather than sport? Exercise rather than games? Or character development and knowledge rather than play? If so, you may see options 2, 3, or 4 as more desirable. These options will be examined in detail in what follows.

Avoiding Sport, Games, and Play?

We have come to the interesting, if unsettling, conclusion that our profession's content, at least as it involves sport, games, and play, may be primarily responsible for doubts about the significance of our work. We may not particularly have to worry about our identity as a profession concerned substantially with the physical aspects of personhood, or with the fact that we teach skills, or even with the fact that we teach muscle- and motor-oriented types of skills. But we may have to worry about our association with sport, games, and play. It is our content that is seen by some as relatively trivial, particularly when it is compared to the arts. It is our content that generates comments like "Relax, it's only a game," "There are many more important things to do than to play soccer all your life," or "Play is for kids; why don't you grow up?" The content of the arts will not support similar statements. It would be strange to hear comments like the following: "Don't worry, it's only a concert," "There are many more important things to do than to paint portraits all your life," or "Performing on a piano is for kids. Why don't you quit fooling around with music and grow up?"

We seem caught in a bind, the same one encountered by Sally McIntyre in the account at the start of this chapter. We want to claim that we can make important changes and improvements in people's lives. But a substantial part of our content involves "fun and games." The goal and the content would seem to be mismatched.

Such thinking has prompted some professionals to give sport, games, and play a lower profile through two strategies. But as we can show from our analysis in previous chapters, such shifts in focus are, at least, misleading.

Fallacy 1: Focus Shifted to Movement

One strategy is to retain muscle- and motor-oriented skill development as a central purpose of the profession but focus on movement, not sport, games, and play. Thus, in physical education we teach generic movement skills (pushing, pulling, lifting, moving rhythmically, and so on) more than baseball, tennis, and football. Some sports and games

Human beings at play: trivial or crucial activity?

are retained, but primarily because they employ basic movement patterns. Consequently, we teach human movement, not idiosyncratic or childish games and play. We do not support participation in sport, games, and play as ends in themselves or as the focal point of the profession.

One problem is that this shift to movement can be nothing more than a verbal ploy to make us sound better. No doubt we might be more comfortable telling a colleague from the philosophy department that we are instructors of human movement, not teachers of sport and play. But if the content remains much the same, we have done nothing more than keep our activities in hiding.

If, however, the shift to movement education is a real one, then our field may compromise its ability to promote satisfaction and a coherent and meaningful life, values that were central features of the good life as we defined it in chapter 5. Consequently, any curriculum that would threaten them or make their enhancement less likely should,

at the very least, be examined carefully and critically.

The argument against generic types of movement education briefly is this. If we are a culture-embedded and a culture-affected people, we need a culture-sensitive curriculum to shape us and change us for the better. Traditional games, play, sport, exercise, and folk dance carry culture and local values, as it were, on their persons. Without knowing why, most students resonate to their implicit messages; because the students resonate, they are engaged; because they are engaged, they are in a situation in which teaching typically goes better; when teaching goes better, students change, grow, improve, and learn faster.

On the other hand, movement curricula that are logically designed to cover all basic movement forms respond more to system and comprehensiveness than meaning. Without knowing why, many students find culturally mismatched movement exercises and experimentation uninteresting once their novelty wears off. Teaching and learning go less well as the students become less engaged with the curriculum.

Fallacy 2: Focus Shifted to Fitness, Knowledge, or Morality

The second strategy is to shift the emphasis in the profession from skill development to physical fitness or cognitive or affective development. Sport, games, and play (to the extent that they still remain in the curriculum) become means to the respective ends of health and fitness, acquisition of knowledge, and personal and moral development. Thus, we teach fitness, theory, and social adjustment. We employ sport, games, and play largely because they can be effective tools in achieving these ends. We do not think that participation in sport, games, and play should be considered ends in themselves.

Unfortunately, this strategy devalues sport, games, and play. It says, in effect, that these are unimportant in themselves but may still be useful as tools. It says that time spent in these activities is inherently wasted time, unless one learns lessons or gains fitness from them. This produces a Pyrrhic victory. It avoids the potential awkwardness of highlighting such supposedly dubious content as sport, games, and play, but at the cost of characterizing the field as one that has little or no intrinsically valuable content of its own. Presumably, if there were other more efficient ways to achieve fitness, knowledge, or social development, physical education could be eliminated altogether—without bringing harm to anyone.

Given these concerns about strategies for de-emphasizing a sizeable portion of our content and thereby dodging concerns over the value of "mere" play and games, it becomes ever more important to understand better the nature of what might be called mainstream education. Once that has been described, we will be in a better position to determine the educational value of sport, games, and play.

Qualities of Mainstream Education

Mainstream education, as I am defining it here, is synonymous with liberal education. Mainstream education is devoted to freeing persons from narrow thinking, ignorance, unexamined biases about other people and other times, a lack of familiarity with literature and the arts, the tendency to act on habit rather than scientific fact or other types of accurate information, and the unwillingness to wonder about, question, and examine one's place in life. It is devoted to freeing a person for a life of informed citizenship, creative work, meaningful interrelationships, and tasteful recreation.

Mainstream education uses a wide lens when focusing on its mission. It aims to improve the whole of a person's life, to elevate all of an individual's living to a higher plane, to recast a person's orientation to life itself. Other forms of education, by way of contrast, use a narrow lens. With *training*, students learn how to perform a specific task—like serving effectively in the military. In *vocational education*, students prepare for a specific job. *Indoctrination* gives people only a single perspective on life. *Service education* teaches people how to manage daily necessities—like practicing good hygiene, driving a car, cooking nutritious meals, maintaining physical fitness, and participating in healthful recreation. Whatever its form and degree of importance, nonliberal education is relatively narrow.

Mainstream education should affect broad aspects of life (not specific jobs, necessities, or occasional duties) and should modify human existence in the direction of greater freedom

Music and sport: two worthy components of mainstream education?

(not toward habit, training, or indoctrination). This freedom that stands at the heart of liberal education can be promoted in two very different ways (Kimball, 1986). Eventually we will want to determine if the development of skill itself in playing and watching sport and games can give our students and clients experiences of both of these freedoms.

The Wisdom Tradition

Education under the **wisdom tradition** (see Table 8.1) is focused on preserving and transmitting the great truths of the humanities, sciences, and social sciences. It is intended to develop civilized people, to prepare leaders, and to teach firm values. It is supposed to put individuals in touch with the finest ideas available and then to prepare people to share them, to express them in public. It typically places an emphasis on classic texts and puts a premium on memorization and recitation. It holds that knowledge is an end in itself, though it can also be used as a means.

The wisdom tradition keeps individuals' feet planted firmly on the ground. It suggests that the good life can be gained by relying heavily on the progress made by one's ancestors—by coming into contact with time-tested wisdom, by noticing that many old truths are still true today, by transmitting facts that deserve preservation.

The Exploration Tradition

Education under the **exploration tradition** is focused on the development of liberating skills that permit exploration. It is intended to develop people who are able to do and to act. This tradition emerged in the Renaissance with the rise of science, and it is grounded in criticism and questionning. Descartes with his systematic doubt, Locke with his attack on innate ideas, and Hume with his belief that the "New Science" could never provide certainty established a need for continuing inquiry and perpetual searching (Kimball, 1986). They also established a foundation for tolerance and egalitarianism.

The exploration tradition provides very little firm footing, for it prepares people for a journey without assuring them of where they will be going or even if they will ever arrive at a satisfying destination. It suggests that the

"At the center of a liberal education is being free"

Table 8.1   Two Traditions in Mainstream Education

	Wisdom tradition	Exploration tradition
Assumptions	World is static, truths can be known and recreated	World is dynamic, truths ever-changing (or at least ever-expanding)
Focus	On the community	On the individual
Its glory	Solidarity with past	Freedom of intellect
Its highest good	Public expression of what is known	Pursuit of knowledge
Current manifestations	Great books curricula, religious education	Modern science, organization of modern research universities

Note. Adapted from Kimball (1986).

good life involves the *pursuit* of knowledge in the absence of bigotry, provincialism, superstition, or any other form of narrow thinking and without the handicap of underdeveloped skills.

The Modern Combination of Traditions

Contemporary education has more the character of the exploration tradition than the old wisdom tradition. Even the use of literary classics is often justified today by noting that they are good tools by which to teach intellectual skills rather than repositories of the truth. Modern education seems to be based on a healthy skepticism about much of our knowledge; there is a great tolerance for different answers, and there is great patience with individuals seeking personal truths. The modern de-emphasis on memorization and the general lack of consensus in identifying the classics and describing their value may be related to a sense that there no longer are any eternal truths worth reading, memorizing, or reciting.

Nevertheless, both traditions have their strengths. Even if the wisdom tradition is partly out of favor, any education that ignores the preservation of knowledge, that turns its back on tradition, that radically doubts everything, and that relies wholly on free flights of the intellect ends up being an unsatisfactory caricature of education. It has little important content to teach, since all content is relative, incomplete, or both, and it is forever unsure of itself.

Conversely, any education that would carry the wisdom tradition to an extreme, that ignores dynamic aspects of the world, that underestimates the complexity of the truth, that glorifies the past, that becomes married to various dogmas, and that promotes rote memorization and recitation likewise ends up being an unsatisfactory caricature of education. It has few important intellectual skills to teach and is dangerously sure of itself.

You may have already concluded that either tradition becomes less defensible the more it is pushed to an extreme. If so, you should be ready to look at sport, games, and play in light of both traditions, not just the currently popular exploration perspective.

Mainstream Education and Sport, Games, and Play

Each tradition needs to be reviewed in terms of physical education's motor skills and activities.

Motor Skill and the Wisdom Tradition

How can physical educators think of themselves as change agents in the Wisdom Tradition? How would they help free their students or clients by sharing great truths or wise sayings? After all, physical education has so little to do with words, and the theory it possesses would hardly pass as comprehensive guidelines for good living.

Sport Performances as a Form of Wisdom

Athletes, dancers, and other skillful individuals, as we noted in chapters 2 and 3, feel the truth more than they know it reflectively. They recognize it when it presents itself even though they may not be able to put it into words before or even after performances. An example of this is described in the box below.

Much sport knowledge and wisdom is inaccessible away from the sport environment. This does not, however, necessarily compromise the quality of the wisdom that athletes encounter, live, and share. Their wisdom simply has not been reflected upon, abstracted, and put into verbal symbols.

When athletes try to make the transition from nonverbal to verbal podiums, they frequently fail. Yogi Berra, the great Yankee catcher and Hall of Fame member, was asked years ago when he was still an active ball player to explain his secret to hitting. Berra, always far more comfortable at home plate than at a microphone, thought for a moment and then blurted out, "I see this white, round thing coming, and I takes a swing at it." The artistry that went into Berra's prowess as a hitter was far more complex and impressive than that, but skilled performers can always do more than they can say. The fact that Berra was inarticulate did not prevent him from

---

Wisdom in Sport

I once asked an advanced table tennis player of mine to explain to a class of beginning students where he held his bat prior to taking his patented forehand loop shot. This young man, who had already played in a number of regional and national tournaments and well knew the feel of the shot, stiffened and looked frightened. He stammered for a moment or two while looking down at the hand that held his bat. He could not say precisely where he held the bat for a top-spin loop.

He then proceeded to do a most remarkable thing. He walked a couple of paces to the end of a nearby table tennis table, imagined a ball coming to his forehand, got into position to make the loop kill and froze his arm, hand, and bat in that position. With more than a little relief he then pointed with his free hand to where he held the bat and announced to the class, "I start my forehand loop shot from here!"

An athlete's wisdom is inaccessible away from the athletic environment.

possessing and sharing a good deal of wisdom, albeit in a nontraditional way.

Sport as a Powerful Language

Wisdom, whether in the abstract verbal form of the orators or the concrete lived form of the athlete and artist, is often opaque, hidden, deep, mysterious, difficult to discern. Much wisdom sounds like a contradiction to those who do not yet possess it. For example, the claim that "those who are last shall be first" may well contain some wisdom, even outside a religious context. But it sounds like a logical contradiction, and it runs against the common-sense advice about promoting ourselves aggressively if we are ever to get ahead. This notion leads us to think more deeply and ask further questions. In what sense "last"? In

what sense "first"? Does life always work that way, or only in special circumstances?

Paradoxically, such insights are often difficult to communicate directly. They resist translation into straightforward sentences. Thus, poets are needed. They resist transmission to listeners' ears through the spoken word. Thus, composers and musicians are needed. They resist being shared through literal pictures or road signs. Thus, artists are needed. And they resist transmission through denotational gestures or hand signals. Thus, dancers, mimes, and athletes are needed. In short, wisdom cannot always be packaged and delivered in literal words, sounds, signs, or signals. It is often served up by fine performers in various crafts through impressionistic and suggestive forms. It is then ingested by spectators and observers through repeated contact with sport and art.

What are some examples of wisdom in sport? Does sport participate in the mysteries of life per se? I think it does, and here are a few possibilities:

1. In order to hit the golf ball harder, you must swing the club easier.
2. If you want to see more in basketball, you should not be so worried about seeing everything.
3. The tennis racquet is an implement I use to hit a ball harder and more efficiently. Yet, after years of practice, the racquet is no longer a thing I manipulate. It is an extension of my arm.
4. The best game plan is no game plan at all.
5. The more skilled I become, and the more I am in control of this game, the more humble I feel in its presence.

PHILOSOPHIC EXERCISE

Try to do two things with the paradoxical statements listed above. First, translate them. That is, try to unravel them, make sense of them—in words. The recommendation about hitting a golfball harder by swinging easier, for example, may be grounded in certain biomechanical principles. The idea about seeing more by looking for less may be based on psychological facts or theories.

Second, try to imagine the experience of living the wisdom captured by these sayings. Reflect on your best sport and try to feel the experiences pointed to by these statements. For instance, what is it like to have a tennis racquet become a part of one's arm? Have you ever had a comparable experience in another sport? Can you remember the experience or, if you have not had one, can you imagine what it would be like?

Sport Spectating as an Encounter With Wisdom

Watching a game as knowledgeable spectators can put us in contact with certain truths or bits of wisdom. Because we care so much for the game and because we cheer with such intensity for our teams, these messages may actually come through more clearly and forcefully in stadiums than they do in lecture halls or churches. Some contemporary thinkers believe that sport has taken the place of religion as an institution that allows us to experience ritual, find inspiration, and become reacquainted with important cultural values. Novak (1976) believes that sport spectators actually see, upon occasion, how the human race should live:

If I had to give one single reason for my love of sports it would be this. I love the tests of the human spirit. I love to see defeated teams refuse to die. I love to see impossible odds confronted. I love to see impossible dares accepted. I love to see the incredible grace lavished on simple plays—the simple flashing beauty of perfect form—but, even more I love to see the heart that refuses to give in, refuses to panic, seizes opportunity, slips through defenses, exerts itself far beyond capacity, forges momentarily of its bodily habitat an instrument of almost perfect will. I love it when the other side is winning and there are only moments left; I love it when it would be reasonable to be reconciled to defeat, but one will not, cannot; I love it when a last set of calculated, reckless, free and impassioned efforts is crowned with success. When I see others play that way, I am full of admiration, of gratitude. That is the way I believe the human race should live. When human beings actually accomplish it, it is for me as if the intentions of the Creator were suddenly limpid before our eyes: as though into the

Sport is a library of sorts for movement wisdom.

fiery heart of the Creator we had momentary insight. (pp. 150-151)

Of course, sport participation and spectating may not always reach as high as wisdom. Those who play casually or only to get fit may be refreshed and healthy but will probably not encounter some of life's deeper mysteries in sport. Those who have little skill and lack creativity in their play may have some fun, but will not experience the power of movement to communicate paradoxical truths. And those who watch games merely to avoid boredom may be sedated or entertained but are unlikely to experience the more profound insights contained in those contests. But here it is enough to see that sport can be regarded as a repository for truths, a library of sorts for movement wisdom. We can gain access to this library in two ways: by becoming skilled performers and knowledgeable and attentive spectators. We can "read the same books" that inspired and informed our predecessors.

SUMMARY BREAK

There are at least two ways to have wisdom and transmit it:

1. to possess a notion reflectively and share it through words, as the classical orators did, and
2. to live wisdom immediately as a fine performer and transmit it through one's craft, as musicians, painters, and athletes do.

When we encounter wisdom as abstract truths and understand and act on them, we are freed in important ways. We avoid errors of narrow thinking, traditional biases, and mindless habit.

When we encounter lived wisdom as skilled performers ourselves, we embody wisdom and experience it firsthand. As spectators who watch others perform, we see wisdom in action, and it may rub off on us. We can be inspired by the excellence we experience or see; it may move us to try harder ourselves; it may remind us of some of our possibilities that are yet unfulfilled; we may return home to rededicate ourselves to practice. We see hard looking easy in a professional golfer's swing, five basketball players performing as one, grace and confidence pushing out fear and timidity in Olympic ski jumping. Again, we are freed in important ways. We avoid errors of narrow thinking, traditional biases, and mindless habits—those suggesting that hard is always hard, that five is forever five, and that jumping into space over ice and snow requires nervous self-concern and caution.

Motor Skill and the Exploration Tradition

This is what we provide to our students

In terms of the exploration tradition, it is easy to see how movement professionals might make contributions as change agents. The freedom found in this tradition has more to do with skills, tendencies, habits, attitudes, orientations, and continuing inquiry than it does with truths, propositions, contemplation, and recitation. Obviously, activity instructors teach skills, tendencies, habits, attitudes, and orientations. And they provide the wherewithal, in a sense, for continuing inquiry, discovery, and growth. So long as they are not disqualified on dualistic grounds (i.e., that their skills are merely physical ones), they would seem to occupy a central position as educators in the exploration tradition.

We can legitimately claim to make measurable contributions in at least five areas that promote human liberation: discovery, exploration, expression, invention, and creation. We may do other things too, but these should be sufficient to show our potential as educators in this tradition.

—freedom to find

Discovery. Human movement is a dialogue between persons and a spatiotemporal world. The dialogue is given life by purposes—to play, to win, to score, to kick, to show. As the dialogue unfolds, discoveries typically trip along one after another. People learn about themselves—their personalities, their capabilities, their intensity, their determination, their generosity, their fears, their tenderness, their prickliness, their capacity for love, their potential for hate. This information does not come inscribed on parchment. It comes as human beings jump, through their victories and defeats, when they swing or pirouette, as they fall or dive, while they pass to a teammate or get shut out of an offensive scheme. This process of discovering can be valued for its own sake.

People also learn about their spatiotemporal world—whether it is friendly or hostile, whether it will hold them up, whether a certain distance can be reached in a short time, what different rhythms feel like, how different grips press upon the hand, what is too high or too far or too heavy or too light, whether a caught baseball can feel like a feather, whether a rapidly approaching tennis ball can be experienced in slow motion, whether a golf club can be experienced as having nerves.

It is not that people stop to think about all these and many other discoveries that they come upon in their movement world. Mostly they simply live through them. Many times they enjoy them or find them irritating or surprising in passing. Occasionally, some discovery is important enough to get people to stop their flow of experience and think about it. They stand and ponder, or recollect some remarkable event later at home. This process of discovering can be appreciated for its own sake. It can provide an important freedom, the freedom to find.

But are these discoveries at a level that might be called impressive or meritorious? This, of course, depends much on a person's level of skill. Primitive skills generate impoverished

Human movement is a dialogue between people and a temporal/spatial world.

discoveries. Beginning tennis capabilities typically provide beginning discoveries about the tennis-engaged self and the tennis-oriented world. More on this will have to be said under inventiveness and creativity.
— freedom to look

Exploration. This speaks to the scope of human discoveries. If exploration skills and tendencies are weak, discoveries will tend to be local, incomplete, narrow, parochial. On the other hand, if exploration capabilities are strong, discoveries will likely be more global and comprehensive.

Performers all know that as movement skills become better, new movement questions are generated in a never-ending stream. When basketball players get better, for example, they encounter new questions about what they can do. When they explore some of these movement uncertainties, their skill improves. In turn, this raises new questions. How far away can performers stand from the person they are guarding and still be effective? How quickly can they jump? How subtly can they fake a move and still get the opponent to react?

There are also questions about nongame space and time and the extent to which they can be explored. How many places have performers seen—to what locations can their walking, climbing, swimming, bicycling, jogging, and skateboarding skills take them? How are their dialogues going with mountains, valleys, rivers, lakes, sand, wind, rocks, textures, and odors? Where have performers been? What have they explored? How many places are they free to visit?

Likewise it can be asked, how much of the temporal world have they experienced—to what rhythms, and durations, and deadlines can their dancing, swinging, jumping, pushing, pulling, batting, and skipping take them? How are their dialogues going with syncopation, even beats, waltz rhythms, jazz time, long times, short times, open time, closed time, slow time, fast time? The process of exploring in these many ways, the process of learning what it involves, can be appreciated and valued for its own sake. It can provide an important freedom, the freedom to look.

But are such explorations at a level that can be regarded as impressive or meritorious? That depends again on the athlete's or dancer's level of skill. Entry-level skill brings with it entry-level explorations. Spend only a short time being introduced to the skills of orienteering, and performers will stay close to home. Live with sport or dance or other movement skills for 20 or 30 or 40 years, and they will not only be leaving "home" but will be venturing off into uncharted movement territory.

— freedom to say.

Expression. All human beings interpret raw experiences, and they all need to tell about them. They have different perspectives, unique histories, particular sets of genes, distinct biceps, and so on. A certain situation in soccer strikes one player differently than it would another. An inside fastball means, at least in part, different things to one baseball player than it does to another. As Eleanor Metheny (1972) was fond of saying and indeed once wrote, sport is "a flow of meanings without speech" and "of as many meanings as of men" (p. 226). Human beings need to tell what their experiences are. They need to have a way of telling their story. They want to get it out of themselves—whether they do it in play or work, by pen or through a football, in prose, music, sculpture, painting, mime, social dance, modern dance, bicycling, or swimming.

The stories people tell and the meanings they express are not always clear, formal, or explicit. Some individuals, at least part of the time, may not even have any clear intention of telling or interpreting. There may not be anyone there to watch or listen. Nevertheless, they are quite unable to move without affixing their unique signature to their actions. To be sure, the more machinelike people are, the more faint the image of their name on their work. But the good news is that people can never become wholly machines; their signature can never disappear entirely. Their cockiness, the way they hold their head, the ease with which they move, the timings they

use to complete a gesture—all these and more say, "Respect is appropriate. Interpretation in progress! Unique perspective being expressed!" Every sport gesture, every dynamic form, every playful movement comes signed by its author whether that person wishes to remain anonymous or not. This process of expressing in unique ways, this learning, can be appreciated and valued for its own sake. It can provide an important freedom, the freedom to say.

But is it possible that this expressiveness through movement is immature or in some other way substandard? Certainly it can be. Practice very little and performers' "vocabularies" will be small, their "syntax" immature, their "sentence structure" elementary. Keep skills at beginning or low intermediate levels and performers will be dancing or competing by the numbers and will not be interpreting much at all. Keep skills underdeveloped,

Every sport gesture comes signed by its author.

and players will be too preoccupied with the mechanics of the activity to say or tell much at all. But become accomplished at something and performers can say the same thing a thousand different ways. They can share subtleties of meaning and insight that perhaps can be put to words only through poetry.

Inventiveness. *Freedom to modify* Polanyi and Prosch (1975) have argued that inventiveness is one of two important hallmarks of any human intellect that is operating at its greatest capacity. (The other is creativity, a concept discussed in the next section.) According to the authors, inventiveness requires the reconciliation of what they call *contraries*. Contraries might be things that are understood to have little or nothing to do with one another. Reconciliation in this case would be the illumination of a hidden relationship. Or contraries might even be commonly understood to be opposed to one another. Reconciliation in this case would be the illumination of a positive relationship where a negative one was thought to exist.

There was a time when no one saw any relationship between little pieces of metal and improved running in baseball—that is, until someone put metal and shoes together in the form of baseball spikes. There was a time when people thought that putting a football up in the air for grabs and retaining possession while improving field position were actually contrary ideas—that is, until Sammy Baugh sent well-directed balls to teammates through an invention called the forward pass. And there was a time when experts in track and field thought that a back-to-the-ground position and gaining optimum height in high jumping were contradictions—that is, until someone named Fosbury put these two things together and showed them to be very compatible indeed.

Inventors are clever, insightful, shrewd. They see relationships that others miss. Inventive souls discover more fully, explore more completely, and express more thoroughly, subtly, and unpredictably. In this sense, inventiveness is a qualifier for the skills of discovery, exploration, and expression. Partly liberated people, in other words, have the capability to discover, explore, and express. Greater freedom comes with the ability to do these things, at least occasionally, with a bit of inventiveness and uncommon insight.

Inventions like the forward pass and Fosbury Flop are high-visibility, historic accomplishments. Most sports have their analogues of these sorts of inventions that end up revolutionizing their games. But inventiveness occurs much less dramatically and much more frequently among all dancers, athletes, and other movers who confront problems in the absence of pat answers. Some experimentation is in order. A modification of some coach's tip or a textbook recommendation is needed. On occasion a modest, local invention takes place. A novel stance is tried out in basketball, a different swing thought is used in golf, a different training regimen is experimented with in field hockey, a distinctive practice technique is employed in football, an unusual feel is focused upon in modifying a swimming stroke. New connections are made and, where these connections hold up, new (though usually small-scale) inventions emerge. This process of inventing can be appreciated for its own sake. It can provide an important freedom, the freedom to modify.

As with discovery, exploration, and expressiveness, inventiveness admits of degrees. There is such a thing as low-level inventiveness where connections or compatibilities between contraries are really quite transparent to most everyone. But again, when skill levels improve and when sense perceptual acuity is greater and movement capabilities more refined, a whole host of new inventive possibilities present themselves. Beginners probably produce only occasional and primitive inventions during an afternoon game. They count on using the script, past instructions, or a few simple game thoughts.

More accomplished performers probably produce regular and more sophisticated inventions during a similar afternoon game. They count, in part, on using spontaneously encountered inventions and are more comfortable in leaving the script at home.

Creativity. — *Freedom to solve a resolve.* The difference between inventiveness and creativity, according to Polanyi and Prosch (1975), is that whereas contraries melt away once an invention takes place, they reemerge once creative behavior has come to an end. For example, with the Fosbury Flop, once the connections between a certain positioning and jumping were pointed out, their compatibility was easy to see. The same with the forward pass, the jump shot in basketball, the hit and run in baseball, new materials for sports equipment, and so on. Once the invention is laid out, the mystery, the apparent unconnectedness, or the possible contrariness dissolves forever.

Not so with creativity. Here there are contraries too, but they are so opaque, so durable, so complex, that their resolution can be only temporary. Performers appreciate the resolution and therefore know that one is possible while they are watching or otherwise experiencing it, but then when the experience comes to an end, the harmonious illusion disappears. They are left wondering once again how these contraries could ever have joined hands and whether they will ever do so again.

Some creativity sounds a bit spooky, mystical, and simply illogical. As we saw previously in this chapter, this is the level at which athletes live wisdom and sport spectators can be inspired by it. We noticed that many of the best examples of this level of play border on the inexplicable. Playing golf with soft hands, or being an effective defensive lineman in football with effortless effort, or running slower to run faster all speak to creative resolutions of contraries that must be experienced by advanced athletes or knowledgeable spectators to be fully appreciated and understood. Getting more skilled

will increase the chances that these resolutions will show up, but performers cannot mandate an appearance. They know that possibilities for harmonized contraries are always there, but they have no fail-safe buttons to push that will make them come forward. They practice, and play or dance, and practice some more. But then they must hope for a bit of grace at the right time. If they are lucky, they fall into remarkable zones of experience where previous contraries, everyday hurdles, and common frustrating experiences melt away. Hard becomes easy, disconnected parts turn into all of one piece, left becomes right, too fast turns into deliciously slow, a struggling or uneven rhythm is now smooth and steady.

At a more global level there are other possibilities for creative experiences. Can an opponent actually be loved, even during periods of fierce competition? Can a longed-for victory be experienced as a profound defeat? Or can a defeat be lived as a fundamental success? Can teammates become so attuned to one another that they know where each person is and where they are going and what they plan to do, even though no word is spoken and no apparent signal is given? Can opponents be so well known that a performer senses where they are, where they are going, and what they plan to do in spite of the fact that these opponents try to keep all of this hidden and a secret?

There is a rough analogy here with music, and perhaps too with some of the other arts. It is said that all accomplished musicians eventually make the transition from merely playing notes to making music. Of course, it is no mean feat to play notes correctly, particularly with demanding pieces of music. Some pianists, for instance, will study for years and years simply to acquire the basic skills needed to play the notes correctly. But it is yet another step, and a most critical one at that, to be able to make music (see Sudnow's magical little book on improvisational piano [1978]).

It is here that creativity comes into play. The limits of musical interpretation are tested, intuited, retested, and resolved. New contraries are put together with an ear for the appearance of fresh musical power and meaning. It is here that the performer and audience alike may be carried away by a new musical illusion. After the performance they are refreshed and grateful. But when those musical contraries (that just moments ago were resolved) are durable, there can be no after-the-performance explanation that fully satisfies the intellect. Even the pianist, if he is honest, will not be able to say just what happened at the keyboard any better than Yogi Berra could describe what occurred in the batter's box. Some artists and athletes—merely to satisfy reporters, newspaper readers, television broadcasters, scientists, and others who have little idea of what it is like to enter the kingdom (Murphy, 1972)—will dutifully and seriously spew out some sentences about what they saw, heard, felt, and thought. They all know that if they really saw and thought all of what they reported, they could not have done what in fact they did. In any case, the process of creativity can be appreciated and valued for its own sake. It can provide a freedom, the freedom to solve and resolve.

Powers of creativity, like those of discovery, exploration, expressiveness, and inventiveness can be relatively well- or poorly developed through an infinite number of degrees. Thus, it is possible that the exploration tradition changes, as regards creativity, can be low-grade, unimpressive, or insignificant. Low powers of creativity put an unfortunate cap on discovery (durable opposites are never found out to be potentially harmonious), on exploration (performers never look in unlikely, contradictory, or unfriendly places), on expressiveness (what is "said" is rarely new or unusual), and on inventiveness

(there is not enough playing around to set the stage for inventions).

PHILOSOPHIC EXERCISE

Are *you* liberally educated in motor- and muscle-oriented ways? Take the short inventory on p. 201 to see how well you have been freed in wisdom and exploration ways.

Motor Skill as Mainstream Education: Strengths and Weaknesses

Do the changes we make in our students as we teach them sport, games, and play matter? Are they significant? Is a human being significantly handicapped for not having those skills? The following dialogue, which outlines the strengths and weaknesses of our arguments about the significance of the wisdom and exploration traditions, should help us draw at least tentative conclusions before proceeding, in the next chapter, to look more closely at the nature of sport, games, and play.

Pro. Arendt (1958) has said that "the earth is the very quintessance of the human condition." People cannot choose to have bodies or not; they cannot choose whether they will need motor- and muscle-oriented skills or not. All that is a given. From the first cell division of their life, to birth, to maturation, to decline, to death, to dust—human beings belong to the earth. If they are to make a mark, do something special, have some fun, or gain a bit of freedom, they always do it, at least partly, by pushing off against the earth, by moving.

Activity Liberation Inventory

Rating Scale:

Strongly Disagree						Strongly Agree
1	2	3	4	5	6	7

1. I am a highly skilled athlete (i.e., at least NCAA Division III, varsity-level capability) or accomplished dancer in at least one sport or dance form. 4

2. I have trained under fine coaches/teachers in a single sport/dance activity for at least 5 years. 6

3. I have advanced intermediate skill (i.e., I have mastered the basics under competent instruction and am a somewhat creative performer) in at least two other sport or dance forms. 6

4. I am a highly knowledgeable spectator of at least two sport or dance forms (i.e., I have spent much of my life following or watching them; I understand the subtle strategies of the activities; I can see slight variations in better and worse performance.)

5. I enjoy a level of strength, skill, and conditioning that allows me to participate fully and play indefinitely (i.e., I am in or near the top 10% of all players or dancers on these factors). 6

Add up your score. A score of 25 or better would give you good credentials as a liberally educated individual in the activity domain. Such a score would indicate that you can experience and transmit wisdom as a performer, see it and appreciate it as a spectator, and make yet additional discoveries as a highly skilled athlete or dancer. A score of 15 or lower would indicate the opposite. As regards activity, you cannot experience, see, or do much. If your score places you somewhere in the middle, your liberal and liberating education is in progress and still needs some attention.

Given the necessity of embodiment and the inescapability of movement, physical education must be central to human growth and liberation.

Con. While it is true that all people are embodied and movement cannot be avoided, not everyone needs to be freed in ways permitted by motor skills. There are many kinds of content and truth that are worth having, and there are many skills that allow people to inquire and discover. In fact, truths about government, religion, philosophy, human relations, and the like traditionally have been regarded as far more significant than lived understandings about time, space, and force relationships in sport. And academic skills having to do with computing, writing, speaking, reflecting, deducing, inducing, speculating, and concluding have been regarded historically as far more important than such skills as moving, gesturing, walking, posturing, spatially exploring, or rhythmically expressing.

Thus, because humans can be liberated through wisdom and skill in many ways, and because freedoms associated with academic subjects may be more important than those we promote, physical education should, at most, be an optional element in liberal education.

Pro. It is true that some people have reasonably good lives in spite of the fact that they are ignorant of kinesthetic truths and that they have very limited abilities to discover, explore, express, invent and create in motor-oriented ways. But it may also be true that these people live under a considerable handicap. Is it conceivable that a person might have a good life without, for example, understanding the important truths of democracy and political freedom and without having the reasoning skills of a knowledgeable citizen? Yes, but even so, nobody would want to place a person under such a handicap if it were not necessary to do so. Why then should human beings be expected to live with the handicap of primitive motor skills, primitive spectating abilities, an inability to encounter the wisdom of the movement domain in sport, dance, play, and games?

Thus, because an inability to move well and observe cultural games and play knowledgeably places people at distinct disadvantages, physical education should be regarded as a critical element of liberal education.

Con. It may be true that broadly conceptualized motor skills taught in the right way could lead to more important liberations than is often admitted. But it is easier to see music, art, and dance as including important lived truths and life-enhancing skills than it is to see the centrality of jogging, baseball, jump rope, table tennis, and square dancing.

If physical education's content became movement education, its stock would go up as a contributor to liberal education. If it were to de-emphasize extrinsic values like physical fitness and recreation and turn away from such narrow subject matter as sport, games, and play, once again it might be seen as more significant educationally.

However, because most physical education is promoted today as a means to health and fitness, and because it still relies on such content as sport, games, and play, physical education does not deserve a place in liberal education.

Pro. It has already been acknowledged that exercise as a health-promoting, extrinsic value is not central to liberal education. However, it is not clear that sport, games, and play are as educationally trivial as some people think they are. Many motor-oriented activities in this modern, push-button world come in the form of games and play. Because not as many people must move vigorously in field or factory today, they invent movement needs and settings (in games), and they spontaneously accept interesting invitations to move (in play). Moreover, much of what is culturally important, many of the meanings and values that are significant in any country, are transmitted and infused with new life through games and play. Much of the glue of life—that which makes peoples' diverse daily activities cohere or form something of a story line—comes from games and play.

Thus, if sport, games, and play have important cultural roles to fulfill, physical education should be an integral part of liberal education. All work and only the study of abstract academics with no games, sport, or play not only make Jack and Jill dull people; it can also make them cultural nomads and misfits.

Con. It has not been shown that cultural development is tied very tightly to such matters as sport, games, and play. Surely growth in cultural meanings and values comes in other ways too.

Pro. Because so much learning occurs at very early ages, and because children are so taken with games, play, and rhythmic activities of various sorts, what alternate methods for cultural education and grounding can be superior to the activities of physical education? Whether or not it can be proven empirically that sport, games, and play have the most influence in promoting and advancing cultural meanings and values for children and youth, they surely have a major impact.

Thus, physical education should be included in liberal education, particularly at the preschool and elementary levels.

Con. Even if the aspects of the wisdom and exploration traditions that come through sport, games, and play are important in some cultural sense, it must be acknowledged that skill in the absence of theory provides only an inferior kind of liberation. Because performers cannot explain what they do, because they do not act on the basis of known principles, they are not truly free. Liberal education promotes skill that is informed with theory, not skill that stands on its own.

Pro. That is not true. Liberal education has a long history of promoting skill in the absence of theory. Students are taught to write without necessarily understanding the principles of paragraph formation. They are taught to read without knowing the psychology of word recognition. They are taught to count without comprehending the arbitrariness of different numerical symbols and systems. Moreover, this is done by choice and design. There simply is not enough time to teach both theory and skill—at least to the levels at which they become powerful. Because having the skill to write, read, and count is the crucial acquisition, it is emphasized. Why then criticize sport, dance, and game performers as being uninformed? For

them too, having the skill is what counts more.

Consequently, physical education deserves a place in liberal education.

Review

Professionals in sport, exercise science, and physical education, like individuals in other fields, have a duty to change people in positive ways. The question becomes, What sort of change can and should physical educators strive to make in their students, athletes, or clients? Should it be relatively narrow, training- and service-oriented change? Or should it be broad, liberating change of the sort traditionally supported in liberal education?

Skeptics doubt that professionals in physical education can make broad or significant educational changes for at least three reasons:

1. They deal with the body-machine only or primarily.
2. Even if they work with the whole person, they deal with relatively narrow issues—as do teachers in the manual arts of woodworking shop, home economics, or auto repair.
3. Even if they deal with whole persons, and teach important movement activities, they train and indoctrinate more than educate; they aim at developing habits, not thoughtful creativity.

Strong counterarguments, many of which were developed at length in previous chapters, can be made for each of these three claims.

A fourth claim that a major portion of the profession's content (sport, games, and play) appears relatively trivial when compared to the fine arts requires a review of the characteristics of liberal education. Based on two interpretations of education—that whole persons are freed by (1) coming in contact with classical truths or wisdom and (2) gaining the skills needed to explore and discover additional or evolving truths—growth and learning in sport, games, and play can be seen as making contributions to both traditions of liberal education.

Sally McIntyre, the junior high school physical education teacher you met at the beginning of this chapter, should be able to counter the claims of her colleague about the triviality of her work and her profession. While her subject matter includes "fun and games," this may take the form of mainstream liberal education. Unless she has other reasons for doing so, she need not hide sport, games, and play in favor of fitness-recreational service functions or redefine her content as movement education.

Looking Ahead

You should now be ready to draw some important conclusions about the nature of your profession as one that serves whole people, promotes important values in sport, games, and play (in addition to dance and exercise) and thus, produces changes that matter. In the next chapter you will take a closer look at sport, games, and play to determine their specific qualities.

Checking Your Understanding

1. In sequence, what are four reasons for placing physical education on one of the lower rungs of the educational ladder?
2. Which of these reasons is most powerful and why?

3. Why is it not wise to trade sport, dance, exercise, play, and games for movement education?
4. Why is it not wise to trade sport, games, and play for fitness, character development, or recreation?
5. What are some examples of the wisdom tradition of education in sport participation and spectating? Of the exploration tradition, through discovery, exploration, expression, inventiveness, and creativity?

Key Terms

Change agents, p. 181

Dualistic idealism, p. 181

Humanism, p. 183

Liberal (mainstream) education, p. 188

Wisdom tradition, p. 189

Exploration tradition, p. 189

Discovery, p. 195

Exploration, p. 196

Expression, p. 197

Inventiveness, p. 198

Creativity, p. 199

Further Reading

For an account of liberal education, see Kimball (1986). Novak (1976), Santayana (1972), and Bellah et al. (1991) give accounts of sport under the wisdom tradition. See Murphy (1972), Slusher (1967), Metheny (1968), Polanyi and Prosch (1975), and Polanyi (1966) for analyses of sport skills under the exploration tradition.

Chapter 9

The Significance of Games and Play

Fred Oliphant is the head of a large suburban sport fitness center in Illinois. He is in the final stages of hiring an activity instructor who will teach sports and games, oversee a fitness program, and run leagues for youngsters between the ages of 6 and 18. Mr. Oliphant has narrowed the pool of candidates to two finalists. Both candidates have just graduated from the same state university with degrees in exercise and sport science.

Candidate A: Jessica Arnold

Hometown: Los Angeles, California

GPA: 3.48

Personal statement: "I took pride in my academics and worked very hard to achieve the grades I received."

Letters of recommendation: An excellent, serious, conscientious student. Good work ethic, trustworthy, reliable. Writes and thinks well. Excellent in science curriculum. Has taken courses to broaden activity background.

Curricular emphasis: Took extra coursework in fitness programming. Wrote a research paper on motivating children to stay fit.

Hobbies: Recreational reading, cooking

Professional philosophy: "I hope to increase the activity levels of children to promote their health and well-being."

Candidate B: Sigmund Claar

Hometown: Moline, Illinois

GPA: 3.17

Personal statement: "It was hard for me to find enough time to do everything in college that I wanted to do. With the time taken by varsity sports and the outing club, my grades occasionally suffered."

Letters of recommendation: A fine athlete and good student. Excellent background in a number of sports. (Father is a high school coach.) Outgoing personality, popular, good sense of humor. Reliable but also innovative, something of a free spirit.

Curricular emphasis: Elected extra courses in performance.

Hobbies: baseball, outing club, personal fitness activities, building model planes, collecting baseball cards

Professional philosophy: "I want to help children enjoy sport and exercise as much as I do."

Fred Oliphant has had interviews with both candidates and regards each one to be competent and qualified. He recognizes the fact that they are quite different in talent and personality, but he also realizes that each candidate has important strengths. He wonders which one will make the best activity instructor.

If Mr. Oliphant wanted to hire the individual who has come into more contact with movement wisdom as a performer, whom would he select? If he were concerned to hire the best playmaker, someone who understood the kids, their background, and their midwestern values, whom would he select?

In the last chapter, you saw that performance skills themselves can meet general criteria of mainstream education in at least two ways. They can liberate individuals by putting them into contact with timeless movement truths and by giving them the capability to explore the movement world for additional insights. While this laid a foundation for the value of sport, games, and play in education, it did not assure it. Questions could still be asked about the significance of liberation in these specific environments. Thus, you still need to examine the specific qualities of sport, games, and play to determine their educational value.

IN THIS CHAPTER, YOU WILL

- **examine the nature and value of games (including sport);**
- **examine the nature and value of play; and**
- **evaluate the practical implications of a game and play philosophy for personnel, curriculum, and methodology.**

At this point in your philosophic travels you know that your field has the potential to liberate people in a number of ways. You have seen that physical education can promote changes that qualify as mainstream education under both of two dominant traditions in Western history. In spite of this, you may still be uneasy about your profession's subject matter—particularly if it is understood to be *mere* games and play (in addition to exercise and dance). You will need to continue your reflective journey in order to see games and play more clearly and then assess their significance.

Why do games exist in every culture, and why have they often received the devoted attention of many citizens—both young and old?

How can something be "only a game" and yet generate million-dollar contracts, cause large stadiums to be built, and attract hundreds of thousands of fans?

Why are children encouraged to play while adults are often told to be more mature and serious? Do you still play regularly? If so, where, how, and with what? Where are your favorite playgrounds?

Can too much play be harmful? Can physical education teachers promote a spirit

of play and still help students achieve other good things—ends like getting physically fit, staying healthy, and developing good character?

Our Profession's Subject Matter

It is safe to say that no professional field is any stronger than its content will allow it to be. We cannot change people in significant ways if our subject matter is not up to the task. No matter how false mind-body dualism is, no matter how much society may need some of the services we offer, no matter how we might rank our traditional values, and no matter how well we fit the general framework of mainstream education, if games and play do not bring with them important intrinsic values (like the freedoms associated with liberal education), we will be relegated to lower rungs of the educational ladder. Thus, if our content cannot carry the load we are asking of it, it is important to find that out now.

Throughout this book I have identified the content of our profession as a portion of the human movement domain—the portion that includes sport, dance, exercise, games, and play. In this chapter, we will focus on two of these items—games and play.

Just how special are games and play? Are we actually living the good life when we are within their grasp, or are we just preparing for future experiences that are intrinsically valuable? Are we somehow doing something particularly and unmistakably significant when we participate in games or become captured by the spirit of play? Or are we merely trifling, recreating, or recharging our batteries for more important things to come?

In order to answer these questions about the significance of games and play, we need to work on some philosophic descriptions. We need to see more clearly what games and play are and why falling under their spell might be a good thing.

Features of Games

Suits's (1972) definition of **games** may still be the clearest and most accurate one available. He said that

> to play a game is to engage in activity directed toward bringing about a specific state of affairs, using only means permitted by specific rules, where the means permitted by the rules are more limited in scope than they would be in the absence of the rules, and where the sole reason for accepting such limitation is to make possible such activity.

Said more simply, ''Playing a game is the voluntary attempt to overcome unnecessary obstacles'' (p. 22).

It may sound strange to say that there are places and times in daily life when people voluntarily search out problems or cultivate difficulties. Problems and difficulties are typically regarded as things to be avoided. Interestingly however, when looking for a game, we take the opposite stance. Problems and difficulties are understood to be good things—so good that we even search them out and voluntarily accept them.

Of course, game problems are usually not the sort of necessary and unwelcome difficulties that people face in daily life. They are not about real health, real financial woes, real marital problems, and real job insecurities. Game problems, in contrast to real-life dilemmas, have to do with things like solving clues for crossword puzzles, getting little white golf balls into small holes using only unwieldy sticks, and jumping over bars that are a challenging distance from the ground. These are fun problems!

Nevertheless, it is important to realize that they are genuine problems nonetheless. Games offer a cure for the blahs, for the boredom we feel when we wake up with no continents to conquer, no plagues to survive, no brave quests to undertake. Games are particularly inviting in the face of routine—the prospect of just more school, or just more work, or just more of the same old thing!

Because there are games, our free time need not be empty time. We wonder if we can bike a certain distance before exhaustion sets in. We set up a tennis match with a worthy opponent. We see if we can take a different route home from work but still arrive in less time. Games lurk everywhere for those who need a little stimulation.

It could be that people function best at certain levels of arousal, and games are a way to modulate arousal—elevate it when bored and lower it when nervous or frightened. It could be that people need to show their competence, and games offer a vehicle for such displays (Ellis, 1973; Levy, 1978). There could be any number of other chemical, physiological, or psychological mechanisms that might help to explain the presence and value of games. But that is not part of our philosophical concern here.

What is of concern are the distinctive characteristics of games, those things that make game challenges different from, say, challenges when we are working or trying to behave ethically. Three features must be highlighted if we are to understand the uniqueness of games (Suits, 1972).

The Presence of Inefficient Means

Games require the adoption of means that are less efficient for completing some task than they could or need to be. This criterion distinguishes games from most of our daily activities, in which it makes no sense to complicate our jobs unnecessarily. We typically want to finish our work as efficiently, quickly, and as well as possible. We pick the most effective means available. When we are driving home from school or work, for example, we do not typically look for ways to make that trip more challenging. We simply want to get home!

In games, however, we knowingly select inefficient means. We understand, for example, that there are more direct and foolproof methods for getting a golf ball into a hole, such as carrying it from the tee to the green and placing it in the cup. But game players adopt a less efficient and far more difficult means of getting the ball there: using a golf club, negotiating a narrow fairway, avoiding trees that can get in the way, and so on.

Yet, the question arises, Are there not other activities that require the use of inefficient means and yet are not games? Morally governed behavior is limited and yet is not a game simply because it is constrained. For example, an ethical person may insist on paying every dime of her federal taxes, feeding every parking meter where she parks, driving no faster than the posted speed limit, and painstakingly teaching her young children right from wrong. Yet, she has not chosen these more challenging and, in some ways, less efficient ways of living her life because she is bored and wants to turn it into a game.

Consequently, some additional characteristic must be identified to distinguish between two things (morality and games), both of which rely on the adoption of inefficient means.

The Voluntary Acceptance of Limited Means

This distinguishing characteristic is related to reasons for accepting longer or more complicated routes to goals when shorter or easier ones are available. Game means are accepted "where the sole reason for accepting such limitation is to make possible such activity" (Suits, 1972, p. 22). That is, longer routes are accepted in order to have the experience of trying to reach the goal while taking these more difficult avenues.

Businesspeople who accept constraints imposed by ethics do not do so for this reason. They do not choose restrictive ethical avenues because they want to have the fun of trying to make profits in spite of them. Rather they accept these limitations because their conscience demands it, or because their religious commitments require it.

This reasoning has led some to think that game playing is not a serious activity. Because game players purposely adopt inefficient means, it is thought, they must not be particularly committed to reaching their goal. Game players, therefore, must be trifling.

The Adoption of Serious and Nonserious Attitudes

It is true that some people play games as if they do not much matter. But others play as if games were all that counted in life. People, in other words, approach games in very different ways. In fact, we frequently hear the comment that he or she took a game too seriously or not seriously enough.

Is it possible to adopt a goal, impose artificially restricted means in achieving that goal, and then dedicate one's very life to reaching the goal? It would seem that it is, and there are any number of elite athletes whose remarkably demanding training programs give testimony to the fact that it can be done. On the other hand, is it possible to adopt a goal, impose artificially restricted means in achieving that goal, and then attempt to reach that goal only halfheartedly? Again, it would seem that it is. In fact, there are any number of reluctant game players who participate as if they would rather be doing something else.

Consequently, to participate in a game is not necessarily to dabble and trifle or halfheartedly and disinterestedly engage oneself in solving a problem. It may, in fact, invite levels of interest and commitment that are not even given to one's daily work. This is an important point, for the potential of games, as we will see later, is only tapped when games are meaningful and captivating and, thus, when they are taken seriously in this sense.

Features of Play

The issues of seriousness and importance help to distinguish games from **play**. We already saw that games can be taken seriously. However, there are two ways in which games encourage intensity and concern: (1) the participating, the experiencing, the doing of a game itself may be important, and (2) the consequence of the doing can be significant. Game participants, in other words, can be serious about the doing itself (it is fun, and they would play even if nothing important ever came of it; traditionally our amateur athletes play this way) or serious regarding the effects of the doing. (It is not fun, and they would not play if nothing important ever

came of it; traditionally our professional athletes play this way.)

Play, in contrast to games, is necessarily unimportant in terms of its effect—that is, in respect to what happens after the doing is over. True players love the doing; they are attracted by the possibility of participating; they give little thought to outcomes or consequences that do not affect the quality of the experience itself. When games are experienced in the spirit of play, it is the striving to solve game problems or win game contests that is important, not the effects of having succeeded or won. Several qualities help to distinguish the play spirit from other things.

Play Is Prerational and Spontaneous

Play is fundamentally **prerational**. Something is prerational when it is done in the absence of calculation, not because of it (rational) and not in spite of it (irrational). This absence of prudent calculation gives play a spontaneous quality. Players throw themselves into sport before they would (or could) ever know why. Players accept play invitations offered by ball fields, rose gardens, mud puddles, and countless other playgrounds as soon as they are received. And they are accepted only because they are provocative, not because they make sense and not because the player is required to pursue them.

If games are for problem seekers, play is for lovers. Players give themselves to their playgrounds, play equipment, and playmates and have been known to forget what time it is, miss dinner, court physical disaster, encounter exhaustion, and get caught doing silly things. Play often carries its own intoxicating momentum, and players frequently find it difficult to stop their activity

Play often carries its own intoxicating momentum.

and return to the world of prudence, sensible planning, and concern about the future.

Play Is Freely Chosen Activity

Play is freely chosen (Huizinga, 1950). It is not the consequence of duty, fear, prudent thinking, or even of courageous self-sacrifice. It is not what good, sensible, or mature people have to do. It is what they (as well as all others) want to do. It is what the mature and immature, young and old, and males and females are invited to do by a world they find interesting.

Any good consequences that come from play are serendipitous. They are not planned for or intended, though after the fact of playing they may be gladly accepted. Bad consequences from play likewise are not intended and, if they occur, are unfortunate. After the fact they must sometimes be endured.

The Relationship Between Play and Games

Play is more a way of doing things, a quality of experience, than a type of event. Consequently, activities like games can be experienced either as play or not play. The boxes on pages 212 and 213 describe such an experience. A game that is experienced as play is one that has importance in the first sense described above—that is, the meeting and solving of the problem is important (it is enjoyed for its own sake), whatever the postgame consequences might be. A game that is not conducted in the play spirit is one that has importance in the second sense—that is, the meeting and solving of the problem is tolerated for the sake of what is really valued—namely, various intended consequences of the completed activity like trophies, money, and fame.

Falling In and Out of Play

Play's spontaneity gives it a fragile and delicate quality. Play may come unexpectedly and quickly, but it can depart just as abruptly. On a single afternoon during one game, it is possible to fall into and out of play many times. Here is an example of such an experience.

I am asked by some friends to play a round of golf. I am tired and preoccupied by some unfinished work, but I reluctantly agree to play because these friends have asked before, and I have turned them down repeatedly. (*Analysis*: This preparticipation scenario is not very promising regarding play, for it appears that my involvement is provoked by a sense of duty to my friends. In other words, I do not anticipate having a good time at golf. I do anticipate feeling some satisfaction over the result of my having played. Regardless I am headed into a game—a specific unnecessarily difficult test called golf.)

I play two holes in a perfunctory way, getting a bogey on the first and a double bogey on the second. While I enjoy being with my colleagues and get involved in an interesting conversation with them, I am merely going through the motions of golf. Yes, I want to get a good score, and I am trying to concentrate on my shots, but it just isn't working. As far as my golfing is concerned, I could take it or leave it. (*Analysis*: I am clearly in a game. I am voluntarily attempting to overcome unnecessary obstacles. But, just as clearly, I am not experiencing golf in the spirit of play. I am putting up with golf in order to reap extrinsic benefits—perhaps renew some friendships, lessen my sense of guilt at having ignored my friends recently, and get some healthful exercise.)

On the third hole, my swing has become more rhythmic. In fact, I hit a remarkable drive down the middle of the fairway and then a 3-iron (and I can never hit those) to the absolute middle of the green. I miss my birdie putt, but golf has begun its beguiling work. I wonder if I can repeat the wonderful feels of my previous two full swings. I move off to the fourth tee with a spring in my step and a number of unanswered questions swirling about. (*Analysis*: Here I am still in golf, just as I was previously. But now I am entering into the realm of play. The doing of golf is beginning to capture me. Even if I weren't renewing friendships, reducing guilt, or getting some healthful exercise, I might be inclined to continue because solving the problems of golf has become interesting itself.)

By the seventh hole, I have experimented with a number of different shots and most of them had their intended result. For one of the first times since I have been involved in today's game, I think that I can actually direct the ball to a specific location on the fairway or green and not just swing toward a general point on the compass. I am fascinated with this sensation of control and by my new relationship with my clubs—close friends nearly all, enemies hardly a one. (*Analysis*: I am now utterly lost in the spirit of play. Earlier motives for coming out to the course are no longer in mind. My friends and our conversations are now just a pleasant background to the theme that has so captured my interest and attention—the ongoing dialogue between me and the game of golf. Get home in time for dinner? Remember the work that needs to get done? At least for the time being, I remember nothing of dinner and nothing of unfinished work. I have taken up temporary residence on an oasis where prerational fascination stands apart from the surrounding desert of sobering and important duties [Schmitz, 1972, p. 28].)

This ecstasy continues for a number of holes, even though I am not scoring particularly well. I am submerged in golf and am enjoying it thoroughly. Unfortunately, when approaching the 12th tee, I see my dean on an adjacent hole. Her mere presence reminds me of the work awaiting me on my desk at home. I find myself in an internal war—one side of me saying that I deserve to enjoy this golfing match and the other not allowing me to do so. I search vainly for the spirit to take over again. But all is lost. I finish out the 18 holes alternating thoughts of my work, my good reasons for being here, and my hope that this match will soon end. (*Analysis*: The delicate spirit of play has disappeared—chased away in fact by a mere dean! I find that I cannot talk myself back into the attitude that I enjoyed only moments before. I will work through the rest of the golf match, feeling some satisfaction that at least I have spent a bit of long-overdue time with my friends and have done something that is probably good for my health.)

Play, therefore, is not the same thing as a game, though there is some overlap and even confusion between the two. Games, as we saw, can be conducted in the play spirit. My own guess is that many games, most of the time, for most people, are truly played.

Games, at least the good ones, are so fascinating that they hook us, get us involved in their problems, have us questing, venturing, experimenting, solving, and gambling. We love the uncertainty inherent in trying to solve game problems, and we relish the satisfactions that come with the resolutions of those tensions. We like to know how well we did. If someone were to tell us that absolutely nothing of concrete worth could or ever would come our way as a result of having participated in this game, we would continue to play anyway.

But it is also obvious that games need not be conducted in the atmosphere of play. Game participants may, for any variety of reasons, find the activity uninteresting and unrewarding. They focus on what comes after participation, apart from the doing itself. Some professional athletes have grown tired of their games and now play for the money. Some insecure children and adults cannot enjoy sport itself because they are too worried about failing and losing. Some little leaguers do not like the competition but participate to please or placate their parents.

SUMMARY BREAK

A game is an activity in which individuals voluntarily attempt to overcome unnecessary obstacles. Games are made by inventing obstacles where previously there were none and trying to overcome those obstacles simply for the sake of seeing if they can be overcome. This activity can be done in the spirit of play (the struggling and overcoming is its own reward), or it can be done in the spirit of work or labor. (The struggling and overcoming is endured for the sake of other things.) During the course of even a single game, people can fall in and out of the spirit of play and experience play with different degrees of intensity.

Games are clever human conventions that provide challenges in a world that, at times, is too tame, well controlled, technologically sterilized, boring, and tedious. Games give us generally safe vehicles by which to inject tests into the world—to see how far we have progressed, how well we have matured, how competent we have become. They prick us when we become complacent, for their problems expand as our skills improve. Most of us do not learn golf, for instance, and then move on to something else. We can never fully learn golf. No matter how good we become, golf's many tests are always there to invite us back and freshly challenge us.

Play, on the other hand, is not a convention. It is not a human construct. It is a "disease," a tendency, a wonderfully human weakness. Play says, "Come! Get involved! Try me out! Kick up your heels! But know that I am addicting and can be hazardous to your health and profession! I have a way of making you forget your worldly duties and responsibilities."

Play reminds people that, as human beings, they are more than rational calculators. This is not to say that objective analysis is a bad thing, but people who only do that, or who are good only at that, are at least partly dead to the world. They are too deliberate, too careful, too analytical. They have lost the ability to fall in love. They feel that they must deduce their commitments! Those who are on their way to totally rational living still receive provocative invitations from life to jump in and get involved, but they often fight them off until a cost-benefit analysis can be completed. Those who have been fatally afflicted with this prudent thinkers' ailment no longer receive any invitations whatsoever. Their world is only quiet, and orderly, and numerical.

PHILOSOPHIC EXERCISE

See if you can identify yourself as a game seeker and playmaker.

1. Regarding games, what kinds of challenges do you like to face? Have you been able to find games that include these kinds of problems? Where do you look for your games? In gyms? At computer terminals? Around card tables? At parties? Are you an active game maker? Have you ever turned a typical nongame activity into a game? Can you give one or two examples of your most clever game making?

2. Regarding play, where are your personal playgrounds? At home? In the kitchen? In the garden? On basketball courts? In front of a video game? Where are you and what are you doing, for instance, when you forget what time it is? When you want to make play happen for yourself or others, what do you do? Is it necessary for you to finish your work first? Are there places you can go and things you can do that almost always end up providing or being their own reward? When you want to make play, does competition spice up a potentially boring activity and make it fun, or does competition create tension in the doing and make you look forward to the end result?

The Significance of Games and Play

With these definitions on the table, you are in position now to determine whether or not games (including sport) and play are trivial, particularly when compared with academic subject matter. You saw in chapter 8 that games and play have the potential to effect liberation in the wisdom and exploration senses. Nevertheless, this new-won freedom could still be regarded as unimportant because it is gained largely in the "fun and games" part of life, not in the more serious day-to-day matters of working, building relationships, raising children, and so on.

The Need for Games

You already know that games are conventions that present people with artificial problems, self-imposed difficulties, provocative and usually nonthreatening puzzles. In biological terms, games might be regarded as safe stressors. They prick human curiosity; they keep people interested; they challenge players; they cast doubt on how good or proficient performers can get individually and collectively. Games cause people to exercise their capacities for achievement—for learning, for improving, for growing, for succeeding and accomplishing. As cultural stressors, games help people keep what might be called their "reaching muscles" in shape. (See Lenk, 1979, for a similar idea.)

But why are these artificial stressors needed? Aren't there enough real problems in the world to give us more than ample achievement exercise? With all of these real problems—like famine, disease, economic woes, the ethical dilemmas surrounding genetic engineering, familial and other interpersonal difficulties, the growing disparity between the haves and have-nots, the threat of war—is it not morally irresponsible to play games? There are at least four responses to this line of criticism, that is, at least four important functions that games fulfill.

1. *Games test, teach, and stimulate those who do not labor.* Children need safe achievement tests and opportunities. In fact, game playing is most often associated with children and youth, with those who have not yet reached an age where they must concern themselves with taking a job and taking on some of the world's problems.

Interestingly, this general rationale has become applicable to America's graying population—those who have, in many ways, become again like children. Even though they have chosen to retire from day-to-day work, and even though society does not hold them as accountable as before for solving the world's problems, they are very much alive and very much in need of challenges. Many of these stressors for them may come in the form of games or gamelike activities.

2. *Games test, teach, and stimulate those whose jobs are routine and tedious.* The day-to-day lives of many adults, in spite of the persistence of more than a few global problems, are relatively routine and unproblematic. These are individuals who may hold a job that is highly repetitive and tedious. And for virtually everyone else, most health problems are kept at arm's length (thanks to modern medicine, nutrition, and physical education), many economic worries can be put on the back burner (thanks to various forms of insurance and other safety nets), and shelter and clothing needs for many individuals are not pressing concerns. There are no plagues to stamp out, no Wests to conquer or homelands to preserve, no emancipation to earn, no fields to plow, no clothes to weave, and hardly any meals to fully prepare and cook. Many historic challenges that pressed in on day-to-day life are gone. Life has gotten a bit tame. Or perhaps more accurately, it is easier to believe today than in yesteryear that life is tame, if not a little boring. Games provide an antidote for a way of life that may have grown too safe and secure or, if not that, at least too routine.

Moreover, sociologists like Bellah et al. (1985, 1991) and Lasch (1979) have noted that many people today (and particularly Americans) are too focused on personal security and survival to be aware of societal needs and challenges. That is, they display avoidance behavior regarding the many real problems that surround them. They even avoid competition because much of their striving is for personal gain and personal security. Defeats are seen as personally threatening. If this is true, games are needed all the more to make it difficult for a competition-avoiding culture to sidestep challenges altogether.

3. *Games refresh those who need refreshment.* Even socially responsible adults who have developed and frequently use their reaching muscles at work find game challenges different than real-world difficulties and, thus, refreshing and stimulating. Game playing for these folks is like a busman's holiday. In their free time, they do more of what occupies them at work. But game challenges, of course, are not just like work problems. They occur in a different setting (say, a golf course instead of an office), and they change the stakes (say, a certain number of strokes instead of a profit-loss graph). Most importantly, the problems of games are voluntarily chosen. This, of course, is not the case at work.

4. *Games highlight and stylize cultural values.* This fourth argument about the human need for games, I believe, is more important than the other three combined. Even if games were not cultural stressors needed by developing children and stimulation-starved older adults, even if they were not an antidote needed by a population whose day-to-day life has grown a little tame, and even if games did not provide free-time alternatives and refreshment for workaholics, they would be still be needed to highlight, stylize, and foster meaning. They would be needed to help human beings develop their unique culture and to carry forward their collective and individual stories.

Games require people not only to deal with things like balls, bats, weights, distances, and directions but also, and more importantly, with meanings and values. In games we not only become familiar with the world of time, space, and force, and we not only make tennis racquets, hockey sticks, and skis a part of our being, we also become familiar with competing purposes, goals, and interests. And we incorporate them into our lives.

In games, people work on their stories. This is not a conscious effort, but it happens nevertheless. In these self-chosen stressor environments, we find out what we like, what we can do, how we react to pressure and adversity, how we relate to friends and opponents, what our capabilities are, what gets our attention, where we like to be.

Games: Wellsprings of Meaning and Stories

In degrees, of course, virtually all of our life experiences can help us find meaning for our lives and further our stories. However, games seem particularly well-suited for doing this. The reasons for this are very straightforward.

Games are Conventions

Games, in contrast to many day-to-day need-based activities, are human conventions. We make them the way we want them to be. If a certain game does not speak to us or otherwise catch our fancy, we simply do not play it, or we modify it to make it better. Over time then, the games of our culture are crafted precisely to fit this distinctive culture—much like a custom-made suit fits a person's body.

This is why it has been said that, if you want to know a people, watch them in their games and play. It is here that they have had the freedom to invent or make activities that are exactly right for them. It is here that they intentionally give themselves problems—but not just any old problems. Rather they create problems that remind them of their orientation to life, of their personal and community values and meanings.

This degree of latitude is not present in our workaday lives. Food and shelter must be secured, profits must be made, bosses must be pleased, children must be taught, families must be raised. Certainly, we make choices in how these things are accomplished, and, most definitely, cultural style is present here too. But there are more constraints. Biological needs are no respectors of different cultures. Your boss might have values different from your own. Economic necessity sometimes urges people to act in ways that make them philosophically uncomfortable. In short, activities based on physical needs, a boss's attitudes, and economic laws are not conventions. They are not games.

To be sure, games are influenced by necessity and outside influences just like day-to-day life. Many books have been written about the domination of sport by economic factors, political systems, hidden psychological needs, and the like. Yet the fact remains that games are malleable. To the extent that human choice and preference can express themselves apart from alienation, control, and locked-in psychological needs, games have the capacity to reflect those interests. Accordingly, as personally crafted conventions, games provide a marvelous place in which to develop personal stories.

Games Create Tension

There is a second important asset enjoyed by games in helping human beings find meaning and develop stories. Challenges produce memorable events. They allow people to learn more about themselves. They allow individuals to learn more about the world.

At their best, games hold a ritualistic power over us. They cast a spell when we enter their temples. The odors of leather, wood, neat's-foot oil; the sounds of motion, of balls hitting

At their best, games hold a ritualistic power over us.

bats or racquets, of bodies splashing in water; the yells of teammates—all of these sensations tend to put us in a special frame of mind. We are transported from our routine world to a special place.

Tension builds as the game proceeds. We struggle, wonder, hope for a bit of luck. A climax may come where some cleverness will win the day or where a mistake will cost us everything. Then the resolution—the exhaustion, the disappointment or celebration, and the turning of attention to the common matters of the day. But the tension and drama of games has provided an opportunity to experience something that is special and memorable. When achievements of note are experienced, they become a part of our unfolding stories. When multiple achievements occur over the years, they begin to build a coherent pattern, a story line that can be followed.

Games are Repetitive

In ritual experiences like these, cultural values and life meanings are put on display over and over again. Key values are placed on the marquees of life; they are lived out; they recede to the background between games; then they are lived again. These values and meanings become familiar; as children, we grow in and through them; as adults, they are reinforced through playing and spectating. Games are like a favorite record that gets played again and again and again. Pretty soon we are humming its tune without even being aware that we are doing so.

Other life activities are repeated, but they often lack the significance and drama of games. How important, for instance, are experiences of daily grooming activities, duties related to hygiene, the consumption of meals, and routine work? How distinctive are we in these activities? How much are we forced to come to grips with competing values? How often does the remarkable event occur? How

often are these times and happenings remembered and passed down to others in our stories?

There are few arenas in society where rituals are sufficiently repetitive to give shape to our lives and unfolding stories. Worship, prayer, and reading religious texts provide drama and ritual meaning for some. Marriages, anniversaries, the birth of children, reunions, graduations, promotions, and other important life events are occasions when many are reminded of some of the mystery and power of life. But these highlights of existence occur infrequently. Sport, by way of contrast, offers drama on a daily basis. It provides an opportunity to experience the liturgy of hoping, striving, achieving, winning, and losing again and again.

Games Send Messages

What messages do games send? What values do they reinforce? Three examples will show the tremendous potential of games to tell us at least something about what counts in life.

• *Success is good.* In games there are many ways to succeed. One is by winning; another is by reaching a personal goal; yet another is by showing improvement. Because many people find game tests to be provocative and fun, they are invited back again and again. This repetition, and the practice that it provides, leads to improvement and greater successes. In games some highly skilled individuals feel most like artists or craftspersons—that is, people who are very good and creative at a given task.

Games are structured to highlight at least occasional successes because they are designed to be difficult but not impossible. If games were impossible or too easy, nobody would find them to be much fun, and few if any would play them. But good games, by nature, offer intriguing challenges that provide for meaningful success—that is, achievement in the face of problems that are neither too difficult nor too easy.

There are many different types of games and different facets to each of them. With this diversity, it is possible for almost anyone to find some game opportunities that will lead to success. If a person does not have the height, quickness, and strength for basketball, perhaps she can succeed at swimming, tennis, or distance running. If a person cannot hit a long, straight drive, perhaps he can become a fine putter.

Games offer an invitation to success—a chance to solve a meaningful problem, to reach a personal goal, to improve, to defeat a worthy opponent. Games send a cultural

There are enough kinds of games that almost anyone can find opportunities that lead to success.

message that it is good to achieve—to become an artist at our craft, or a good player, or at least a better one. Thus, each time we put on our gear or tee it up, we pay homage to success.

• *Freedom (opportunity) is good*. In games all participants usually have a chance, even if the odds are stacked against them. Everyone has at least a narrow opportunity to succeed, to improve, to gain a bit of fame or at least respect, even if the game cannot be won. In games, the future holds promise, if only to a degree.

Most of our games are structured to give everyone a chance. Some have high components of luck or chance. Thus, even those without great talent can, from time to time, taste success. Games have adaptable rules so that individuals with different levels of skill can play and succeed. Beginners can play with rules different from those used by experts so that each group can enjoy opportunities. Games require opponents to play by the same rules. Thus, initial advantages, reputations, past honors, power, status—all of these things are of minimal importance once the game begins. The average rookie stands at home plate under the same testing conditions as the future hall-of-famer.

• *Justice is good*. In games everyone is expected to play fair. Those who play better usually win more often than those who do not. Those who work harder at developing their skills will typically improve faster than those who are less diligent. Those who care more will normally perform better than those who are more lackadaisical. Justice is usually, but not always, served in games.

The rule-bound structure of games sends strong messages about justice as fairness. In running events, game rules assure that everyone starts at the same place, begins at the same time, runs the same distance under virtually identical conditions, and finishes at the same imaginary plane. There are few other occasions in life when tasks are so clearly defined, and the *do*s and *don't*s for taking them on are so well spelled out.

Games say that there is equal opportunity here. Even if rules are made by the powerful to favor themselves in day-to-day life, and even if our neighbors break rules in the real world, on the field of play things are supposed to be different. Each time we say, "Yes, let's have a game," we reinforce the value of justice.

SUMMARY BREAK

Games are needed for stimulation among those who do not labor or whose work is tedious, for refreshment and relaxation by those whose work is demanding, and for the enhancement of value and meaning for all human beings.

Games are powerful. They are conventions and thus can be crafted to reinforce and modify a specific culture's values. They create tension, provide repetition, and send messages. They provide a stern testing place at which people are required to use their uniquely human capabilities and show themselves as able, if not also creative. By nature, games provide a dramatic stage on which to rehearse and promote values and meanings. In and through games, we are likely to be culturally reminded and oriented, if not also motivated and inspired. Games by their very nature enjoy some advantages shared perhaps only by other activities that have the qualities and characteristics of drama and ritual—for example, activities in religion and the arts.

PHILOSOPHIC EXERCISE

Try to remember the most wonderful experience you ever had in a game. Where were you, what happened, and how did you feel? What does this event say about things that matter to you most and how you would like your life story to go? Be specific both in recalling this event and identifying particular values.

The Need for Play

In chapter 4 you learned that many of the ills in today's society, according to some modern thinkers, are related to our current cultural emphasis on survivalism and our relative neglect of play. Lasch (1979) argues that many people fear competition because they are so psychologically fragile and thus concerned that they cannot survive a loss. Bellah et al. (1985, 1991) claim that human beings retreat to "lifestyle enclaves" in part because such places are comfortable and safe. Gruneau (1983) and Sage (1990) suggest that workers are influenced by those in power to consume goods, recreate, and otherwise merely persist and survive as workers. By these accounts, life today is decidedly unplayful. Thus, an infusion of the play spirit might be able to cure any number of related ills.

Paradoxically, according to some writers (e.g., von Schiller, 1972), nothing less than human survival is dependent on the presence of a healthy component of play in people's lives. Here, the emphasis is on the word "human." Biological survival may well be possible without play; it may even be fostered by sobriety and prudence. But human survival is cast into doubt when individuals do not (or, worse yet, can no longer) play. What is special about human life is somehow compromised or threatened when the play spirit is extinguished. Likewise, human society or culture is somehow compromised or threatened when people interact with one another through their organizations and in their institutions in the absence of play.

Play is good for children *and* adults.

Play may well be needed to keep the world fresh, life interesting, tomorrow worth living. When we become too calculating and rational, one opportunity begins to look like the next, one benefit begins to feel like the last one. A world that is only organized, proper, healthful, useful, important, tidy, and good changes color on us. It becomes gray!

Play may also be needed in order to keep people fresh and interesting. When we become too calculating and rational, we begin to look and act too much like computers or other machines. People who are only rational, calculating, prudent, careful, studied, and worried about the future begin to lose their childlike nature. They become responsible and possibly even successful; but they also turn humanly comatose!

Just as there are underrated players in every sport, there are underrated human activities. And play is one of them. Play is not just good for children. It is also good for adults. In fact, some of its most remarkable power is witnessed in the adult world. But wherever play does its work, its effects are unmistakable and of life-changing significance.

1. *Play produces givers, not takers* (Harper, 1972). In some religious traditions, people are taught that it is more blessed to give than to receive. Players come to understand that there is an important secular truth that parallels this theological principle. Giving, in fact, is something of a prerequisite to taking.

Play, I noted earlier, is for lovers. It is for those who are willing and able to give themselves to something of interest. If this giving can occur with few or no strings attached, play is more likely to occur and be fully rewarding. On the other hand, when the emphasis is on the taking, play often does not work.

Many of us have, on occasion, tried too hard to have a good time. We have worked at it; we have told ourselves that we deserve it; we have gone to traditional playgrounds and spent considerable amounts of money trying to find play. We have shoved our books aside and run over to the gymnasium absolutely determined to have a great time. But the more we aim at orchestrating fun, the less likely we are to experience it, at least in its full form.

Why not run a few cost-benefit analyses before giving ourselves to baseball, or a piano keyboard, or a gourmet dinner, or a kite and

The less orchestrated our fun, the more rewarding it can be.

some wind? Is it not more human to do that? Are we not rational animals who should run a few prudent calculations before we act?

In many cases that may be good advice. But it threatens to cheapen and reduce both the giving and the eventual taking. The giving is no longer complete, unconditional, spontaneous, loving. It is already expecting a certain return on its investment. Because it has anticipated and preselected specific benefits, it is more likely to miss other ones—perhaps even better ones. There will probably be no pleasant surprises. Because we insisted on calculating beforehand, we have solidified the terms of the deal and have undersold ourselves in the process.

Through the ability to give ourselves to others and to play possibilities in the world, we paradoxically stand to take more than we could have anticipated. Those who are good givers are not just noble, kind, or nice. They

are also playful. They receive invitations to get involved, and they say "Yes!"

2. *Play preserves human unpredictability.* There is nothing sacred about unpredictability. In fact, it is often a bad characteristic. We want our friends to be reliable when it comes to keeping promises and helping us when we are in need. We want them to be predictable about showing up at work or school. Nevertheless, as we saw in chapter 3, the development of human levels of intelligence allows us to be insightfully inventive and creative. We are at the plate in baseball when common practice would have us bunting, but we unpredictably swing away.

Play nourishes such unpredictability because, when in the spirit of play, we are interested in the doing and not nervous over the result. When we fret over consequences, when we feel that we have to win, when there are others to please—we are likely to become conservative. We are compelled to do what usually works. If we fail then, we reason, at least we will not be so open to criticism.

Play, as so many have said, reminds us of our possibilities (Meier, 1980). Play widens our future. It allows us to show, once and for all, that we are not programmable and predictable machines. Play keeps us from cynically thinking that we have seen everything before, or from brashly suggesting that we know exactly what we will get out of some experience. Thus, in play, we act freshly, hopefully, humbly, unpredictably.

3. *Play allows meaning to count.* In play, we can relish such values as success, freedom, and justice, as well as beauty, excitement, danger, improvement, tenderness, love, family, individuality, community, and so on—without asking what they are good for. That is, we experience and celebrate them simply because they speak to us, simply because they are meaningful, simply because they are right for our stories, for the ongoing account of who we are and who we are becoming.

We do not always let this happen. In fact, we sometimes equate growing up with growing out of intrinsic meaning. I once saw a group of seven- and eight-year-olds gathered by a fence on the side of a baseball field. They were waiting expectantly for the arrival of their coach for their first-ever official baseball practice. They were literally jumping with excitement—perhaps with some nervousness over how they would do, with visions of playing like their heroes they had seen on television, with the anticipation of receiving a uniform (actually a T-shirt and cap), and who knows what else. The situation was packed with personal meaning for these youngsters, and they could barely contain themselves. The anticipated event promised to be more than sufficient reward. Play would win the day at this first practice, and it would be memorable.

When the coach arrived, he immediately sat the boys down and proceeded to talk with them about making all the practices, about caring for the equipment, about other responsibilities and duties, about becoming men, and (he finished on this point for emphasis) about the importance of winning! By the time he had finished his speech, some of the boys had become bored and were gazing across the field; others were getting restless and shifted uneasily on the ground, and the few who were listening showed some anxiety over the sobering message they were receiving. This coach, without intending to do any harm, did not allow meaning to count—at least not the intrinsically satisfying meanings these youngsters were hoping for at that first practice. Play did not win the day, for the coach had effectively killed it.

Play gives testimony to the fact that, perhaps above all else, human beings are meaning-seeking creatures. We can live for a time without food, without security, without comfort, even without friends. But we cannot endure existence if it does not mean anything. We struggle to make sense out of tragic or chaotic events. We flee boredom like the plague. We need a world that is interesting and meaningful, and in play we find it.

SUMMARY BREAK

Several arguments counter the claim that play is trivial, that it is ''mere'' play. People need play both to keep the world fresh and interesting and to keep themselves unique and unpredictable. Play produces givers and allows people to reap the many benefits of uncalculated, spontaneous commitment. Play preserves human unpredictability and helps individuals to appreciate their unique possibilities. And, perhaps most important of all, play allows meaning to count.

Practical Applications

Our philosophic journey has put us in a position to identify some guidelines for professional practice. These guidelines can be deduced from some of the philosophic conclusions reached in the previous pages. So that we do not lose track of these insights and so you can more easily locate the source of my practical suggestions, I have gathered some of the most important conclusions in what follows.

Body Philosophy

We had to know what a person is before we could determine how persons can be freed or otherwise changed for the better. Specifically, we had to wrestle with dualisms that separate body from mind and thereby reduce the significance of motor- and muscle-oriented activities. I proposed the following conclusions:

1. Persons are whole beings with their thoughtful and motor aspects thoroughly integrated.
2. The higher powers of intelligence are needed in successful advanced performance. In other words, nonverbal movement activities, by themselves, can reflect impressive levels of insight, inventiveness, and creativity.
3. Thus, neither the mind, the mental, the reflective, nor the verbal are needed to dignify or otherwise elevate fine motor- and muscle-oriented performance.
4. Given this integration, human beings can be changed in important ways as moving beings per se; the good life (inasmuch as this rests on human beings using their highest or most powerful capacities) can be pursued by enhancing nonverbal and nonreflective skills themselves. To teach a nonverbal craft like sport or dance, particularly at the higher skill levels, is to change a person in profound ways.

Value Philosophy

We needed to take two steps here—first to check on what values are currently needed by contemporary society; second to examine objectively (apart from current conditions) the power of four basic goods that can be promoted by physical education. The underlying questions here were, What is the nature of the good life? and, How can we, with our unique subject matter, best help people to achieve it? Some conclusions:

1. Sociologists claim that our society suffers from excess individualism and survivalism; from an absence of meaning and shared value; from the utilization of sport and exercise more to divert and subdue the self, stimulate and recreate, entertain oneself, cope, and biologically survive than to promote any sort of educational growth or liberation.
2. The good life is composed of experiences that are appreciated for their own sake. The good life must be meaningful or have purpose. One event must be connected to another, and these events must be headed somewhere important as in the development of a story line. Survival and long life, by themselves, do little to assure good living.
3. Among four traditional categories of objectives in physical education (organic, psychomotor, cognitive, and affective), skill and pleasure should be ranked above fitness and knowledge on their capacity to help individuals experience the good life.
4. Attention should not be diverted from the development of higher levels of motor skill—not for reasons of gaining academic respectability, solving health problems, or providing a broad array of recreational activities for later life. Artistic movement is experienced as satisfying in its own right and thus can contribute to the good life.
5. Attention should not be diverted from developing this skill in an environment of interest and meaning. When sport, dance, and exercise are experienced, in the spirit of play, for example, the experience will be pleasurable. Much of the good life may well be lived in an atmosphere of play whether one is engaged in sport or something else.

Practical Philosophy

Here we needed to look at the practical matter of changing people for the better, particularly in traditional educational terms. We needed to understand whether or not and on what grounds we might be considered as important change agents. Of particular concern was the common bias held against a portion of our subject matter—specifically, games and play. Should we be taken seriously and considered a part of mainstream education if we are the profession (at least in part) that promotes "fun and games"? The following were some additional conclusions:

1. There are two ways in which skillful performance in games and play can, in principle, liberate people. Wisdom liberation comes with the insights and meanings encountered as accomplished performers or knowledgeable and devoted spectators. Exploration liberation comes with the actual development of high-level motor skill and concomitant abilities to explore, discover, express, invent, and create.

2. Games perform the important function of providing challenging opportunities for individuals across the lifespan. In so doing, they serve as a stage on which cultural values can be transmitted, preserved, modified, and, most importantly, relived, shared with others, and appreciated.

3. Play performs the important function of keeping the world interesting, reminding human beings of their human possibilities, and breaking the chain of predictable behavior—from stimulus-response reactions to the constraining patterns of logical and prudent living.

4. If physical educators want to be mainstream change agents, they need not flee from game skills and play environments to movement education, theory, fitness objectives, or lifetime recreation. In fact, they should excel precisely at being teachers of games and the skills that allow people to play them well, and at creating the spirit of play.

PHILOSOPHIC EXERCISE

What kinds of decisions should be made regarding such practical matters as (1) hiring policies, (2) curriculum development, and (3) teaching methodology? Specifically, what kinds of people should be hired to promote the brand of physical education described above? How should curriculum be molded to meet the implications of this philosophy? And by what methods should teachers deal with their students and clients?

You may want to write down your own ideas on these three areas before looking at my deductions in the following sections. Compare your ideas with mine. If any of your recommendations contradict mine, can you find the specific philosophic conclusion listed previously from which you derived your idea and then argue for the validity of your own viewpoint?

Personnel-Related Dilemmas

Issue 1. If you had to choose between one prospective employee who was passionate about activity but lacked some professional training and another person who was technically competent but less personally involved in a movement-oriented lifestyle, which one would you choose?

Professionals should be lovers of activity (games, dance, sport, exercise) first and foremost and technicians second. Anyone entering the field who is to provide instruction or other activity-related services should be a true believer; an unredeemable mover or exerciser or dancer; a person who has trouble going two days in a row without a workout, a game, some practice, a performance; someone who has trouble saying no to any invitation to play.

Most anyone can become technically competent, and such competence is obviously important. But competence alone is not sufficient if human lives are to be changed, if meaning is to be fostered, if sport, dance, exercise, and games are to be portrayed as far more than useful tools for recreation and fitness. Loving commitment is needed. Students, athletes, and fitness clients find it fun and exhilarating to be around "true believers" who provide a model, a living invitation to others to give themselves to activity. Their enthusiasm is often contagious.

I would be suspicious of any employee who talks a good game but does not live it; of new (job and financial security seeking) converts to a movement-oriented life, of those who say they are in the profession primarily because an active lifestyle "makes sense," or because physical fitness is "important"—no matter how technically competent they might be.

The professional I have in mind is one who is giving "keys to a kingdom" more than providing a service or imparting a bit of scientifically correct information, though the two are not mutually exclusive. It is the same difference that exists in other fields that can contribute to the good life, for example, the discipline of English literature. It is the difference between the English teacher who would present the works of Hemingway and Steinbeck merely as samples of good writing and the lover of literature who invites students into a beautiful world of words and human meaning.

Issue 2. If you had to choose between one prospective employee who attended an average exercise–sport science majors program but who had participated in sport and exercise activities throughout her lifetime and was a member of a varsity team at her college,

and another individual who attended a highly regarded majors program but lacked the activity background and varsity-level skill of the other candidate, which one would you select?

Professionals should have rich and lengthy personal histories in movement activities. Because much of the liberation and meaning available in the movement domain comes at beyond-beginner levels of skill and knowledge, professionals need to focus on that level of performance and spectating competence for their students. Those who have not been there, who do not have at least a modest array of intermediate skills and one or two at an advanced level, will not be inclined to embrace such a focus. They will be far more comfortable with introducing students to a variety of sport, dance, and exercise skills only at beginning levels.

Advanced activity literacy cannot be gained quickly. It definitely cannot be secured in the four or five years during which a person is in college. The lore, the stories, the traditions, the heroes and villains, the evolution of strategy—all that makes up a movement craft—is grown into, not taught in a three-credit college course.

While I realize that a person does not have to possess advanced skill in order to teach it, I would hesitate to hire someone who had not personally tasted the fruits of higher levels of performance, who had no particular movement attachment or identity, who had trouble telling movement stories about herself, who had not begun her activity initiation rites at an early age.

Issue 3. You are hiring a physical therapist, and one prospective employee describes himself as a "people person" and the other finalist says that he is a "sport and exercise person." Which would you choose?

Professionals, first and foremost, should have a deep respect for their subject matter. While it may be important in most activity-related

Professionals need to have a deep respect for their subject matter.

professions to be a so-called people person, it is more important to be a sport, dance, or exercise person. The crucial relationship in the movement professions is not between the teacher and student, coach and athlete, or physical therapist and client. It is between the professional and the subject matter. The subject matter is what sustains, regenerates, excites, inspires, and puts passion into one's work. If the subject matter is not embraced and respected, all the personal skills in the world will not make up for it.

If someone told me in an interview that she was a people person, I would ask her why she did not select any one of the hundreds of other professions that require good person-to-person skills. If, upon further questioning I found out that she had not sustained a relationship with some sport, dance, or exercise form in her past, or if I sensed that she (only rationally or logically) regarded activity as a means to such ends as health and fitness, I would doubt the appropriateness of her decision—not the part about helping people, but about helping people in our unique field.

Issue 4. You have a choice between two equally qualified candidates, one of whom is local and one of whom was raised and educated in another part of the country. Would this difference in geographical and cultural upbringing give you any reason for favoring one applicant over the other?

Professionals should know the culture, traditions, and history of the area in which they are working. This is not to say that professionals cannot adapt to different cultures or that a given tradition might not benefit from new ideas and outside influences. However, if movement activities are to mean more than fitness and provide more than shallow diversion or recreation, it is better to work at home than in a culturally or historically strange land. Ideally, instructors would have grown up in and experienced the culture of the students or clients with whom they will be working. They would know the games and dances of that place. They would know the history and values of those people. They would personally know and share many of their aspirations. They would be able to help them become better embedded in their culture, or at least its good aspects.

This is particularly important if professionals are to be good playmakers. Different people, different sexes, different ages, different subcultures, different nationalities, and people of different religions have different "play buttons." To make play happen among people of one part of the country will be different, at least in some ways, from making it happen with other people elsewhere. What is it that intrigues, interests, and awes here, in this place, among these people? Movement educators need to be local in spirit and heart if they are to manufacture play the only way it can be made, which is locally, one historically planted group of play converts at a time.

I would not look favorably on individuals who would espouse a national or world curriculum or who think that science provides both necessary and sufficient information on how and what to teach. I would be skeptical of outsiders who show little interest in local ways or anyone who thinks there is one generic or right way to do things.

Issue 5. Of two candidates, one is more playful and fun loving while the other is the opposite—serious and overly responsible. Who would you tend to favor?

Professionals should be playful. This does not mean that they should be silly or irrational, irresponsible or whimsical, or that they should act entirely like children. It means that they should be full of the play spirit. In practice, this means that they should be willing to let go, to allow a special moment to be a special moment, to refrain from overorganizing classes or exercise sessions, to be searching for interest among their students or clients, to be forever on the lookout for the special or surprising, and to show a personal fascination with their subject matter.

I would be suspicious of those who were highly regimented, who like to line children up on numbers, who tell them that sport is serious business because it builds character, who see sport as a personality testing ground for developing real men or women, and who treat activity sessions as if they were endurance contests.

Curriculum-Related Dilemmas

Issue 1. Should you develop a curriculum that includes a broad array of aims or one that is more limited?

The curriculum should be keyed to motor skill acquisition and improvement as the preeminent aim of the program. If we are to be members of mainstream education and teach things that will actually be part of the good life (not just lead to it), we must liberate people in the motor and muscle world, make them highly movement-literate, free them to express and explore in ways that transcend words, allow them to develop their personal stories in games and play. For this to happen, we must teach skill and teach it well. Physical fitness, knowledge acquisition, the development of leisure-time activities, the improvement of character, and the enhancement of personal health may (and probably should) all be present, but only as secondary or subsidiary aims.

Any curriculum that is ambivalent, that tries to be all things to all people should be held suspect. Any curriculum that is keyed to one of the subsidiary purposes, such as fitness or knowledge acquisition, is selling itself short. Any curriculum that is primarily recreational, that is nothing more than supervised recess, does not deserve a place at the education table. In short, I would opt for a more limited set of aims.

Issue 2. Given the primary aim of skill instruction, should a curriculum be designed for a balanced introduction to many dance, game, and exercise activities or should it limit the breadth of different skills taught? For example, would you prefer a ninth-grade curriculum that introduced students to about 15 different activities taught in two-week modules (two periods of 35 minutes each), or one that included about 6 skills taught in four- to six-week units?

The curriculum should be intellectually rigorous by aiming at skill acquisition beyond beginner levels. Students need to be challenged to reach good levels of grace and cleverness and the pleasure that goes with it; they must be required to go well beyond stilted, awkward, halting, noncreative movement and the lack of satisfaction that goes with it. Students must be expected to use their higher powers of sense perceptual intellect to become inventive, insightful, meaning-filled movers—to become more like pianists who can improvise and less like machines that have a limited and predictable repertoire of actions; to become more like craftspersons who are proud of their creations and less like alienated assembly-line workers who put in their time and have very little of which to be proud.

Consequently, I would look unfavorably on any curriculum or program that provides only survey or introductory experiences, that promises to teach skill in a short time, or that promises to teach too many skills, that is preoccupied with its obligation to provide students with a large variety of lifetime sports. I would wonder about any curriculum that has no clear progression for skills, that does not encourage students to get good at *something*—even if it is only one form of dance, one type of exercise, or one sport.

Issue 3. What is the highest value promoted by a curriculum that favors depth over breadth? For example, is it more excellence or meaning?

The curriculum should promote meaning over excellence. This does not mean that excellence is not a worthy objective, or that some individuals should not strive to attain it. But excellence can be mechanical, and cold, and very exclusive if it is defined in absolute terms. In other words, not many of us can be truly or absolutely excellent at anything. On the other hand, when excellence is humanized, when

We need not excel to experience competence and self-satisfaction.

movements become emotional, expression-filled, idea-modified, story-fortifying, personality-related—then it is special. It is the meaning that makes the difference.

All of us want to feel that we are unique, special, effective and would like our activity lives to contribute to these feelings and recognitions. We do not have to be particularly excellent (let alone perfect or number one) to experience competence and self-satisfaction. All of this can happen if we gain modest or good levels of skill. All of this can happen if we have enough skill to dance out our feelings, compete out our values, and play out our curiosity.

I would look unfavorably on any curriculum that relies heavily on national norms, badges, or other forms of extrinsic motivation to indicate what counts, any school system that reveres its varsity athletes and looks down on its intramural and service classes, or any program that is too much focused on numbers—on being first, on having a certain number of people above the norm, on being the best. Any curriculum that counts heart rates more diligently than students' interest in activity is suspect.

Issue 4.   You have a potentially broad array of movement activities that can be included in the curriculum, such as traditional games, new games, folk dance, social and modern dance, sport, exercise, posture, daily movements (including work-related movements), mime, flexibility and reaction enhancers, self-defense activities, and relaxation and stress-reduction movements. Which should you emphasize?

The curriculum should emphasize dance, games, and sport. These are the most powerful activities that can be enjoyed for their own sake, that have intrinsic value. Dance is an art form and shares in the worth of all the fine arts. Games (including sports), while not art, nevertheless have an important cultural significance, particularly when experienced in the spirit of play.

People say, "I could have danced all night," or, "I wanted to play golf all day." The freedom, meaning, challenge that individuals find in these activities is captivating. Such experiences can make significant portions of our lives go well. On the other hand, one does not often hear, "I wish I could have exercised all day," or, "I could have displayed healthful posture all night." These things have lesser intrinsic value, whatever their important extrinsic worth might be. Good things like fitness and posture are not to be abandoned, but they must be pursued as by-products of dance, sport, and games.

I would be suspicious of any curriculum that underplays the power and significance of dance, that focuses on routine exercise or that uses fitness testing as a focal part of the curriculum, that too strongly downplays the importance of game challenges. I would have doubts about any generic or culture-free movement curriculum or any new-games curriculum that systematically discourages competition.

Issue 5.   You are familiar with curriculum guides that suggest a variety of activities, some of which are compatible with your climate, facilities, traditions, and geography. You wonder if you should emphasize local conditions in choosing dances, games, and outdoor activities or follow national trends and professional curriculum guides.

The curriculum should be at least partly local and idiosyncratic. The curriculum should reflect the history and values of the people in a country, a region of the country, a state, a town or village, perhaps even a neighborhood.

If a physical education program exists next to a mountain, a stream, or a field of snow it should see them as opportunities. If a town has a long history of fine soccer teams, the physical education program should not operate as if that tradition did not exist. If a neighborhood has a long-standing rivalry with another neighborhood across town, that is useful and relevant information when building a curriculum. If a school has a significant Hispanic population, for example, the physical education teacher needs to know that in deciding what is likely to work in the curriculum.

People do not come from outer space. They come from specific ancestors, from a specific time, from within a specific heritage. Education and services must align themselves with that history, approach their students and clients in terms of it, and lead them forward from there. This is not, in the least, to say that everything that is or has been is good. It is not to say that progress and change are not needed. But it is to say that human and humane education take heed of tradition both by relishing it for its own sake and by using it for the purposes of improving or transcending it.

I would have doubts about any curriculum that refuses to include local activities simply because they are scientifically inferior, any uniform national or international curriculum that does not make great allowances for local modification. I would wonder about any curriculum designers who laugh at horseshoes, table tennis, quoits, kite flying, juggling, pantomime, or any other locally popular activities, however quaint they might be. I would question any decision to eliminate softball simply because it does not provide sufficient aerobic fitness.

Methodology-Related Dilemmas

Issue 1.   When new skills are introduced and new drills attempted, the instructor usually needs to provide some explanation and verbal analysis. But how much is best? If the goal is to improve performance, is it better to explain for conceptual clarity and understanding prior to practicing, or is it better to provide only enough explanation to get the exercise and practice under way?

Involvement should take precedence over explanation. The emphasis must be on jumping in and practicing rather than talking about the skill. While theory is important, we also know that its usefulness is limited. Skill level and sensitivity improve with practice, not with talk. Expression and exploration and creativity are promoted by developing beyond beginner level skills, not by thinking about these things. It is far more important to have students actually encounter a sport, some meaning, or a unique challenge in activity than to tell them that it is there.

There are always good reasons for doing things, and these good reasons can be put into words and drummed into students' or clients' heads. But people are not simply rational machines. If they were, everyone would use seat belts; everyone would have stopped smoking; nobody would take undue risks. If all individuals were rational, trainers could get everyone exercising simply by explaining all of the health benefits that come with it. But play-oriented instructors know that it is far more important to hook people on activity than logically and rationally to back them into some active-lifestyle corner.

Consequently, I wonder about instructors who begin classes or workout sessions with lengthy discussions, teachers who like to talk rather than point, individuals who use too many handouts, people who think that students and clients play because it is rational to do so, anyone who doubts that movement is mightier than the pen (or at least as mighty).

Issue 2.   What kind of tone should be used in introducing a new unit or activity? For instance, would you use a more matter-of-fact tone or one that communicates keen anticipation?

Each activity should be treated as special. It is never merely time for the badminton unit, for example. It is time for BADMINTON! There is the chance that some students or

As physical educators, we should treat every activity as special.

clients will end up being its captive. There is a chance that some students or clients will be able to enter the realm of unique movement experience in badminton.

It is difficult to find any activity that does not have its following. Those games that do not capture the human imagination probably fade away before many people learn about them. In any case, virtually any sport or form of dance has its true believers, its guild members, those who have dedicated time, money, energy, and themselves to it. Virtually any sport or form of dance generates its stories about great performers, great feats or performances or memorable failures. They have been special, and can again be special for subsequent generations.

Thus, I wonder about any who would treat an activity as merely the next unit in the curriculum, instructors who would make fun of an activity simply because they themselves are not familiar with it; any who doubt the power of dances, games, and sports to grab and take hold of people; and any who express the attitude to students that activities are only play or just a game.

Issue 3.   As a skill instructor you are caught in a dilemma of needing high numbers of repetitions in order to teach the good habits that free performers but also of trying to keep activity sessions interesting. Do you emphasize novelty, variety, and interest at the expense of repetition, or should you emphasize repetition even though there may be times when this is not much fun?

Repetition should be regarded as a friend of play, not its enemy. The play atmosphere is more likely to surround those who are comfortable, competent, skillful, and creative in a given activity. Awkwardness, fear, incompetence, and the embarrassment that often accompanies these experiences drive away play—at least for most of us.

These play-inducing higher levels of skill are grounded on good reflexes and a variety of sound habits. Reflexes are honed and habits are developed through repetitions, variations on repetitions, and yet more repetitions. Thus, paradoxically, if a teacher wants to be a good playmaker, he had better be demanding in terms of repetitions required and clever in how he goes about achieving them.

I would question methodologies that avoid the work of repetitive activity, that promote free expression without a foundation of good habit and skill, or that regard habits as inferior or unimportant. I would wonder about anyone who rolls out the ball and thus allows for uncorrected repetition to occur. I would doubt the effectiveness of any methodology that emphasizes novelty and variety at the expense of high-quality repetitive practice.

Issue 4. You are interested in getting good results from your teaching efforts but are not sure if you should emphasize individual or group responsibility in attaining them. Should you picture your class more as individuals responsible for reaching their separate destinations or as a community attempting to achieve a mostly common goal?

The values of fine movement are so great a prize that everyone should want to achieve them and help their neighbor achieve them as well. The methodologies of teachers have often reinforced the primacy and isolation of the individual—individual goals, individual rates of learning, individual differences, individual needs, individual progress. Overlooked is what we may achieve and hold in common. In this profession, we have a treasure house of marvelous activities that are ready to delight any who can reach them. They are so marvelous, in fact, that they are likely to be attractive to almost everyone in our classes. To be sure, it is an achievement to have helped one or two students enter the treasure house. But what a greater success it would be to have most of a class, pulling one another along, enter together.

I would be suspicious of methods that aim at differences while overlooking equally obvious similarities. I would wonder about teachers who doubt the value of a game or dance to reach and speak to nearly everyone in a class. I would question methods that turn students into competitors with one another rather than helpmates on a common journey.

Review

Play and games are two different things. To take part in a game is to voluntarily attempt to solve unnecessarily difficult problems. Play, on the other hand, is a way of experiencing games when the participation is enjoyed for its own sake, not for any good reasons, not for what participation may produce afterwards.

Not only are games and play different. They are both needed and valuable. Games are safe stressors that can effectively highlight such cultural values and meanings as success, freedom, and justice. Play makes the game, dance, and sport worlds interesting and fresh. It allows people to relish and enjoy meaningful moments in these activities for their own sake. Play requires spontaneous giving prior to taking, it fosters human unpredictability, and it allows meaning to count.

This defense of games and play; earlier discussions of mind-body holism; the health of contemporary society; the relative importance of activity- and health-related fitness, knowledge, skill, and pleasure; and activity instruction seen as mainstream education hold any number of implications related to personnel, curriculum, and methodology. Solutions to practical problems can be deduced from these philosophic insights.

The hiring dilemma faced by Fred Oliphant in the example presented at the start of this chapter can be addressed by returning to philosophic judgments. Jessica Arnold, on paper, would seem to be the hands-down favorite. She has the better academic record and stronger letters of recommendation. She seems to possess more maturity and would appear to be more conscientious. However, Sigmund Claar is a lover of games and play, he possesses the more spontaneous spirit, he pursues a number of activity hobbies himself, he is a product of the local culture, and he has the professional philosophy of a reverent (and playfully irreverent) game player. Thus, if Mr. Oliphant wants an activity instructor who will recreate and educate clients in mainstream educational ways, he should select Sigmund Claar for the position.

Looking Ahead

In chapter 10 you will examine the ethics of professionals and participants in a field that promotes mainstream educational change in sport, dance, exercise, games, and play. You will look at *do*s and *don't*s of people in the activity world and learn a method for making difficult moral decisions.

Checking Your Understanding

1. Describe at least two defining characteristics that distinguish games from problems that are faced in everyday life.
2. Distinguish the spirit of play from the mood or attitude of obligation or work.

Can both be done seriously? Why or why not?
3. Why are games needed, and what is their power? Why is play needed, and what can it do for us?
4. What are some implications of the philosophic conclusions reached in the present and preceding chapters for such practical matters as hiring policies, curriculum development, and instructional methodology?

Key Terms

Game, p. 208

Inefficient means, p. 209

Serious and nonserious attitudes, p. 209

Play, p. 210

Prerational, p. 210

Conventions, p. 216

Personnel, p. 225

Curriculum, p. 228

Methodology, p. 231

Further Reading

For a discussion on the nature and value of games see Suits (1978), Bellah et al. (1991), Lasch (1979), and Morgan (1982). For analyses of play see Ellis (1973), Levy (1978), Huizinga (1950), Harper (1972), Meier (1980), and von Schiller (1972).

Chapter 10

Making Sound Ethical Decisions

Case 1.   Helen and Artis are playing a game of tennis at a local court. This is an informal contest, though they are keeping score and have decided to play the best of three sets. Because there is no umpire, they will have to call all of the shots themselves.

Early in the first set, Helen returns a ball to Artis that hits very near the baseline. Artis, who is leading at this time, honestly does not know if the ball hit "in" or "out." She finds herself in something of a moral dilemma. On the one hand, she does not want to appear noncompetitive or condescending by giving points away. But on the other, she wants to be a good sport and not claim points that she did not clearly win. Her promise to be competitive would seem to suggest that she call the shot "out" and take the point. But her commitment to be a good sport would seem to suggest that she give her opponent the benefit of the doubt and call the shot "in." She wonders what she should do.

Case 2. John McClintock, the head football coach at Smith High School, studied the rules, the opposing teams' tendencies, his own players' traits, the playing conditions—everything he could—in order to get an edge for his squad. Just before the start of the season during his third year at Smith High, McClintock stumbled upon what seemed to be a brilliant idea.

Near the end of an evening practice, just as the sun was disappearing over the western horizon, McClintock was standing behind his defensive line watching the offense run various dive plays over center, off guard, and off tackle. He noticed that it was very difficult to pick out the player with the ball, given the fact that it was growing dark. All he could see were the two white stripes that are painted on the ball, one at each end.

He knew that the lights at Smith High field were not adequate. In fact, other coaches and teams had complained for years that they could not see well when playing night games at Smith. McClintock figured that with this poor lighting he could make it even more difficult for defensive players of visiting teams to see which Smith High player had the ball. He would tape white bands around the arms of his quarterback and all his running backs and would teach them to hold their arms in such a way that the two stripes would be the same distance apart as those on the football. When these offensive players ran into the line, the defense would not be able to tell if they really had the ball or if they were only seeing the white bands on the players' forearms. McClintock figured that this would give his team just one more advantage in upcoming games.

It did. Opposing linemen and linebackers were frequently fooled into thinking that the wrong person had the ball. Smith won all its home games that season even though it went one and five on the road, where better lighting conditions rendered this practice useless.

Coach McClintock's strategy was effective. But was it morally acceptable?

Is there any right answer to the dilemma faced by Artis in the tennis game? Can she change her options from lose-lose to win-win choices? How would she do that?

Where does strategy end and cheating begin? Should coach McClintock be praised for devising a shrewd and effective plan for winning or criticized for compromising the letter or at least the spirit of the rules?

Much of your journey to this point has been devoted to answering so-called big questions—questions having to do with the nature of persons, the needs of society, and physical education's contributions to the good life and its ability to participate in mainstream, liberal education. In this chapter you will learn a procedure for making sound ethical decisions about relatively small issues—about day-to-day actions as an athlete, coach, teacher, or fitness specialist. Here the focus narrows as we attempt to understand how to behave morally.

IN THIS CHAPTER, YOU WILL

- **gain sensitivity to the presence of moral issues,**
- **learn the significance of attitudes toward yourself in moral decision making,**
- **learn how to find win-win solutions for many dilemmas,**
- **come to understand the importance of respecting your craft, and**
- **learn why it is important to strive for moral excellence.**

This philosophic journey would not be complete without looking at an important aspect of philosophy: ethics. Ethics involves judgments about what is good and worth pursuing in life and decisions about how we should act or behave. We worked with ethics in chapters 6 and 7, where we identified and ranked four values that should be promoted by our profession. But we have not yet looked carefully at questions related to our behavior. Many of the most fascinating and difficult problems of ethics in our field are found in sport:

Is it possible to distinguish between strategy, rule bending, and cheating?

Is sport a selfish activity? Do most ethically correct solutions to problems require you to deny yourself in some way?

Is ethics in sport worse today than it was in the past? If you think so, how could you go about demonstrating this? What are the key elements that make ethics become better or worse?

Why do we hear so much about athletic excellence and so little about moral excellence? Has something gone wrong in our society, or is this the way things should be?

What Are Ethics?

In this chapter, I use the terms **ethics** and **morality** synonymously. They have to do with decision making where right and wrong, should and should not, help and harm are at stake. The terms *ethics* and *morality* define an area of human responsibility and, by themselves, are value neutral. That is, all human beings have ethics and morals (all human beings have values and make judgments based on them), but not everyone has good ethics or high morals. The issue for professionals then is not to have ethics but to have good ethics, or high standards of morality. Good ethics involves at least two things: (1) identifying what is worthwhile or valuable and (2) distributing that good fairly. (justice)

The five steps presented here should provide you with a technique for achieving these two objectives of ethics and dealing with moral dilemmas like the ones posed in the examples at the beginning of the chapter. You will learn the ethical benefits of

1. becoming sensitive to moral issues,
2. respecting and loving yourself,
3. looking for win-win solutions,

4. respecting and loving your craft, and
5. searching for moral excellence.

Step 1: Becoming Sensitive to Moral Issues

Our society promotes moral insensitivity in a number of ways. Because of this, a first step in moral decision making involves regaining an ability to identify moral dilemmas and to be concerned about them.

How Moral Callouses Develop

While we may not be innately morally good creatures and know from first-hand experience that even youngsters can be robustly selfish, it does seem that children are generally compassionate. Yet, they are encouraged in our culture to grow from greater moral sensitivity to lesser care and concern.

This pattern can be seen in sport. An example has been provided in the box below.

Moral Sensitivity vs. Moral Callouses

Setting: A girl's soccer game

Date: July 1978

Location: Upstate New York, on a makeshift, sun-baked soccer field

Participants: Seven- and eight-year-old girls

Coaches: Volunteer parents

Officials: Two male high school soccer players paid $3/game

Weather conditions: Dry and uncomfortably hot

For most of the girls in this contest, it was their first summer of soccer and, for many, their first experience with organized competition of any sort. Their soccer skills might best be described as primitive, and they had not yet been highly socialized into any contemporary soccer ethic. In short, these young girls, at this very early point in their athletic lives, were not so much soccer players as they were youngsters who happened to be playing a game that vaguely resembled soccer.

The movement of these players was nothing short of remarkable. Except for the two goalies, they traveled in a pack chasing the elusive ball. It was as if they were all tied together on short tethers. Had they not been wearing different colored shirts, it would have been difficult for an onlooker to tell one team from the other.

Frequently, the ball would become somewhat trapped in the middle of this mass of girls with those closest to this frustrating object of interest kicking furiously to dislodge it. On one of these occasions, an eight-year-old contacted the ball solidly and sent it about two yards squarely into the stomach of a pony-tailed opponent. There was an audible thud, and the victim dropped to the ground gasping and sobbing.

No whistle was blown, but spontaneously and instantly the action stopped. Girls from both teams gathered around the temporarily injured player, some of them rubbing her back and asking if she was all right, others watching with

> interest and concern. The soccer ball, still officially in play, lay motionless and unattended somewhere around midfield.
>
> The two high school–aged officials, never having been told what to do when play stops while time is "in," looked genuinely nonplussed, but one of them finally blew his whistle. The officials retrieved the ball and walked over to the huddle of girls. The injured player had nearly regained her breath and was rising to her feet.
>
> She wiped away the few tears that remained and told her coach that she still wanted to play. Shortly, the game resumed and once again the girls, as if a single unit, began following the ball around the hot field (Kretchmar, 1990b, pp. 5, 27).

It is quite a distance, morally speaking, from a spontaneous gesture of concern for the welfare of an opponent to some of the acts of intimidation, rule bending, and general insensitivity we witness in the play of many athletes. How long does it take for young girls, or any youthful athletes, to become sophisticated players who exhibit rough play and think little or nothing of an opponent's injury or discomfort?

The anecdote about the girl's soccer game suggests that human beings develop something I have called **moral callouses** (Kretchmar, 1990). Just as callouses on our hands prevent us from feeling what we touch with much sensitivity, moral callouses that form around our hearts keep us from feeling issues of ethical right and wrong. To remove such callouses, we must be aware of how they formed and how they affect the way we think, perceive, and behave.

Common symptoms of the presence of moral callouses include

- frequent appeals to the fact that "everyone is doing it" (therefore, how could it be wrong?);
- an inability to distinguish between what is part of the game and what is not (if there are no penalties in the rulebook for behavior x, behavior x must be part of the game);
- difficulty in telling morally sound strategy from win-at-all-costs trickery (some

blatant rule breaking is now referred to by TV commentators, for example, as shrewd strategy); and

- a sense that if one is not caught, nothing wrong happened (whatever works is right).

We develop moral callouses in part by observing those we look up to.

PHILOSOPHIC EXERCISE

Below, I have identified five common behaviors that are regarded by many as morally acceptable. Do you think that their acceptability is the result of moral callouses, or do you think that they are actually OK? For help in getting answers to this question, ask yourself in each case, Do these behaviors cause any harm?

1. A coach who works officials at a basketball game (such as by yelling at an official with extra vigor to improve his team's chances of getting the next call)
2. A physical education teacher who calls in sick but uses the day for family responsibilities, justifying this as mental rest and relaxation
3. A hockey player who intentionally goes after an opponent who is known to be only partly recovered from an injury
4. A coach who teaches a basketball player to exaggerate or fake contact in order to draw a foul
5. Fans who intentionally interfere with communication among visiting team members (such as by producing a deafening roar at a football game so that the players cannot hear their quarterback's signals)

How to Remove Moral Callouses

If the development of moral callouses is a problem for many in our modern world, including those of us in the exercise sciences, how are we to soften or remove our moral callouses? We can begin by focusing on some important issues that are closely related to good ethics.

Making Promises

One fundamental method used by human beings for mutual protection and well-being is making promises. What promises should we make when we enter a game with another person?

- To play hard?
- To play by the rules?
- All the rules?
- All the time?
- What else?

What promises should teachers, physical therapists, or athletic trainers make?

- To work only when they feel like it?
- To honor the letter and spirit of their contracts?
- To keep the interests of their clients and students foremost in their thoughts?
- Anything else?

Looking Out for Harm

Ethical people are always on the lookout for harm, particularly harm to others that can be prevented by their own actions.

- Are we careful enough in looking for all sorts of harm in sport, and not just physical injury?
- Do we shove too much responsibility on the game officials and umpires for preventing harm, and thereby hide from this obligation ourselves?
- Does too strong a focus on winning or attaining excellence harm anyone?

As professionals,

- Are we aware that our actions affect not only our students and clients, but others

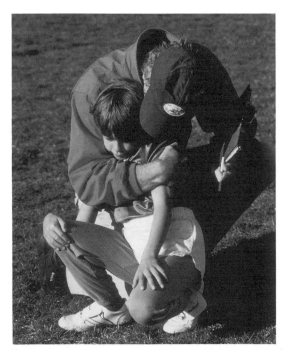

Are we careful in looking for all kinds of potential harm in sport?

as well, such as parents, taxpayers, and local residents?

• Are we so busy in our daily activities that we do not see many opportunities to prevent harm?

• Do we even harm ourselves by not doing a job as well as we can?

Looking Out for Selfishness

Excellent moral agents are careful not to act selfishly. They are aware of various rationalizations for essentially greedy behavior, and they refuse to use them. Are we tough enough on ourselves today in this regard? Do we use the following twin tests commonly employed to uncover selfishness?

1. Will I honestly be able to recommend this action for everyone in a similar situation? (Always act as if you are acting for everyone.)

2. Would I be willing to have others know of my actions and motives? (Always act in ways that you would be willing, in principle, to make public.)

Callouses take time to develop, and they take time to dissolve. The techniques of making and keeping promises, looking out for harm, and being alert for selfishness can start the process of increasing one's moral sensitivity. They can be used for virtually all situations that require moral treatment.

Step 2: Respecting and Loving Yourself

We tend to underestimate the importance of ourselves in the area of ethics for at least two reasons. First, some think that ethics has to do fundamentally with helping others to at least the partial exclusion of caring for ourselves. People who are highly ethical, it is often believed, are those who consistently deny themselves and even sacrifice personal wants for the good of their neighbors. This is called altruism, and individuals who are highly moral will often adopt this stance.

Second, much ethics is carried on without paying attention to how much we approve of ourselves. Whether or not we regard ourselves as precious or unique in some sense is not thought to be an ethically relevant question. What matters, it is said, is whether or not we regard our neighbors as precious.

Both of these beliefs about ethics are incomplete and thus ultimately inaccurate. An important early step in doing good ethics involves getting control of ourselves, respecting ourselves, and placing our needs and interests in a proper perspective. As we will see, many individuals in sport- and activity-related professions have trouble with ethics not because they dislike others but because they have problems of one sort or another with themselves.

Ethics has more to do with promoting the good and celebrating it than with giving things away and denying ourselves, though on occasion an altruistic attitude is required. In the first example at the beginning of the chapter, Artis faces a dilemma in which her rights appear to stand against those of Helen. Only one person can get the point. But who deserves it? And how should the problem of uncertain information about the shot be resolved? In truth, a resolution may present itself if Artis is capable of managing *herself* properly. Three types of self-management are worth examining: cooling out, loving oneself psychologically, and loving oneself philosophically.

Cooling Out

It is risky to make ethical decisions in a highly emotional state. For one thing, it is difficult to see and assess the various options that may be at your disposal if you are disturbed, highly excited, or too interested in some specific outcome.

In highly emotional states, you may be more inclined to be selfish without, perhaps, intending to be so. If Artis is excited about a big point and the possibility of finally winning a match against her long-time rival, she may be inclined automatically to favor herself with her decision. Or if she has been taught that it is far better to give than to receive, in an emotionally charged moment she may, in rote fashion, give the point away without understanding whether this is the most appropriate thing to do.

You will do ethics better if you **cool out**, that is, if you have the quiet and calm to look and see, to put at least some of your emotional involvement out of play, to reflectively review any obligations you might have, and to imagine the consequences of various actions on both yourself and others. It is best, of course, if you can take the time needed to relax and assess. But, in the heat of the game, such time is not always available. You cannot stop a contest for 15 minutes in order to make a good moral decision. You must gain this more objective perspective quickly and make a decision now—a decision that is neither blindly selfish nor automatically altruistic or sacrificial.

Thus, it would be wise for Artis to do some of her thinking beforehand. She might even want to discuss such situations with Helen before the contest begins. This would give them a chance to decide how close calls are to be dealt with before the first serve is hit, before emotions rise, before it becomes more difficult to make ethical decisions that would be maximally helpful. Perhaps the two players, under these conditions, would agree to replay any rallies where the winner cannot be determined. Or, if they feel that keeping the game going is more important than determining a winner accurately, they might agree to call all close shots "in."

Many of the things we say and do that we come to regret are done under the impulses of such strong emotions as anger, fear, jealousy, and disappointment. It is often important, therefore, to call a timeout in order to do good ethics consistently. Where lengthy timeouts are not feasible, it is important to think through options before emotions rise and a quick decision is needed.

Cooling out and thinking through a problem with some calmness, however, will do little good if a second crucial matter related to the self is not in place. It has to do with how you value yourself psychologically.

Loving Yourself Psychologically

It is often believed that the more highly we think of ourselves, the more likely we are to be selfish or egotistical. High self-regard, on this line of thought, leads to self-preoccupation and any number of behaviors that promote self-satisfaction, often at the expense of others' feelings or rights. Therefore the role of ethics, it is commonly believed, is to depress or check self-love, to downplay any feelings of entitlement to wealth and happiness, to promote giving more than receiving, to encourage one to love others more than oneself. Self-love and other-love are thought to stand in some sort of zero-sum relationship to one another. The more we love ourselves, the less we will be able (or inclined) to love others.

A more common view today, however, suggests that precisely the opposite is true. High self-regard is not only compatible with a healthy concern for others but may be a prerequisite for reaching out in morally good ways (Fromm, 1947, 1956). It stands to reason that if you are preoccupied with yourself—with your own fears and concerns and needs—you will be less likely to notice your neighbor's situation. Even less will you be

inclined to help this person. High self-regard, according to this theory, actually allows for and promotes self-forgetting. It is accompanied with the experiences of self-comfort and self-confidence, not self-preoccupation. Self-concern is actually a symptom of poor self-regard, weak ego strength, perhaps even self-hate. Consequently, if you want to be a good sportsperson, an early step would be to achieve a degree of peace with yourself, learn to like yourself, get to the point where you participate with a self that is OK.

High self-esteem, of course, is not something that people can simply talk themselves into. It is something that probably has chemical and genetic roots and that develops slowly from infancy on into adulthood. Nevertheless, it is useful and important to understand its role in ethics and the place it might have in your own experience as a moral agent.

PHILOSOPHIC EXERCISE

The self-test on p. 244 contains several activity-related statements that will help you get a rough reading on your self-regard and thus your ability to forget yourself. Respond to each statement using the number that corresponds to how frequently you experience the feelings described.

Drawing Conclusions About High and Low Self-Esteem

Everyone, to one extent or another, has the sorts of feelings reflected in the self-test. Nevertheless, people with higher levels of self-regard are less likely to be preoccupied with such thoughts and should be better able to

Self-Regard Self-Test

Rating Scale:	Very often	Often	Sometimes	Infrequently	Never
	1	2	3	4	5

1. I experience anger when I fall behind in sport contests.
2. I am impatient with myself when I cannot get a new move right.
3. When I was younger, I would lose my temper if I lost a big game or made mistakes.
4. I feel that it is very important to win.
5. I am self-conscious when I perform in front of a crowd.
6. I tend to focus on how well others are playing or performing and sometimes am jealous if they are doing well.
7. I wonder if I will ever be satisfied with the way I play or perform.
8. I worry about how skilled I am in comparison to others in my sport.
9. Before competing or performing I think about what it would be like to fail.
10. My sense of well-being rises and falls dramatically with how well I am playing or performing at the moment.

Add up your score. If your total score falls between 10 and 20, it is likely that you miss some moral opportunities because of your level of self-interest and self-concern. It may even be that you intentionally bring some harm to others because of the amount of psychological time and energy you spend on yourself. If your total score falls between 40 and 50, it is likely that you are largely free of yourself when you play or perform. You are in a better position to see and assess opportunities to promote the good, and you are probably more inclined to act accordingly. If you scored in the middle—somewhere between 20 and 40—your results are mixed. You probably have good days (when you are self-confident and largely free of self-concern) and bad days (when you doubt your worth or competence and spend too much time focused on your feelings and needs).

notice what is going on around them, what needs their teammates (and opponents) might have. And they should be more available to act in ways that prevent harm and promote good.

Self-esteem affects everything that we do at work and play. Of course, it affects the way we approach competitive situations. Table 10.1 lists a few typical effects of high and low self-esteem on attitudes toward winning, cheating, opponents, teammates, and the activity itself.

Loving Yourself Philosophically

Why be ethical at all? Why not do what we want to do and not worry about the conventions of society that would tell us that our actions are morally right or wrong? One answer to this question is provided by looking at human capability and potential, much as you did in establishing criteria for the good life in chapter 5 (MacIntyre, 1984). Briefly, the argument goes like this:

Table 10.1   Effects of High and Low Self-Regard

	High self-regard	Low self-regard
Winning and losing	Participants have the experience of trying to win or wanting to win: winning is desirable	Participants have the experience of needing or having to win: winning is a litmus test for worth or status
Cheating	Less inclination to seek shortcuts for sake of victory; no need to cheat to win.	Cheating and rule bending are seen as sensible, and sometimes necessary, means to a victory
Opponents	Less likely to fear, dislike, or distrust opponents; opponents are seen as helpful partners who provide desirable opportunities	Opponents often disliked because they stand in the way of what is needed—victory
Teammates	Less likely to have experiences of jealousy; less likely to blame teammates for a loss	Often see teammates as a threat or roadblock to one's own success; more likely to have negative feelings toward teammates after a loss
The game	More likely to enjoy the game for its own sake—win or lose	Enjoyment of the game is dependent on winning; focus is frequently on extrinsic factors like fame, trophies, notoriety

1. We can tell humans at their best from humans at their worst, just as we can tell good cars, books, and restaurants from bad ones. Further, just as we can describe many of the features and qualities that distinguish good cars, books, or restaurants from bad ones, we can describe many of the features and qualities that distinguish humanity at its best from humanity at its worst.

2. While we may not be able to agree on every feature of humans who have reached their full human potential, we can (across cultures, time, religions, and other variables) come to at least a rough consensus on this.

3. Knowledge of what humanity is at its best brings with it a call for action, a mandate that all people should aim at achieving this status. This is so because it would be contradictory to say that this is what people are like when they are their finest but that there is no reason for anyone to strive to be this way. It would be like saying that we can tell good cars from bad ones, but this gives us absolutely no reason to build or buy the better varieties. It is to claim, for example, that model X, gives a smooth, safe ride in contrast to model Y, but that is still no reason for building or buying model X.

To know what it is to be an outstanding human being, or a good car, or a fine restaurant, is to have strong reasons for pursuing those ends. To understand what the finest human capabilities are is to have a rational basis for organizing one's behavior in that direction.

As you have already discovered, coming up with an agreeable description of humanity at its best is not a simple assignment. But some such description is necessary if you are to have a philosophic foundation for high self-regard.

Humans at Their Best

There are many competing descriptions of humanity at its best. A recent one that has gained some popularity (MacIntyre, 1984) includes three recommendations, discussed in detail as follows.

People Should Seek Internal Goods

Human beings are capable of understanding the distinction between succeeding by means of artistry and skill, on the one hand, and through luck, undisciplined force, cheating, or treachery, on the other. We are also capable of objectively valuing the former over the latter. We are able to judge confidently, in other words, that it would be better to show skill, creativity, meaningful achievement, and other forms of excellence than it would be to benefit merely from luck, brute force, questionable ethics, and hollow successes. In sport, we can judge that it would be better, for example, to show admirable artistry in a losing cause than it would be to display a reliance on blind luck, intimidation, and cheating to produce a victory. The **internal goods** of any practice—be it playing football, sculpting, doing research, coaching, running a fitness center, raising children, or performing in a dance company—are those achievements or excellences that are available only to those who confront the problems of the practice head-on, honestly, with their own personal capabilities.

The internal goods of any practice are available only to those who confront the problems of the practice head-on with their own personal capabilities.

The pursuit of internal goods, unfortunately can be (and often is) traded for external ones—things like victories, fame, and fortune. These can be had in any number of ways—legally and illegally, by means of displaying skill or by means of intimidation or luck, creatively or unimaginatively, insightfully or blindly. Because fame and fortune have their own value that some regard highly, there is always the temptation to pursue and take them in whatever way one can. But, of course, this threatens opportunities to achieve those higher goods that are internal to a practice. If you were to rely on cheating or intimidation, for example, in order to win, you will diminish your chances to show grace, fine timing, touch, endurance, and so on.

If you love yourself in this way (if you hold yourself primarily to the pursuit of internal goods), you will develop various character traits that will guide your daily actions. You will develop honesty and integrity, for example, for you realize that you cannot achieve genuine artistic goals by looking for tricks or shortcuts or by relying on luck or good fortune. You will develop perseverance because you realize that internal goods are not usually easy to come by. You will develop a sense of justice and fair play, for you know that victories under certain illegal or unjust circumstances have little or nothing to do with internal goods.

People Should Develop a Coherent Life Story

Human beings are capable of comprehending and living their lives as connected, meaningful stages in the development of a story rather than a number of largely isolated events that have nothing more in common than their contribution to making it or surviving. We are able to survey opportunities we encounter and to determine whether or not they are consistent with personal goals and values, whether or not they are right based on our personal history and previous life experiences.

Individuals who exemplify the species at its best insist on making this discrimination between what is right for their unique life story and what is not, and on acting accordingly. Even when exciting opportunities are presented, they are able to say no if, for some reason, these options move these people off course or into a job or profession for which they cannot generate much excitement. Flattery, money, advancement, and security, of course, might make opportunities attractive. But these features, as seductive as they are, are kept in perspective. They are considered in conjunction with concerns about being true to oneself, about choosing options that will be personally meaningful and, for that reason, right.

Individuals who do not reach this higher level of lifespan coherence are often referred to as opportunistic. They jump at advancements; they are distracted by glitter; they do what is convenient or what is immediately enjoyable or presently gratifying. When they look back on a career or a lifetime, they see very little pattern in past events.

If you respect yourself in this second philosophic sense (if you insist on pursuing a coherent and meaningful lifecourse), you will develop yet additional virtues. You will find that you need the virtue of constancy or persistence because it takes singleness of purpose to find your story and your values in the face of various distractions. You will find that you need the virtue of patience because any number of attractive opportunities may come your way that are not right for you. You may think, at times, that the right job, the right person, the right opportunity, the right break will never show up. You will need to continue to look and pursue and wait, rather than abandon your dream.

People Should Promote Good and Avoid Harm

Human beings who operate at their highest levels are capable of making yet another discrimination and commitment. This has to do with identifying good and harm and acting in accordance with this perception (Frankena, 1973). It also has to do with a recognition that these actions have consequences for others as well as oneself and that goods should be distributed justly.

The best examples of the human species do not live as if they are blind to good and harm. They can identify any number of intrinsic and extrinsic values—as we did in chapters 6 and 7. Nor do the best examples of the human species live as if they are blind to the existence of others and their own interest in living good lives.

This aspect of high self-regard can be illustrated by returning to one of the fictional characters at the beginning of the chapter, John McClintock, the clever high school football coach who devised the scheme for gaining a competitive edge on a poorly lit home football field. What if he were to claim that he has high self-regard in the two senses we have already discussed? What if he were to claim that he is committed to a practice—that of being a most devious, clever, win-at-all-cost football coach? Other coaches, most of whom do not like McClintock or his methods, still begrudgingly recognize him for being excellent at what he does.

And what if McClintock were to claim that he was following a coherent life course? He truly believes that winning is the only thing that matters, and he has chosen his profession and his way of developing his skills accordingly. When he looks back over his life of coaching, he sees a consistent pattern of development as a no-holds-barred winner.

Many thoughtful people, however, would not regard individuals like McClintock as prototypes of humanity at its best—in spite of his excellence as a devious, manipulative coach and in spite of the remarkable consistency and coherence of the win-at-all-costs narrative that tells the story of his life. Our third criterion for high human standards,

however, provides a way of highlighting the shortcomings of a person like McClintock. He is not able to (or chooses not to) discriminate between promoting good and harm and between distributing goods fairly and unfairly. There are signs that McClintock was at least a bit callous (he wasn't terribly concerned that he was bringing certain harm to everyone who played the game), nor was he apparently concerned that he and perhaps his players were reaping benefits that they did not earn or otherwise deserve. (He was willing to take advantage of poor lighting through an overt act of deception when he knew that other schools, given the better lighting on their fields, could not reciprocate.)

What harm did he bring to the game and its participants? By placing the deceptive stripes on his running backs and taking advantage of unfortunately poor lighting conditions, he reduced the emphasis that football places on the testing of skills (including legal deception). His own players were deprived of the chance to beat their opponents (show their superior skill) by running, blocking, cutting, and faking better. His players would always be open to the charge that they won because they had bad lights and deceptive uniforms, not because they played better football.

There are also problems with McClintock's insensitivity to questions of distribution. Is he claiming goods for himself (and possibly his team) that should be more evenly available to his opponents and their coach? Is he not saying, in effect, "I will take advantage of our poor lighting, and I will reap all the benefits associated with winning and success, even though the playing field is not level tonight, and even though I know that the good lighting at your field will not allow you to turn the tables on us next year"? Is this attitude not a little myopic if not blatantly selfish? Is there not some sense in which justice has been violated here?

If you think of yourself as a person who can distinguish good from evil, better from worse, and fair distribution from its counterpart, you will develop additional virtues. You will need to become conscientious in looking for the good in each situation and in finding ways to maximize the good for the greatest number of people. You may need to become courageous, because some of your decisions about promoting the good will undoubtedly contradict common practice. Regarding equalitarian justice, you will need to develop the virtue of fairness. It is also likely that you will have to be industrious, for it usually takes extra time and energy to assure that goods are distributed fairly.

SUMMARY BREAK

Good ethics are highly dependent on the self and require self-control (and cooling out, when necessary), good feelings about oneself (self-respect and self-love in a psychological sense), and high human standards (self-respect and self-love in a philosophical sense).

If you are impetuous, if you let emotions like anger, frustration, and fear guide your decisions, you run a particular risk of displaying bad ethics. If you are not comfortable with yourself and who you are, you are more likely to display bad ethics. And if you do not see human beings as special creatures with unique powers to seek internal goods over external ones, choose a coherent life course or story line, and promote good over evil, you run a higher risk of displaying bad ethics. These differences promote the development of diverse character traits and virtues. Table 10.2 provides a comparison of good and bad traits that are associated with good and bad ethics.

Step 3: Looking for Win-Win Solutions

Ethics does not always require that you sacrifice for the benefit of others. In many situations, there are choices that are actually **win-win solutions**. They are good for others and you. Therefore, it is wise first to examine dilemmas for solutions that benefit everyone. If none are available, then you may be faced with the possibility of suspending your own interests or even of sacrificing something for the good of others.

You will recall that in the tennis game between Artis and Helen, Artis faced an apparent lose-lose situation. No matter what she did (called the shot "in" or "out"), she would violate some obligation. If she called the shot "in" and thereby gave away a point she might have actually deserved, she would not be meeting her obligation as a competitor. She might even appear to be patronizing Helen. If she called the shot "out" and thereby took a point she might not have actually deserved, she would not be meeting her obligation as a sportsperson. She might even appear to be selfishly interested in winning at the cost of stealing points.

Is there a win-win moral option here? The chances of finding one are enhanced if some agreements are made before the match begins. Imagine the following conversation, one that has the effect of clarifying the interests that the two women have in playing on that day:

> *Helen*: "Let's keep score today and play three sets."
>
> *Artis*: "OK."

This is already a win-win move. Both want to play competitively today. Both regard the keeping of a score and the attempt to outdo one another as meeting their interests. Both realize, in coming to this agreement, that they could end up the loser in what will be a competitive match rather than recreation or practice. But they also know that this possibility is necessary if the added excitement and interest of a true contest is to be had.

Table 10.2   Contrasting Ethical Traits

Traits that promote good ethics	Traits that promote bad ethics
Self-control, rationality, an ability to gain some distance from an emotional event or issue	Recklessness, emotionalism, a tendency to act with emotion and self-interest
Honesty and integrity; an interest in achieving something of value	Drive and desire; an interest in succeeding by whatever means
A sense of fair play	A win-at-all-costs attitude
Patience, a willingness to wait for the right opportunity	Opportunism, a tendency to jump at the first attractive offer one receives
Constancy, singleness of purpose, the development of a life and career guided by clear values	Adaptability, vacillation, a tendency to adopt values that work or that are currently popular
Conscientiousness, thoroughness	Efficiency, productivity
Courage, a willingness to stand by one's values in the face of difficulty	Strategic shrewdness, an unwillingness to let extraneous values stand in the way of success
Altruism, a tendency to look out for the rights and interests of others	Survivalism, a tendency to take care of oneself and let others take care of their own problems

During the second rally, Artis intentionally plays the disputed shot from Helen that might have been out. At the end of the rally, one that Helen ends up winning, the conversation goes like this:

Helen: "That ball you hit a moment ago looked like it might have been out."

Artis: "I wasn't sure, so I played it."

Helen: "Do you want to play the point over?"

Artis: "No. It delays the game to do that. Why don't we both call any questionable shots 'in' and play them?"

Helen: "I agree. Let's keep the game moving."

Again, this is a win-win decision because both parties found out that they shared common interests, and a solution was found that meets those interests. Artis did not have to sacrifice something to Helen by calling the shot "in." Both gained something because this call kept the game going. Moreover, fairness was reasonably well assured because they made a promise that all such close calls will be played. Helen, in other words, will behave exactly as Artis did when a questionable shot lands on her side of the net.

But what if Helen and Artis had different interests? What if Helen wanted to play recreationally (no score would be kept, and she would not expend much effort to play her best), and Artis wanted to have a true contest? It appears that a compromise would be in order, particularly if the women enjoy each other's company in spite of their differing interests. For example, instead of playing three sets, they could play one and then spend another hour just hitting the ball around. Each side would make a partial sacrifice, and each side would receive a partial benefit while enjoying the other's company.

Step 4: Respecting and Loving Our Crafts

We all know that there are certain situations in which there is no clear win-win option. There are times when every choice has some distasteful aspect to it. Here, it would seem, is where self-denial comes into ethics. Here, some might claim, highly ethical people are required to downplay personal interests in favor of others' interests. While there is an element of truth to this, and while courageous, sacrificial acts are among the most honored forms of behavior in human history, ethics does not lead directly and irrevocably to self-denial—even where no win-win solutions would seem to be readily available.

Sometimes ethics are made more difficult than they need to be because we focus on the rights and interests of different *people*. This promotes a me-versus-you kind of thinking and too often ends up in a moral stalemate. We both have legitimate rights, and sometimes we have no way to decide whose rights take priority.

Perhaps our focus should be on the activity instead! It could be that we would end up being more ethical if we made sport, dance, or exercise the objects of our concern first and people second! After all, it is sport, dance, and exercise that stand between us. These are what we share, and relish, and learn from, and grow by. If we nurtured and protected them, perhaps many other things (morally speaking) would fall into place. In fact, some ethical questions do turn out to be more easily answerable by reference to the integrity of the game than to the players, as we shall see.

What if we were to consider our tests and contests (whether they involve dance, sport, or exercise) as precious jewels that need to be safeguarded and polished and then thoroughly enjoyed? What if we regarded them

so highly that we dedicated ourselves to their preservation and enhancement? This deflects attention and concern from what I get in contrast to what you get. It puts the spotlight on what we share—an art form in dance, a game, a sport, a type of play, some special kind of exercise. In order to investigate this possibility, we need to review some ideas about preserving and enhancing tests and contests. The game test is the problem presented by the activity. As noted in chapter 9, it includes a goal and a set of limited means for achieving it. The contest comes into existence when two or more parties confront the same game test and attempt to reach its goal in a superior way.

What if we consider our contests as precious jewels?

Preserving Tests

1. *Care must be taken to retain the difficulties or hurdles of game tests.* If a testing problem becomes too easy, the test will be boring and probably uninteresting.

2. *Care must be taken to retain chances for success in game tests.* If a testing problem becomes too difficult, the test will be frustratingly hard and probably uninteresting.

3. *Care must be taken to preserve an active, creative role for the performer.* If a testing problem is solved only or primarily on the basis of chance or luck, the test will not sufficiently allow for the exercise of skill, cunning, inventiveness, and creativity. The participant will become a passive spectator and a beneficiary or victim of blind fate.

4. *Care must be taken to provide flexible rules that accommodate people of different ages, maturation levels, and skills and, in some cases, of both genders.* If a testing problem is inflexible, the test will be appropriate for only a narrow range of individuals. Those whose maturity and skills do not match the demands of the game problem will be disinterested in it.

5. *Care must be taken to structure games so that both challenges and skill improvement are open-ended.* If a test is not complex and does not offer new challenges to performers as they improve their skills, the test will lack durability. People will quickly grow out of tests and turn to different activities.

There are a number of other characteristics of good tests that could have been discussed here. For example, there are a host of practical considerations having to do with time, cost, and safety. But the list here gets at many of the central factors that make for good tests. If these characteristics were kept in mind and preserved, the future of our sport, dance, and exercise tests would be well assured.

Preserving Contests

There are also important factors to consider in preserving competition and the contests in which competition takes place. As was the case with tests, contests can be damaged and otherwise harmed. Their characteristics need to be understood so that proper diagnoses can be made when problems emerge. Here are a few suggestions regarding the health and well-being of contests.

1. *Care must be taken to make sure that rules are the same for all competitors so that fair competition and an ability to compare results meaningfully are preserved.* If the two or more competitors are not taking the same test (e.g., they are not playing by the same rules), it will be difficult, if not impossible, to compare their results. If one person cheats or misinterprets a rule and consequently faces an easier test than his opponent, the final result will probably not reflect the actual differences in their skills and abilities.

2. *Care must be taken to preserve an appropriate level of difficulty in the tests faced by competitors.* If game tests are too easy or difficult, the related contest will be endangered. If all competitors can solve the problem quickly and easily or, conversely, if no competitors can solve a game problem, the result (in principle, and probably in practice) will be a tie.

3. *Care must be taken to assure that commitment is in place prior to all competition.* If contestants are not committed to outdoing the other side, the resulting competition will lose its integrity and the results are likely to be misleading or meaningless.

4. *Care should be taken to make sure that competitors are members of the "same testing families"* (Kretchmar, 1975). If contestants do not have comparable skill, chances for satisfactory competition are decreased. In

interactive sports like football and basketball, incomparable skills usually lead to tests that are too easy and too difficult for the opposing teams. In noninteractive sports like bowling, swimming, and skiing, incomparable skills lead to contests that are lopsided and uninteresting.

This is only a brief sketch of tests and contests, but it serves to identify some of the characteristics of sport that make it the enduring and fascinating activity it is. It gives us an idea of what sport looks like when it is healthy and when it is ill.

An Example

The dilemma described in the box below was actually faced by table tennis players and rule makers a few years ago. I will use this example to demonstrate how to work through an ethical problem.

Preserving Table Tennis

Some very clever table tennis players once devised a novel technique that was entirely legal but one that virtually assured victory, even against superior opponents. What they did was this. Like many table tennis players, they put very different types of sponge rubber on the two sides of their bats (paddles). The rubber on one side was tacky and would grab the ball, often imparting a tremendous spin to it in the direction of the arm swing. The rubber on the other side of the bat would have precisely the opposite effect on the ball. It would allow the ball to skid and retain its original spin, even though the arm action would make it look as if the spin had been reversed. The two sheets of rubber were the same color, so an opponent could not tell which type of rubber had contacted the ball on any given shot. Up to this time, players kept the same grip on their bats for an entire rally. Thus, an opponent would know that all forehand shots were hit with the same rubber, as were all the backhands. They could adjust their return accordingly.

These clever players, however, developed the technique of flipping their bats beneath the surface of the table between shots. The rubber that was on the backhand side on one shot might be on the forehand side on the next swing. This technique was not easy to master. Players had to know by feel alone which type of rubber sheet was currently on their forehand and backhand sides, and they would have to recognize this in an instant.

Opponents who faced this new technique simply could not tell which type of rubber sheet was being used on each stroke. Not knowing this, they could not adjust for the spin of the ball and make an effective return. They were virtually reduced to guessing which side of the bat had hit the ball. If they guessed wrong, their own shot would almost always go astray. As a result, top world players who had not mastered (or even seen) this new technique were losing to much lesser opponents.

Finding the Best Question. I suggest that we might find a potential solution to this problem by focusing on what is best or good for the art of table tennis rather than trying to determine the rights and interests of the players who developed the new technique versus the rights and interests of their opponents. Therefore, the best question to ask may be this: What decision will do the most to protect the richness and integrity of table tennis and thus do the most to bring good to table tennis players now and in the future?

Finding a Good Answer. While we may never find the single best solution to any moral dilemma, we must have confidence that we can discover a good answer. With that limitation acknowledged, we must ask if better answers lie in the direction of continuing to permit the technique, prohibiting it, or something in between. What effect, in short, does this technique have on the game?

The bat-flipping technique threatens to diminish the craft, art, or practice of table tennis. Balls hit with this novel technique cannot be returned. Or more accurately put, opponents are reduced to guessing which side of the bat had, in fact, contacted the ball. If they guess right, they might be successful in returning the shot. If they guess wrong, the ball has virtually no chance of striking the table. The defensive aspect of the game, because of this technique, is turned, for all practical purposes, into a 50-50 game of roulette.

This unavoidable consequence dramatically and unequivocally impoverishes the activity. It simplifies the problem; it reduces the significance of skill in playing the game; it replaces creative responses, in part, with the table tennis equivalent of flipping a coin; it threatens to make the defensive side of the game boring. And moreover, those in the table tennis family, those who know best, say there is no realistic possibility for a defensive adjustment.

It becomes clear that this new technique damages the test of table tennis on at least three of the five criteria of good tests that were listed previously and on at least one of the guidelines for good contests.

- In this case it was virtually impossible to tell which type of rubber had contacted the ball and thus what kind of spin was on it. The best players in the world could not determine the spin. The test was too difficult and thus was experienced as frustrating and uninteresting.

- The new technique, while it required the development of some skill for its effective utilization, actually eliminated many more skill opportunities in the defensive half of the game. Returning shots was reduced, in part, to a guessing game about which side of the opponent's bat had hit the ball.

- This new technique made table tennis a far less complex and interesting activity. It eliminated possibilities for making clever returns of shots that arrive with a number of different spins on them. Because one could not tell the spin, one could not react to it.

- The level of opportunity, regarding the guessing part of the activity, is the same, and this reduces the ability of opponents to show skill and superiority. Over the long term, the law of averages dictates that everybody ties in games of pure chance. An excess element of chance, therefore, is not a good thing in a contest where the purpose is to compare capabilities and show differences.

On the basis of this evidence, and assuming that there is no realistic expectation that a defense can be invented for this new technique, the morally superior answer is clear. The new strategy should not become part of the game. Even if it is technically legal, players who respect the craft of table tennis should voluntarily not use it. They would quickly see its negative impact and choose not to harm the activity that is the home of their artistry, indeed the very condition for it.

This resolution is a partial win-win solution because it protects the game and thereby assures untold amounts of good for present and future table tennis players. Everyone who receives internal goods from table tennis (the excellence of timing, touch, creativity, speed, etc.) wins because the source of that good (a valid game test) is preserved. Only those who focus on external goods could be losers.

Not surprisingly, much the same resolution was actually mandated by rule makers at the International Table Tennis Federation. While they permitted the technique of spinning the bat, they eliminated its game-harming effects by requiring that all players use different-colored rubber on each side of their bat. Players could still flip their bats below the level of the table, but now as they raised their arm to take a swing, opponents could tell which side of the bat struck the ball. This allowed them to read the spin and adjust for a skillful return.

Step 5: Looking for Moral Excellence

It is a curious fact that people will work overtime and make all manner of sacrifice to achieve dance, athletic, and exercise excellence, but do not seem to be interested in doing the same in the arena of ethics. Athletes will practice for months, maybe years, to get a certain move right in gymnastics, but they will hardly apply themselves at all to nagging moral questions about the overspecialization or neglect of other duties that this practice requires. It could be, therefore, that we are socialized to set our moral goals too low. If this is true, how should we go about raising our standards?

One recommendation is that we should be vigilant in looking for actions that are optional rather than required, surprising rather than expected, unusual rather than routine. A number of years ago I read a newspaper account of a high school cross-country meet and was struck by the fine gesture made by one of the coaches. This account is included in the box on p. 256 (Patrick, 1981).

Of significance here is the fact that this coach did not have to give up the championship trophy. He could have accepted his team's good fortune at the disqualification of the opposing runner and taken the award back to his school's trophy case. Who would have faulted him for this? But he held himself to higher standards. He looked for the optional, not just the expected!

PHILOSOPHIC EXERCISE

To determine if you can see the difference between acting in morally high versus average ways, analyze the following situations. Which have a larger duty component to them, and which are morally optional or high?

1. After a poor call that went against the home team at a championship basketball game, fans shout their displeasure but refrain from throwing objects at the officials or onto the court.
2. Basketball fans, before the start of a championship game, applaud respectfully when the officials' names are announced over the public address system.
3. A baseball coach, angry at an umpire for a bad call, questions his ability orally but does not physically bump or hit him.
4. A high school soccer player quickly commends a nearby official for an accurate call that helped her own team win an important game.

An Example of Moral Excellence

Bob Bradley is giving up the trophy it took him 20 years to win.

His McQuaid Jesuit High School cross-country team was declared state champion Saturday through a disqualification in the annual intersectional meet at Malone. But Bradley turned over the trophy to Corcoran High of Syracuse, a team his runners defeated twice during the season.

Bradley said the team didn't think the trophy would have looked right in the McQuaid trophy case.

The official score of the meet was McQuaid, 96. Corcoran, Kingston, Clarkstown South and Hauppaque all tied for second with 97. The low score wins. But McQuaid didn't like the way it won the title.

The Knights were declared winners after Corcoran's Steve Loretz, the apparent individual winner, was disqualified. Loretz and Grant Whitney of Penfield were disqualified for making a wrong turn on a poorly marked section of the snow-covered course.

The two leaders cut the course by 15-30 yards but had a greater margin of victory over the rest of the field. Bradley and his runners didn't feel Loretz and Whitney should have been penalized. Bradley called the home of Corcoran Coach John Hohm Sunday night, but Hohm wasn't in. Bradley left a message that the McQuaid team felt Corcoran had run the best race of the day and deserved to be champions.

"That call meant more to me than anything in the world," said Hohm. "I couldn't sleep that night."

Hohm was more overwhelmed when he learned yesterday that McQuaid was mailing the trophy.

"It's something you don't see in sports," he said. "It's a very noble gesture. I can't say enough about Bradley. It forces other coaches to ask themselves, 'In the same situation, could I do something so noble?'"

Bradley chose to downplay the matter. "We don't want to make a big deal over this," he said. "It just seemed like the thing to do."

---

5. A tennis player applauds an outstanding return made by an opponent, even though that shot decided an important game in the match.

If we are to concern ourselves with ethics, why should we not make a commitment to do it well? Why not make a commitment to seek out acts that are not just morally expected but also those that are unusually fine, surprising, and thus memorable? Is there not more than a little inconsistency in the commitment of any person who aspires to be a fine athlete or dancer by displaying excellent motor skill but only average ethics?

Have you heard of the Heisman Trophy? The Stanley Cup? The Super Bowl? The Final Four? The Rider Cup? The World Series? The Olympics? Have you ever seen these things featured on the front pages of newspapers and at prime time on your television?

How about the International Fair Play Award? Do you remember who won it last year? Do you know what that person did? Did you see it reported in the headlines of your local paper or watch film clips of those morally excellent actions on television? Unless you teach ethics of sport at a college or university, you probably do not even know that such an award exists.

In order to promote a better balance between respect for fine play and excellent behavior, we need to focus on going beyond the call of duty in looking for those options that have some moral height to them. Perhaps you learned from the exercise above that you have no trouble in finding them. If so, the only issue that remains is whether or not you have the will, energy, and courage to pursue them.

Review

Ethics is about promoting good living and distributing benefits fairly. One procedure for promoting good moral behavior includes five steps:

1. Becoming sensitive to moral issues
2. Respecting and loving yourself
3. Looking for win-win solutions
4. Respecting and loving your craft
5. Searching for moral excellence

Good ethics requires that we are able to find ethical issues and remove any moral callouses that may have developed. Good ethics is more likely to come about when we are comfortable with ourselves and hold ourselves to high standards, when we cool off when under duress and when we plan ahead in looking for common interests. Some of the best ethical decisions come from loving one's craft rather than focusing on competing rights of people and from looking for fine

or optional actions rather than merely what is expected.

Looking Ahead

You have covered a considerable amount of philosophic territory and should now attempt to summarize the highlights of this journey. In the next chapter, I will give you some guidelines for developing a personal philosophy of sport, exercise science, and physical education.

Checking Your Understanding

1. What is it like to develop moral callouses in sport? What are some symptoms of this problem in contemporary sport?
2. Why is the self an issue in ethics? What are three issues regarding the self that affect good ethics?
3. Can you give an example of a win-win solution in ethics? Can you provide any practical tips for finding such an outcome?
4. Explain how it is possible to solve an ethics problem between people by doing what is right for the sport these people are playing.
5. What are some examples of moral heroism in sport?

Key Terms

Ethics/morality, p. 237

Moral callouses, p. 238

Cool out, p. 242

Loving oneself psychologically, p. 243

Further Reading

For a good overview of ethics see Frankena (1973). For treatments of ethics in sports, see Fraleigh (1984), Simon (1992), and the "Fair Play" column in *Strategies*.

Chapter 11

Writing a Personal Philosophy

In one sense you have come to the end of your philosophic journey. But in another you have only begun. It is time both to take stock of what happened to you along this philosophic trail and to look ahead.

Professional Traveling and Philosophic Road Maps

In the Introduction I mentioned that many young professionals are encouraged to do

259

their jobs without undue delays caused by philosophic reflection and without the effort needed to consult philosophic road maps to find superior destinations. You may well be encouraged to get on with your life—to get a job, to pull out onto some professional highway and simply follow the car ahead of you. Someone up there, you could reason, must know where they are going.

College education, for many individuals, has become something of a vocational prep school where the right majors, right courses, right certifications, right internships, and right GPAs culminate in a right résumé—right, that is, for getting a job. We are socialized to pull out into the traffic, earn our paychecks, and equate all this with success.

Yet we wonder why there are so few fresh thoughts in our profession, why our field does not advance more quickly, why we seem to be reacting to external conditions rather than acting boldly and with vision, why the various health and fitness needs of the world are not catapulting us into the educational and service limelights! Perhaps too many professionals have been overly concerned with developing right résumés rather than right ideas and practices.

If the philosophic traveling described in this book has affected you in a personal way, you will hesitate before pulling out into any of the traffic lanes established for your vocation. You will check your philosophic road map for good destinations before you begin traveling. You will require reasons for selecting one itinerary over another. You may end up going someplace alone, but the journey should be most satisfying and might even inspire others to follow.

If this journey has affected you in a personal way, you are now more a questioner, a critic, a "why" person than when you began. You are less likely to accept the status quo. You may even be thoughtfully irreverent by raising questions that make some of your colleagues uncomfortable.

You may question the sufficiency of science to solve all human dilemmas, or even just the major ones.

You may question the scientific assumptions about human beings as machines and about the distinction between mind and body.

You may question the superior value traditionally assigned to the so-called intellect—to thinking as a prerequisite for doing, to speaking and writing over gesturing and moving, to thinking propositionally or abstractly (even when it is done unimaginatively) over performing in fleshy-motor ways (even when it is done insightfully and creatively).

You may question the traditionally assigned and often readily accepted role of physical educators as body mechanics and repair persons.

You may question the values and overall well-being of contemporary society and wonder about your field's potential to cure society's ills rather than perpetuate its problems.

You may question traditional rankings of values—like fitness, skill, knowledge, and pleasure—and wonder about the extrinsic and intrinsic power of these values to promote the good life.

You may question typical understandings of human movement that miss the cultural power of sport, games, and play—power that shows up in skill to participate in and build interesting lives, power that shows up in a capacity to play within and experience significance in culture's better traditions.

You may question physical education's typical exclusion from mainstream education and the common assumption that coaches, fitness instructors, and teachers cannot be liberal change agents.

You may question the facts that morally uncertain practices today pass for strategy, that many professionals believe that there are no objective ways to solve dilemmas in ethics, that loving one's activity (in contrast to people) has supposedly little to do with morality.

If these issues and others like them get in your way and delay you, that is good. The time used to ponder, evaluate, understand, choose, and commit yourself will be time well spent!

Relying on Philosophy to Provide a Road Map

As a result of reading this book and working through its exercises, you should be more inclined to find philosophic questions in your profession. Some of my own students teasingly tell me, years after taking my courses, that I have contaminated them. They can't watch games on television or walk down the street without being reminded of a philosophic issue. They hear the slogan, "A mind is a terrible thing to waste," or see a sign that reads, "The Body Shop," or learn that physical education has been dropped from a local school district's required curriculum, or notice a TV sports commentator claiming that as long as you are not caught it is not illegal, or watch their own national organization promoting physical fitness as if it were the primary or only value in the field. Their philosophic curiosity is aroused; their philosophic hackles are raised. They have been "contaminated" by philosophy. As a result they are more thoughtful professionals, more interesting, better guided, more dangerous to any establishment that would like them to be docile workers, more powerful, better prepared to be faithful to the marvelous potential for human change their profession offers.

Before I had much of a chance to "contaminate" you regarding the importance of philosophy, you took the Philosophic Readiness Inventory. Do you remember your score on the PRI in chapter 1? If you were to take it again, would you score any higher? Have your attitudes related to philosophic curiosity, confidence, and commitment changed? How interested are you in becoming a thinker and questioner?

PHILOSOPHIC EXERCISE

Take the PRI again *without looking at your previous answers.* Add up the score and compare your three subtotals and your final scores with your earlier ones. Attempt to interpret these results. If your PRI scores stayed fairly constant, try to account for this. For example, was the time you spent on this book too short to effect a change in attitudes? If your scores remained low, did the topics covered on this journey seem irrelevant? Vague? Unimportant? If your scores remained high, did the book merely reinforce what you already believed?

On the other hand, if your scores changed in either direction, try to identify reasons for this change by comparing specific answers and describing the attitudes that led to those responses. For example, if your scores declined, did something in particular discourage you about the work of philosophy? If your scores improved, was there a particular experience that convinced you of the importance of philosophic reflection?

Writing a Personal Philosophy

In this book I emphasized the importance of doubting, asking, and thinking as an ongoing process. I recommended that you incorporate the habits of philosophizing into your professional life. I speculated that you would need to use the philosophic skills that you developed here for countless other day-to-day decisions in the years ahead. Indeed, you gained some practice in using the philosophic skills of induction, deduction, and direct intuition by thinking through the analyses I provided and by completing the exercises provided throughout the book.

I also emphasized the importance of finding truths, or at least partial truths. I provided some philosophic information about people as thoroughly embodied creatures; about different forms of intelligence and high movement IQs; about growing into a meaningful, culturally embedded life through games and play; about the wisdom that can be encountered and the freedom won by people who can move skillfully; and about the nature of moral excellence and its curious absence from much of contemporary sport.

The question now becomes, What will you do with your newly won skill and this additional information? I suggest that you test your skills and commit yourself to some conclusions. This can be done by writing something down. Putting words on paper forces you to organize your ideas and defend your position; it allows you to see if you really understand these ideas and can effectively think through them. You should write your philosophy in pencil, not ink, because your reflections should be refined throughout your career. Then sign your work. This is a symbolic step that indicates that this is not just an academic exercise, that these conclusions are not just anybody's, that they are yours. Then share them with others. This makes a private commitment public and consequently more binding.

There are any number of ways to write philosophic statements, but I will suggest two of them here. The first is to write a comprehensive philosophy of your profession.

The second is to develop a philosophic position for some specific purpose.

A Comprehensive Philosophic Statement

I will not presume to present the philosophic claims that should comprise your statement, but I will remind you of the vantage points that we adopted during the course of this journey. Then you will have to decide if you will want to write one or more statements from each of these perspectives.

The Importance of Philosophy for the Profession

Does it bother you that some people think that science has answers for virtually all of our problems and needs? Are you concerned that some professionals merely assume that fitness or skill, for instance, is valuable? Does it matter that we have had considerable difficulty articulating the significance of our field and convincing others that our work is central to human education and development? What if professionals relied wholly on taking the empirical turn and never took the reflective, philosophic turn?

Thus, do you want to write something in your personal philosophy about the place and importance of philosophy in a profession? What actions are needed to address this issue? For example, what kinds of philosophic questions should you be able to address?

The Nature of the Profession's Clientele

Does it bother you that some professionals look upon human bodies as machines? Why is it professionally dangerous and philosophically inaccurate to separate bodies from persons? Are you concerned that object, value, behavior, and language dualism continue to have a powerful effect on our programs—even on how we think and what we say? Do you believe we still have a problem with modern "holistic" philosophies that continue to present a vertical image of persons by placing mind over body? Do you believe it is important to describe the operations of high intelligence in the artistic, nonverbal actions of sport and dance? Are you worried that this profession has yet to fully embrace a holistic, horizontal image of persons and generate respect for multiple forms of intelligence?

Thus, do you want to write something about the dangers of dualistic interpretations of persons and the various forms that they take in our culture? How can you change the way you talk and behave in order to undo the four forms of dualism? What implications does a horizontal image of persons have for the respect given to physical education, the status of performance, the practice of using sport to promote "academic" education, and traditional definitions of intelligence?

The Mission of the Profession

Are you convinced that your profession understands the contemporary needs of society and is attempting to address them? Are you concerned that your profession tries too hard to be all things to all people? Does it bother you that many professionals report very little sense of mission and excitement—of a dedication to a few important goals? To any goals? Do you think it is enough to list four, safe, traditional aims— like organic, cognitive, psychomotor, and affective ends—and leave it at that? Does it matter if professionals picture their field more as a service profession in which they provide means to the good life rather than a life-changing profession in which they teach meaningful activities and advanced skills that are part of the good life?

Thus, do you want to write something about the mission of your field? Do you want to write something in your personal philosophy about the condition of contemporary society and how your profession might address its needs? Do you want to identify and describe your profession's most powerful values and describe its aims in terms of those values? What can you do to combat the excessive survivalism, individualism, and meaninglessness that some individuals experience today? How would you prioritize the contributions your profession can make?

What can we do to combat the excessive survivalism, individualism, and meaninglessness that many athletes experience today?

Practices and Ethics in the Profession

Does it bother you that, apart from promoting fitness and providing a few lifetime sport skills, the changes your profession can bring about are often considered relatively trivial? Are you concerned that very few people think of high-level movement skill in terms of human wisdom and freedom—albeit nonverbal and nonsedentary in nature? Does it concern you that many contemporary children achieve only a small portion of their human potential because schools emphasize reflective, sedentary liberation and generally neglect the active, embodied freedom to discover, explore, express, invent, and create? Does it matter that many people badly underestimate the power of games, sport, and play to provide delightful and meaningful moments in life? Do you care if ethical behavior in your field is often mediocre, at best?

Thus, do you want to write about the importance of skillful performance as a source of human freedom and as a legitimate component of mainstream, liberal education? On what grounds would you stake out the centrality of performance in education? How would you describe the human need for games and play and the power that these activities have to contribute to the good life? How can your profession bring more good to more people on a consistent basis? Do you want to write about the nature and importance of high ethical standards?

A Function-Specific Philosophic Statement

In contrast to the comprehensive statement that would result from addressing each of the areas identified above, you may want to write a statement geared to a specific context or purpose. I will describe three such contexts

below; you and your instructor should be able to identify others.

Defending Physical Education in a School District

The school district in which you work is experiencing financial difficulties and is thinking of cutting music, art, and physical education from the curriculum. You are the head of the physical education department and have been asked to provide a brief presentation at the next school board meeting on the importance of your field's contributions to the district's educational offerings.

Writing a Philosophic Statement for an Athletic Policy Manual

You are member of a committee that has been asked to write an athletic policy manual for your school district. Your athletic program has had some difficulties with win-at-all-costs attitudes and related behavior. You are told that the philosophic statement is to come first in this manual and that it must set the direction and tone for the specific policies that follow.

Writing an Oath for an Activity-Related Profession

You have heard of the Hippocratic Oath that medical doctors take. You have been asked by the head of your unit to write a similar statement that would guide your profession's practices. You are told that this should be a short statement (no longer than one page) so that it can be displayed publicly. You are requested to identify those promises or commitments that are most important for practitioners in your field to make.

In order to write any of these context specific philosophic statements, you should go

265 of MWwriting a Personal Philosophy

back to the suggestions made above for the comprehensive statement. You will find elements there that you will want to incorporate into your particular philosophy. But in contrast to writing the general statement, you will need to keep your audience in mind. You will be writing for them (not yourself), and will have to adjust your terminology and other communication strategies accordingly.

What Happens Now?

I don't know about you, but I'm going out for a jog, a round of golf, or a pickup basketball game over at the gym. I want to find one of those places that this book is all about—places where words, word processors, and written sentences do not hold sway.

References

Arendt, H. (1958). *The human condition.* Chicago: University of Chicago Press.

Arnold, P. (1988). *Education, movement and the curriculm.* New York: Falmer Press.

Arnold, P. (1991, April). The preeminence of skill as an educational value in the movement curriculum. *Quest, 43,* 66-77.

Baier, K. (1958). *The moral point of view: A rational basis of ethics.* Ithaca, NY: Cornell University Press.

Bellah, R., Madsen, R., Sullivan, W., Swidler, A., & Tipton, S. (1985). *Habits of the heart: Individualism and commitment in American life.* Berkeley: University of California Press.

Bellah, R., Madsen, R., Sullivan, W., Swidler, A., & Tipton, S. (1991). *The good society.* New York: Knopf.

Best, D. (1974). Expression in movement of the arts: A philosophical enquiry. London: Lepus.

Bloom, A. (1987). *The closing of the American mind.* New York: Simon & Schuster.

Buber, M. (1958). *I and thou.* (2nd ed.) (R.G. Smith, Trans.). New York: Scribner's.

Buber, M. (1965). *The knowledge of man.* New York: Harper & Row.

Cassirer, R. (1944). *An essay on man: An introduction to a philosophy of human culture.* New Haven, CT: Yale University Press.

Coakley, J. (1990). *Sport in society: Issues and controversies.* St. Louis: Times Mirror/Mosby.

Cremin, L. (1961). *The transformation of the school: Progressivism in American education, 1876-1957.* New York: Random House.

Crepeau, R. (1985). Where have you gone, Frank Merriwell? The decline of the American sports hero. In W. Umphlett (Ed.), *American sport culture: The humanistic dimensions* (pp. 76-82). Lewisburg, PA: Bucknell University Press.

Csikszentmihalyi, M. (1975). *Beyond boredom and anxiety.* San Francisco: Jossey-Bass.

Descartes, R. (1960). *Discourse on method and meditations* (L.J. Lafleur, Trans.). Indianapolis: Bobbs-Merrill. (Original work published 1641)

Dewey, J. (1970). Soul and body. In S.F. Spicker (Ed.), *The philosophy of the body: Rejections of Cartesian dualism* (pp. 101-120). Chicago: Quadrangle Books.

Dodds, P. (Ed.) (1987). *Basic stuff series I.* Reston, VA: American Alliance for Health, Physical Education, Recreation and Dance.

Ellis, M. (1973). Why people play. Englewood Cliffs, NJ: Prentice Hall.

Fraleigh, S. (1987). *Dance and the lived body: A descriptive aesthetics.* Pittsburgh: University of Pittsburgh Press.

Fraleigh, W. (1984). *Right actions in sport: Ethics for contestants.* Champaign, IL: Human Kinetics.

Fraleigh, W. (1986). The sports contest and value priorities. *Journal of the Philosophy of Sport, 8,* 65-77.

Fraleigh, W. (1989, April). *The supremacy of knowledge as a value of physical education.* Paper presented at the National Convention of the American Alliance for Health, Physical Education, Recreation and Dance, Boston.

Fraleigh, W. (1990, April). Different educational purposes: Different sport values. *Quest, 42,* 77-92.

Frankena, W. (1973). *Ethics* (2nd ed.). Englewood Cliffs, NJ: Prentice Hall.

Fromm, E. (1947). *Man for himself: An inquiry into the psychology of ethics.* New York: Fawcett World Library.

Fromm, E. (1956). *The art of loving: An enquiry into the nature of love*. New York: Harper & Row.

Fulghum, R. (1989). *All I really needed to know I learned in kindergarten: Uncommon thoughts on common things*. New York: Villard Books.

Gardner, H. (1985). *Frames of mind: The theory of multiple intelligences*. New York: Basic Books.

Gleick, J. (1987). *Chaos: Making a new science*. New York: Penguin Books.

Griffith, R. (1970). Anthropodology: Man a-foot. In S.F. Spicker (Ed.), *The philosophy of the body: Rejections of Cartesian dualism* (pp. 273-292). Chicago: Quadrangle Books.

Gruneau, R. (1983). *Class, sports, and social development*. Amherst, MA: University of Massachusetts Press.

Hanna, T. (1970). *Bodies in revolt: A primer in somatic thinking*. New York: Dell Publishing.

Harper, W. (1969, May). Man alone. *Quest*, **12**, 57-60.

Harper, W. (1972, February). *Giving and taking*. Paper presented at the meeting of the Philosophic Society for the Study of Sport, Brockport, NY.

Harper, W. (1973-1976). *The play factory advocate* (Vols. I-IV). Emporia, KS: William A. Harper.

Harper, W. (1985). The philosopher in us. In D. Vanderwerken and S. Wertz (Eds.), *Sport inside out: Readings in literature and philosophy* (pp. 449-454). Fort Worth, TX: Texas Christian University Press.

Hellison, D. (1973). *Humanistic physical education*. Englewood Cliffs, NJ: Prentice Hall.

Herrigel, E. (1971). *Zen in the art of archery*. New York: Vintage Books.

Hetherington, C. (1910). Fundamental education. *Journal of Proceedings and Addresses of the National Education Association*, **XLVIII**, 350-357.

Hoberman, J. (1992). *Mortal engines: The science of performance and the dehumanization of sport*. New York: Free Press.

Huizinga, J. (1950). *Homo ludens: A study of the play element in culture*. Boston: Beacon Press.

Hyland, D. (1990). *Philosophy of sport*. New York: Paragon House.

Kapleau, P. (1965). *The three pillars of Zen: Teaching, practice, enlightenment*. Boston: Beacon Press.

Kimball, B. (1986). *Orators and philosophers: A history of the idea of liberal education*. New York: Teachers College Press.

Kirk, D. (1983, July). *Understanding: A Focus for our conceptualisation of physical performance in games*. Paper presented at the meeting of the Philosophic Society for the Study of Sport, London.

Kleinman, S. (Ed.) (1986). *Mind and body: East meets west*. Champaign, IL: Human Kinetics Publishers.

Kretchmar, S. (1975). From test to contest: An analysis of two kinds of counterpoint in sport. *Journal of the Philosophy of Sport*, **II**, 23-30.

Kretchmar, S. (1985). "Distancing": An essay on abstract thinking in sport performances. In D. Vanderwerken & S. Wertz (Eds.), *Sport inside out: Readings in literature and philosophy* (pp. 87-102). Fort Worth, TX: Texas Christian University Press.

Kretchmar, S. (1988, April). Toward a stronger position for physical education in higher education: Three recommendations. *Quest*, **40**, 47-55.

Kretchmar, S. (1990a). The naming debate: Exercise and sport science. *Journal of Physical Education, Recreation and Dance*, **60**, 68-69.

Kretchmar, S. (1990b). Values, passion, and the expected lifespan of physical education. *Quest*, **42**, 95-112.

Kretchmar, S. (1990c, September/October). Moral callouses in sport. *Strategies*, **4**, 5, 27.

Kretchmar, S., & Gerber, E. (1983). Jesse Feiring Williams. *Journal of Physical Education, Recreation and Dance*, **54**, 16-20.

Lasch, C. (1979). *The culture of narcissism: American life in an age of diminishing expectations.* New York: Warner Books.

Lasch, C. (1984). The minimal self: Psychic survival in troubled times. New York: Norton.

Lenk, H. (1979). *Social philosophy of athletics.* Champaign, IL: Stipes.

Levy, J. (1978). *Play behavior.* New York: Wiley.

MacIntyre, A. (1984). *After virtue* (2nd ed.). Notre Dame, IN: University of Notre Dame Press.

Marcel, G. (1950). *The mystery of being* (Vol. 1) (G.S. Fraser, Trans.). Chicago: Henry Regnery.

Maslow, A. (1962). *Toward a psychology of being.* Princeton, NJ: Van Nostrand.

McCloy, C. (1966). How about some muscle? In H.S. Slusher & A.S. Lockhart (Eds.), *Anthology of contemporary readings: An introduction to physical education* (pp. 13-17). Dubuque, IA: Brown.

McCloy, C. (1940). *Philosophical bases for physical education.* New York: Appleton-Century-Crofts.

Meier, K. (1975). Cartesian and phenomenological anthropology: The radical shift and its meaning for sport. *Journal of the Philosophy of Sport,* **2**, 51-73.

Meier, K. (1980). An affair of flutes: An appreciation of play. *Journal of the Philosophy of Sport,* **7**, 24-45.

Meier, K. (1988). Embodiment, sport, and meaning. In W. Morgan and K. Meier (Eds.), *Philosophic inquiry in sport* (pp. 93-101). Champaign, IL: Human Kinetics.

Metheny, E. (1965). *Connotations of movement in sport and dance.* Dubuque, IA: Brown.

Metheny, E. (1968). *Movement and meaning.* New York: McGraw-Hill.

Metheny, E. (1972). The symbolic power of sport. In E. Gerber (Ed.), *Sport and the body: A philosophical symposium* (pp. 221-226). Philadelphia: Lea & Febiger.

Morgan, W. (1982). Play, utopia, and dystopia: Prologue to a ludic theory of the state. *Journal of the Philosophy of Sport,* **9**, 30-42.

Morgan, W., & Meier, K. (Eds.) (1988). *Philosophic inquiry in sport.* Champaign, IL: Human Kinetics.

Murphy, M. (1972). *Golf in the kingdom.* New York: Viking.

Nash, J. (Ed.) (1931). *Interpretations of physical education: Mind-body relationships.* New York: Barnes.

National Association for Sport and Physical Education (NASPE). (1992). *Outcomes of quality physical education programs.* Reston, VA: American Alliance for Health, Physical Education, Recreation and Dance.

Novak, M. (1976). *The joy of sports: End zones, bases, baskets, balls, and the consecration of the American spirit.* New York: Basic Books.

Osterhoudt, R. (1991). *The philosophy of sport: An overview.* Champaign, IL: Stipes.

Parker, D. (1957). *The philosophy of value.* Ann Arbor: University of Michigan Press.

Parry, J. (1988). Physical education, justification, and the national curriculum. *Physical Education Review,* **11**, 106-118.

Patrick, D. (1981, November 12). McQuaid turns down #1. *Rochester Times-Union.*

Penrose, R. (1989). *The emperor's new mind: Concerning computers, minds, and the laws of physics.* New York: Penguin Books.

Pieper, J. (1952). *Leisure: The basis of culture.* New York: Pantheon Books.

Plato (1951). *Phaedo* (F.J. Church, Trans.) New York: The Liberal Arts Press.

Polanyi, M. (1958). *Personal knowledge: Towards a post-critical philosophy.* Chicago: University of Chicago Press.

Polanyi, M. (1966). *The tacit dimension.* Garden City, NY: Doubleday.

Polanyi, M., & Prosch, H. (1975). *Meaning.* Chicago: University of Chicago Press.

Rue, L. (1989). *Amythia*: Crisis in the natural history of western culture. Tuscaloosa, AL: University of Alabama.

Rey, H. (1952). *Curious George rides a bike*. Boston: Houghton Mifflin.

Ryle, G. (1949). *The concept of mind*. New York: Barnes & Noble.

Sage, G. (1986). Social development. In Y. Seefeldt (Ed.), *Physical activity and well-being* (pp. 343-371). Reston, VA: American Alliance for Health, Physical Education, Recreation and Dance.

Sage, G. (1990). *Power and ideology in American sport: A critical perspective*. Champaign, IL: Human Kinetics.

Santayana, G. (1972). Philosophy on the bleachers. In E. Gerber (Ed.), *Sport and the body: A philosophical symposium* (pp. 230-234). Philadelphia: Lea & Febiger.

Scheffler, I. (1965). *The conditions of knowledge*. Glenview, IL: Scott, Foresman.

Schmitz, K. (1972). Sport and play: Suspension of the ordinary. In E. Gerber (Ed.), *Sport and the body: A philosophical symposium* (pp. 25-32). Philadelphia: Lea & Febiger.

Schrag, C. (1972). The lived body as phenomenological datum. In E. Gerber (Ed.), *Sport and the body: A philosophical symposium* (pp. 142-149). Philadelphia: Lea & Febiger.

Seefeldt, V. (Ed.) (1986). *Physical activity & well-being*. Reston, VA: American Alliance for Health, Physical Education, Recreation and Dance.

Simon, R. (1985). *Sports and social values*. Englewood Cliffs, NJ: Prentice Hall.

Simon, R. (1991). *Fair play: Sports, values, & society*. San Francisco: Westview Press.

Slusher, H. (1967). *Man, sport and existence: A critical analysis*. Philadelphia: Lea & Febiger.

Smith, A. (1985). Sport is a western yoga. In D. Vanderwerken & S. Wertz (Eds.), *Sport inside out: Readings in literature and philosophy* (pp. 63-78). Fort Worth, TX: Texas Christian University Press.

Spicker, S.F. (Ed.) (1970). *The philosophy of the body: Rejections of Cartesian dualism*. Chicago: Quadrangle Books.

Steel, M. (1985). What we know when we know a game. In D. Vanderwerken & S. Wertz (Eds.), *Sport inside out: Readings in literature and philosophy* (pp. 78-86). Fort Worth, TX: Texas Christian University Press.

Sudnow, D. (1978). *Ways of the hand: The organization of improvised conduct*. Cambridge, MA: Harvard University Press.

Suits, B. (1972). What is a game? In E. Gerber (Ed.), *Sport and the body: A philosophical symposium* (pp. 16-22). Philadelphia: Lea & Febiger.

Suits, B. (1978). *The grasshopper: Games, life and utopia*. Toronto: University of Toronto Press.

Thomas, C. (1983). *Sport in a philosophic context*. Philadelphia: Lea & Febiger.

Vanderwerken, D., & Wertz, S. (Eds.) (1985). *Sport inside out: Readings in literature and philosophy*. Fort Worth, TX: Texas Christian University Press.

Vogel, P. (1986). Effects of physical education programs on children. In V. Seefeldt (Ed.), *Physical activity & well-being* (pp. 455-509). Reston, VA: American Alliance for Health, Physical Education, Recreation and Dance.

von Schiller, F. (1972). Play and beauty. In E. Gerber (Ed.), *Sport and the body: A philosophical symposium* (pp. 299-301). Philadelphia: Lea & Febiger.

Weiss, M., & Bredemeier, B. (1986). Moral development. In V. Seefeldt (Ed.), *Physical activity & well-being* (pp. 373-390). Reston, VA: American Alliance for Health, Physical Education, Recreation and Dance.

Weiss, P. (1969). *Sport: A philosophic inquiry*. Carbondale, IL: Southern Illinois University Press.

Wertz, S. (1991). *Talking a good game: Inquiries into the principles of sport*. Dallas: Southern Methodist University Press.

Willard, D. (1973). The absurdity of thinking in language. *The Southwestern Journal of Philosophy*, **4**, 125-132.

Williams, J.F. (1948). *The principles of physical education* (5th ed.). Philadelphia: Saunders.

Williams, J.F. (1964). *The principles of physical education* (8th ed.). Philadelphia: Saunders.

Williams, J.F. (1965). Education through the physical. In A. Paterson & E.C. Hallberg (Eds.), *Background readings for physical education* (pp. 191-196). New York: Holt, Rinehart & Winston.

Wood, T., & Cassidy, R. (1927). *The new physical education: A program of naturalized activities for education toward citizenship*. New York: Macmillan.

Zeigler, E. (1977). *Physical education and sport philosophy*. Englewood Cliffs, NJ: Prentice Hall.

Photo Credits

Source	Photo on page(s)
Casa Colina/Teresa Whitehead (909) 596-7733	153
Cleo Freelance Photo, St. Paul, MN	3, 129, 149
Mark Cowan, *The Daily Illini*, Champaign, IL	140, 229
The Daily Illini Photo Staff	15, 16, 35, 51, 61, 101, 120, 131, 172, 196, 197, 259
Chad Ehlers/Photo Network, Tustin, CA	97
Beth Hulina, Champaign, IL	170
Bob Kalmbach, University of Michigan, Ann Arbor	44, *right*
John Kilroy, Champaign, IL (217) 352-0213	31, 67, 75 (top), 77 (top), 109, 114
John Konstantaras, *The Daily Illini*	103
Jean Lachat, *The Daily Illini*	251
Bill Luthy, *The Daily Illini*	72
Dennis MacDonald/Photo Network, Tustin, CA	241
Del Munroe/Photo Network, Tustin, CA	119
Marilyn Nolt, Souderton, PA (215) 721-9055	vvii, 112
Oregon Tourism Division, Salem, OR	162
Purdue CIS Photographic Services, West Lafayette, IN	44, *left*
Connie Springer, Cincinnati, OH (513) 871-1677	58, 169, 222
Brian Stocker, Champaign, IL	143
Steve Warmowski, *The Daily Illini*	102, 205
James Wentworth, Thorton, CO	148, 187
Rick Widmer, *The Daily Illini*	192, 219
Lloyd Young, *The Daily Illini*	263

Index

A

Activity, types of
 criticism of physical education and, 184
 in holism, 74, 75-76, 78-80, 83-84
Activity Liberation Inventory, 201
Activity-related fitness, definition of, 137. *See also* Fitness; Fitness values
Activity-related knowledge. *See* Health- and activity-related knowledge
Activity skill, as mainstream education, 200-203. *See also* Skill; Skill values
Aerobic fitness, 138
Aesthetic pleasure, 147
Aesthetics, 17
Affective ends of physical education, 113, 115
Agility, 138
Anaerobic fitness, 138
Answers. *See* Philosophic answers; Philosophic questions
Applications. *See* Practical application
Arendt, Hannah, 96, 200
Arts (high culture)
 criticism of physical education from, 184, 186, 203
 response to criticism from, 186-188, 203-204
Ascetic pleasure, 147
Athletic policy manuals, 264
Attention, in holism, 76, 77
Attitudes, serious vs. nonserious, in games, 209-210
Axiology, 16

B

Baier, K., 126
Basic Stuff curriculum, 161
Beauty, philosophy of (aesthetics), 17
Behavioral changes, for defeating dualism, 40-42, 48-49, 53-56, 63-64
Behavior dualism, 37, 49-56
Bellah, R., 96, 99, 104, 216, 220
Berra, Yogi, 191-192
Biases, vs. insights, 94
Biological values, 113-114
Bodies, definition of, 33. *See also* Embodiment; Machines, bodies as
Body composition, 138-139
Body image, dualism and, 32

Body-person separation. *See* Dualism (body-person separation)
Body-person unity. *See* Holism
Body philosophy, practical application of, 223-224. *See also* Dualism (body-person separation); Holism
Body shape and size, 139
Buber, Martin, 45

C

Change agents
 definition of, 181
 in exploration tradition of education, 195-200
 in wisdom tradition of education, 191-195
Christianity, muscular, 103-104
Citius, altius, fortius, 106
Clientele, in philosophic statements, 262-263
Cognitive ends of physical education, 113. *See also* Health- and activity-related knowledge
Coherence
 ethics and, 247, 248
 knowledge values and, 163-164
 pleasure values and, 170-171
 priority ranking of values and, 130-133, 156
 skill values and, 166-167
Coherent life story, in ethics, 247
Commitment
 to contests, ethical aspects of, 252
 philosophic readiness and, 9-10
Competition. *See* Contests
Competitive performance knowledge, 141
Comprehensive philosophic statements, 262-264
Conclusions, evaluating validity of, 25-28. *See also* Philosophic answers
Confidence
 philosophic readiness and, 9, 14-15
 skill and, 165
Contests
 ethics and, 252-255
 knowledge (intrinsic) value of, 160
 pleasure (extrinsic) values of, 147
Contraries, 198
Conventions, games as, 216-217
Cooling out, for ethical decisions, 242-243
Corollary of durability, 129, 130, 155
Corollary of purity, 128-129, 130, 155

Local values
curriculum decisions and, 230-231
personnel decisions and, 227-228, 233-234
rationalism and, 104-105
value choices and, 124
Logic. *See also* Rationalism
object dualism and, 38
value dualism and, 43
Loving yourself. *See also* Self-concept; Self-esteem; Self-respect
philosophical self-love, 244-245
psychological self-love, 243
Ludic pleasure, 147

M

Machines, bodies as
behavior dualism and, 49, 50, 51
dualism in general and, 34-35
object dualism and, 38
in rationalism, 103, 106
Madsen, R., 96
Mainstream education. *See* Liberal education (mainstream education)
McCloy, Charles, 72-73
Meaning, in life
curricular emphasis on, 229-230
definition of, 130
ethics and, 247, 248
games and, 216-220
knowledge and, 163-164
play and, 222-223
pleasure and, 169-171
in practical application, 224
priority ranking of values and, 130-131, 132, 150, 156
skill and, 166-167, 171
Means, and games, 209
Means values. *See* Extrinsic values (means values)
Metaphysics, 16
Metheny, Eleanor, 197
Methods, instructional, applying philosophy to, 231-233. *See also* Practical application
Military preparedness, fitness for, 103-104
Mind-body separation. *See also* Dualism (body-person separation)
in object dualism, 36, 37, 38-42
in value dualism, 37, 42-49
Mind-body unity. *See* Holism
Mission of physical education
personal philosophic statements on, 263
social values and, 100-101
Military preparedness, fitness for, 103-104
Moral callouses, 238-241
Moral excellence, 255-257. *See also* Ethics (morality)

Moral values. *See also* Ethics (morality)
definition of, 111-112
in response to criticism of physical education, 188
Motor active activity. *See also* Skillful behavior
criticism of physical education and, 184
holistic view of, 74, 75, 76, 78-80, 83-84
Motor skill. *See* Skill; Skill values
Movement skills, generic, 186-188
Muscular Christianity, 103-104

N

National Association of Sport and Physical Education (NASPE), 123
Nature of things, philosophy of (metaphysics), 16
Needs
for games, 215-216, 225
for play, 220-223, 225
priority ranking of, 94
Nonmoral values, definition of, 112
Nonserious attitudes, in games and play, 209-210
Nonverbal symbols. *See also* Expression skill
language dualism and, 37, 49-56
wisdom tradition of education and, 192-193
Novak, M., 193-194

O

Oaths, professional, 264-265
Object dualism, 36, 37, 38-42
Objectives of physical education
four prime ends, 113
mission, 100-101, 263
Organic ends of physical education, 113

P

Pain, fitness and absence of, 156
Peak experiences, 165
Performance. *See also* Skill; Skill values
holistic implications for, 83-84
knowledge of, 141
Personal philosophy, development and writing of, xx-xxi, 261-265
Person-body separation. *See* Dualism (body-person separation)
Personhood
in behavior dualism, 50
definition of, 33
dualism in general and, 34
holistic images of, 70-74, 77-81
horizontal image of, 77-81
object dualism and, 39
in value dualism, 46
vertical image of, 73-74
Personnel decisions, applying philosophy to, 225-228, 233-234

Value dualism, 37, 42-49. *See also* Dualistic idealism
Values. *See also* Ethics (morality); Fitness values; Health- and activity-related knowledge; Health- and activity-related pleasure; Intrinsic values (end values); Knowledge values; Local values; Pleasure (enjoyment, fun) values; Skill values; Value choices; Values, of physical education; Values, priority ranking of
  affective, 113, 115
  biological, 113-114
  choice of, method for, 124-126
  common, and skill instruction, 233
  common, lack of, 100-101
  games in reinforcing, 218-220
  the good life and, 111-115, 224
  individualist, 99-102
  moral vs. nonmoral, 111-112
  overview of, 110-111
  practical application of, 224
  rationalist, 102-106
  survivalist, 95-99
Values, of physical education. *See also* Fitness values; Health- and activity-related knowledge; Health- and activity-related pleasure; Skill values
  four prime, 113-115
  the good life and, 113-115, 224
  individualist, 100-102
  knowledge values, 113, 114, 117-118
  rationalist, 104-106
  survivalist, 96-99
Values, priority ranking of
  of extrinsic values, 127-128, 136, 137, 148-152, 173, 174
  of extrinsic vs. intrinsic values, 173, 174

  of fitness values, 149-150, 172-173, 224
  of intrinsic values, 127-128, 133, 155, 171-173, 174
  of knowledge values, 151, 173, 224
  meaning in, 130-131, 132, 150, 156
  overall, 173, 174, 224
  of pleasure values, 150-151, 173, 224
  procedure for, 124-134
  rationale for, 115-123
  satisfaction in, 128-130, 172
  of skill values, 150-151, 224
  social influences on, 92, 117-121, 131
  tolerance/intolerance in, 124-126
Verbal skills, and language dualism, 37, 49-56
Vertical image of personhood, 73-74
Vocation, of physical education, xviii
Vocational education, definition of, 188
Vogel, P., 123

W
Weighing the reasons, procedure for, 126-133
Williams, J.F., 71-72, 73
Winning
  games for reinforcing value of, 218
  in survivalism, 98
Win-win solutions, 249-250, 255
Wisdom tradition, in education
  description of, 189, 190
  in physical vs. mainstream education debate, 203, 225
  skill in, 191-193, 194-195, 225
  spectator knowledge in, 193-194
Words, defining, in philosophic process, 18
Workouts, in survivalism, 97. *See also* Exercise
Work/recreation cycle, 97-98

Z
Zone, living in the, 165